THE STORY OF
THE PANAMA CANAL

The Story of
The Panama Canal

THE WONDERFUL ACCOUNT OF THE GIGANTIC
UNDERTAKING COMMENCED BY THE
FRENCH, AND BROUGHT TO
TRIUMPHANT COMPLETION
BY THE UNITED STATES

WITH

A HISTORY OF PANAMA FROM THE DAYS
OF BALBOA TO THE PRESENT TIME

By
LOGAN MARSHALL
Author of "The Story of Polar Conquest;"
"The Universal Handbook," Etc., Etc.

Illustrated

COPYRIGHT, 1913
BY L. T. MYERS

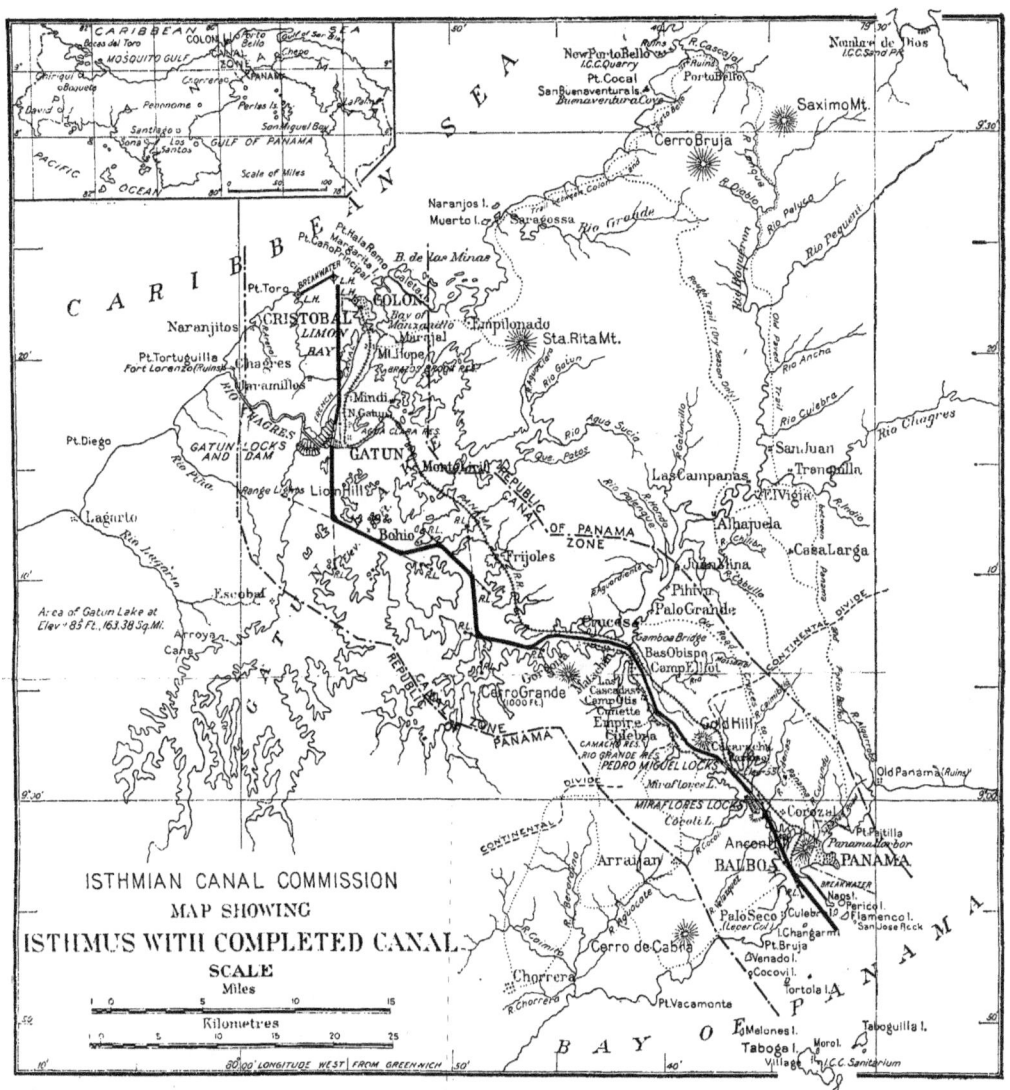

THE ISTHMUS WITH COMPLETED CANAL.

The dotted lines show the boundary of the territory known as the Canal Zone, a strip ten miles wide, from deep water in the Atlantic to deep water in the Pacific, and extending five miles on each side of the center line of the Canal, which was purchased by the United States from the Republic of Panama. The heavy line shows the Canal, and the crossed line just above it the relocated Panama Railroad. The cities of Colon and Panama, though included in the limits of the Zone, are reserved to the Republic of Panama. The sanitation of these cities is however, under the control of the United States.

GATUN SPILLWAY.

Flood water is being discharged from Gatun Lake at the rate of 15,000 cubic feet per second.

THE GREAT LOCK GATES AT GATUN DURING CONSTRUCTION.

These huge gates weigh from 390 to 730 tons each and are built with air chambers so that they will float, to save weight on the hinges.

PREFACE

No material work of man since the creation of the world has had so deep and widespread an influence upon the affairs of mankind in general as that which may calculably be expected to ensue from the achievement of the Panama Canal. The results will be seen in commercial, political, social, and even religious, effects. It will make and mar the fortunes of nations. Cousin, the French philosopher, has said: "Tell me the geography of a country and I will tell you its destiny." By creating important modifications in the geographical relations of certain communities the Canal will be the means of bringing about great and lasting changes which are beyond the range of accurate forethought. We can, however, predict an enormous gain to this country from the stupendous enterprise which has been brought to a brilliant and successful conclusion.

No task has ever been undertaken before which can compare with it either in magnitude or difficulty, and the great waterway will stand forever a monument to the dauntless courage, infinite resourcefulness, ingenuity and administrative ability of the American people. Ten years have passed since the United States undertook the work, years of struggling against all the forces of nature, hardships and disease which would have tried the patience and resources of any other nation to the breaking point. In that time a huge cut has been dug and blasted across the Isthmus of Panama, a mountain range has been pierced and a smaller range made thirty miles away in the form of Gatun Dam. Huge locks, the largest in the world, have been built of enduring concrete, great rivers have been dammed and an inland sea created in what was a tropic jungle. In short, the American people have accomplished the greatest and most important engineering enterprise in the history of the world.

All the available data at the command of the Isthmian Canal Commission have been placed at the disposal of the author, together with official photographs, maps, plans, etc., and this volume is now presented as a complete history and practical exposition in simple language of the great enterprise, covering every noteworthy aspect and feature of the work from its inception in the days of Columbus to its completion.

LOGAN MARSHALL.

CONTENTS

CHAPTER I
The American Isthmus under Spain 13

CHAPTER II
Canal Exploration 28

CHAPTER III
The Panama Railroad 44

CHAPTER IV
The Isthmian Country 59

CHAPTER V
Colon and Panama 76

CHAPTER VI
The French Panama Canal Company 91

CHAPTER VII
The New Panama Canal Company 110

CHAPTER VIII
The American Enterprise 124

CHAPTER IX
The Health Problem 137

CHAPTER X
The Labor Problem. 148

CONTENTS

CHAPTER XI
Plan and Operation of the Canal 157

CHAPTER XII
Military and Political Aspects 198

CHAPTER XIII
The Results of Opening the Canal 208

APPENDICES

I
Great Canals of the World 239

II
Economic Effects of Ship Canals 254

III
History of Traffic on Great Canals 265

IV
The Canal System of India 273

V
Canals in China 283

An important epoch in the history of the Canal was marked when the steam shovels shown met opposite the town of Culebra, both working on the floor of the Canal and completing a channel at its bottom level extending the entire length of Culebra Cut.

CHAPTER I

The American Isthmus Under Spain

On the early morning of the twenty-fifth of September, in 1513, a small party of men made their laborious way up the densely covered face of a steep ridge. One, keen of eye and with determined countenance, pressed forward eagerly ahead of his companions. When, at length, he reached the summit, a vast expanse of water stretched before him on either hand. Balboa had discovered the Pacific Ocean. Vasco Nuñez de Balboa was a man of extraordinary intellect, and it is not improbable that something of the true significance of this new knowledge dawned upon his mind even in these first moments of discovery. Perhaps he, first of all contemporary explorers, realized that the Tierra Firma of Columbus was not the Ultima Thule of sixteenth century endeavor, and that the land of mystic legend lay away toward the setting sun, beyond the sparkling sea whose placid waters washed the shores of the bay below the height upon which he stood. It was an age of splendid achievements in geographical science. Bold and ardent adventurers were fast dispersing the haze that had obscured more than half the earth, and disclosing new lands almost as rapidly as geographers could map them. In the last year of the fifteenth century, Vasco da Gama, returning home from his eventful voyage to India, re-rounded the cape which Bartholomew Diaz had discovered and which King John had named Good Hope. A waterway to the East was thus opened up, and this circuitous route remained the main means of direct ocean communication between Europe and Asia until the opening of the Suez Canal, nearly four hundred years later. Columbus, with the vaguest ideas of the extent of the globe, and with none but the most faulty charts for guide, thought to find Cipango, where he ran across Cuba and died without knowing that he had added an enormous continent to the map. First in the West Indies and later on the mainland of America he hoped to reach the capital of the Grand Khan, to whom he bore letters from Ferdinand of Spain. When, upon his last disastrous voyage, Columbus beat down the coast from Honduras to Darien seeking a strait through the massive barrier that stayed his farther progress to the west, he little dreamed that at a point which he passed in his disheartening search a caudal cut would one day separate two great continents and unite two vast oceans. Though Columbus was not actually the discoverer of the Isthmus, yet his matchless courage in sailing into uncharted seas in 1492 was chiefly responsible for its subsequent discovery. It is altogether fitting that the great bronze statue of Columbus and the Indian maiden should stand at Cristobal overlooking the Atlantic entrance to the canal which is to materialize his vision of a direct route to Asia. The statue is life size and stands upon a marble pedestal ten feet high, an imposing tribute to the great discoverer. It was the gift of the Empress Eugenie to the Republic of Colombia in 1868 and stood for a time in the railroad yards at Colon. Count de Lesseps, however, had it removed and placed it in front of his palace, where it now stands, beholding at last the New Route to India! That to his dying day Columbus persisted in his belief that there was a strait through to the Western waters and the lands he sought is shown in the map inspired by him which was published soon after his death. Balboa, who followed Columbus, also believed this legend of the Indians. Explorers who followed them failed to find the strait, but out of this idea grew the project of cutting a canal across the Isthmus first proposed by Hernando Cortez, Spanish conqueror of Mexico to King Charles V of Spain in 1523, about two hundred and fifty years before the birth of the United

PEDRO MIGUEL LOCKS.

Showing center wall and intakes, looking north. In the upper right hand corner are the great berm cranes used to carry the concrete from the mixers to the locks.

States of America, the nation destined to complete the project.

EARLY SETTLEMENTS OF THE SPANISH MAIN

Amongst the horde of adventurers who followed in the wake of the Great Discoverer was Rodrigo Bastidas. He was in command of an expedition that, in 1500, coasted the Spanish Main from some point on the Venezuelan littoral to almost as far south as Porto Bello. Balboa, a lad of twenty-five, received his first taste of adventure upon this occasion. On the return voyage the weather-worn and worm-eaten ships of Bastidas were barely able to make Hispanola before they sank. Balboa, who possessed little or no means, turned his attention to agriculture on the island. The spirit of the rover was strong in him, however, and, in order to indulge his desire as well as to escape his creditors, he concealed himself in a cask and caused it to be carried on board a ship bound for Tierra Firma. At this time Spain had two sparsely settled provinces on the Isthmus of Darien and an important stronghold at Cartagena.

Balboa was successful in his scheme of escaping his creditors and seeking once more the new lands which had aroused his curiosity and love of adventure. The ship upon which his cask happened to be carried was that of Encisco, which was bound on a relief expedition to the Gulf of Darien. As soon as the ship reached the open sea Balboa was discovered and had difficulty in persuading Encisco not to throw him overboard, thus ending a very promising career. The fact that he had previously visited the Isthmus and would probably be of value to Encisco through his knowledge of the country, turned the tide in his favor, however, and he was made a member of the expedition. During the year before, 1509, an unlucky expedition had been undertaken by Ojeda and Niqueza, who had been appointed governors of all the mainland from Cape de la Vela on the Venezuelan coast to Cape Gracias á Dios on the coast of Honduras. The Gulf of

Darien was the line of division between them and they held dominion over the entire region. Ojeda had preceded Niqueza on this expedition with four ships and three hundred soldiers. When Niqueza arrived with seven ships and eight hundred soldiers he found Ojeda suffering greatly from attacks by Indians. Joining forces they routed the natives and then proceeded to occupy the region, founding several towns, among them Nombre de Dios. This town, though unhealthful and having but a poor harbor, remained the chief port on the Atlantic side of the Isthmus for nearly a hundred years. Ojeda and Niqueza both died during this enterprise and were succeeded by Pizarro, who later on was destined for an important role in Isthmian affairs.

At the time of the arrival of Balboa and Encisco, Pizarro was in desperate straits and the town of San Sebastian almost destroyed. Encisco was proclaimed as governor to succeed Niqueza and established the town of Santa Maria de la Antigua del Darien. It had the distinction of being the first Episcopal see upon the mainland and of containing the oldest church on the American continent. Balboa was made *alcalde* of the new town. Soon afterward he quarreled with Encisco and managing to gain the upper hand, deported the former governor to Spain.

Balboa soon rose to a position of importance among the colonists of Tierra Firma. He learned from the Indians that a great sea lay beyond the range of mountains that traversed the Isthmus, and lost no time in investigating the statement. With a small force of Spaniards and Indian guides Balboa succeeded, not without great difficulty, for the whole way was through dense jungle and over swamps, in reaching the ocean, of which he formally took possession in the name of the King of Spain. During this journey across the isthmus the Spaniards heard of a rich land to the south abounding in precious metals. Balboa planned the conquest of this country, and it is more than probable that Pizarro, who was his companion on this occasion, shared his designs. Had the former lived to pursue his energetic and ambitious career Pizarro might never have found the heroic place which he occupies in history.

In 1515, Balboa received the reward of his enterprise in the form of the appointment of Adelantado of the Southern Sea, as the Pacific had been named. The same ship which brought this news, unfortunately for Balboa, carried also the new governor, Pedro Arias de Avila, better known as Pedrarias. Of this monster and his atrocities so much has been written that it need not be dwelt upon here. As soon as he arrived Pedrarias had arrested Balboa, but had failed to convict him. So a truce was arranged between them, giving Pedrarias the governorship of the Atlantic side and Balboa the Pacific or "South Sea" with freedom to continue his explorations.

PREPARATIONS FOR EXPLORING THE PACIFIC COAST

In the following year he prepared to organize an expedition to the south by way of the newly discovered ocean. The problem involved in the undertaking was one to daunt a less bold spirit. Trees suitable to the construction of ships were to be found only upon the Atlantic side of the divide, which necessitated the tremendous task of transporting timbers over a route that presented great difficulties to the passage of an unencumbered man. The terribly onerous labor of collecting the material and carrying it on their backs to its destination was imposed upon the Indians, of whom thousands were gathered together for the purpose, and impelled to the unaccustomed work by the merciless severity of their taskmasters. Many months were consumed in this grim struggle for a passage of the Isthmus, which, in many respects, foreshadowed the endeavors of the modern successors of these hardy pioneers. Hundreds of the wretched aborigines, Las Casas says their number fell little short of two thousand, lost their lives in the undertaking, but it succeeded, and four brigantines were carried piecemeal from sea to sea and put together on the Pacific coast.

The work of fitting out the ships proceeded rapidly and Balboa was upon the eve of departure when his arrest was effected by order of the Governor.

Pedrarias had entertained a jealous hatred of Balboa for years and could not endure the thought of his achieving the further successes that promised to follow his expedition to the south. The Governor pretended to have received information that Balboa purposed the creation of an independent kingdom in the countries that he might discover. Balboa was tried, condemned on evidence of an *ex parte* character, and executed. Thus fell, in the prime of life, the first of that trio of Spanish explorers whose brave deeds excite our admiration whilst we deplore the cruelties with which they were accompanied. Balboa, more than any of the early explorers except Columbus, deserves recognition in this day. It is altogether fitting that the name of the Pacific entrance to the canal should have been changed from La Boca to Balboa in tardy appreciation of his great achievements.

THE SEARCH FOR A STRAIT THROUGH THE ISTHMUS

Three years after the death of Balboa, Magellan passed through the Straits of Tierra del Fuego and opened up a western waterway to the Orient. The attempts to find a strait through the continent were not abandoned, however, Charles the Fifth taking a keen interest in the prosecution of these efforts. He instructed the governors of all his American provinces to have the coast lines of their respective territories thoroughly examined and every river and inlet explored. The orders addressed to Cortes were especially explicit and urgent, for at this time the hope began to prevail that a solution to the problem would be found in the territory of Mexico. It was in accordance with this idea that Gil Gonzales was despatched from Spain to the New World. Gonzales had authority to use the vessels which had been built by Balboa, but Pedrarias refused to deliver them to him. Gonzales was not to be balked by this denial, however. He immediately took to pieces the two caravels with which he had arrived and transported them to the Pacific coast by the route which Balboa had when out. The reconstructed ships were soon lost and the party built others, in which they proceeded north in January, 1522, to Fonseca Bay. At this point the leader, with one hundred men, continued the exploration by land. Lake Nicaragua was discovered and a settlement was shortly afterwards made upon its shore, the Indians having been subjected. The new discovery awakened fresh ideas and projects relating to the much desired interocean route. It was at first reported that an opening existed from the lake to the South Sea, but an immediate examination failed to reveal any water connection. In 1529, Diego Machuca, in command of a considerable force, carefully explored Lake Nicaragua and its eastern outlet. He found the navigation of the San Juan River, at that time called the Desaguadero, extremely difficult, but eventually emerged from its mouth with his ships and continued down the coast to Nombre de Dios. At a later period an important commerce was conducted over this route by vessels making ports in Spain, the West Indies and South America. Thomas Gage, the English priest who visited Nicaragua in 1637, mentions this traffic as in existence at that time.

The early exploration of the Isthmus was quickly followed by settlements and then the establishment of towns inhabited by traders and connected by trade routes, for this was the beginning of Spain's golden age in her colonies, and for more than a hundred years a constant stream of gold, pearls, and other products of Spain's island possessions flowed across the Isthmus. The towns became cities with royal storehouses guarded by slaves, merchants' warehouses, great stone stables for the mules of the treasure trains, beautiful convents and monasteries and residences built in the Moorish style either of stone or carved native cedar. Soon the necessity for a permanent highway to take the place of the Indian trails which were poorly adapted to the traffic which had now begun to move over them became apparent.

THE ESTABLISHMENT OF OVERLAND COMMUNICATION

Pending the discovery of a maritime channel between the two oceans, the Spanish authorities had decided to establish permanent land communication across the Isthmus of Darien. Under Charles the Fifth a line of posts was maintained from coast to coast. Nombre de Dios was made the Atlantic port and the Pacific terminus was located at Old Panama, which was created a city in 1521. A road was at once constructed between these two points, which crossed the Chagres at Las Cruces. Great difficulties were surmounted in building this highway. Much of the route lay over swamps that had to be filled in. Several streams were spanned by bridges and vast masses of rock were removed to facilitate the passage over the mountains. The way was paved and, according to Peter Martyr, was wide enough to accommodate two carts abreast. There is little left of this road, once the richest highway in the world, but it is still possible to catch a glimpse of it at Old Panama, though it is quickly lost in the deep jungle before the visitor has followed it more than a few yards. The city of Old Panama, which is now marked solely by ruins, was erected about five miles from the modern city of Panama. Founded in 1519 by Pedrarias, it quickly attained the position of the most important Spanish city in the New World, and at the time of its destruction by Morgan had a population of about thirty thousand.

About ten years after the establishment of this route a modification of it came into use. Light draft vessels began to sail from Nombre de Dios along the coast and up the Chagres as far as Cruces, where the road met the stream, and thence the journey was completed by land. In the closing years of the sixteenth century, Nombre de Dios, which had been repeatedly condemned in memorials to the Crown, as "the sepulcher of Spaniards," was abandoned in favor of Porto Bello, with a location and other natural

Copyright by Harris & Ewing.

COLONEL GEORGE WASHINGTON GOETHALS, U. S. A.

The genius of the Canal. After the successive resignations of John F. Wallace and John F. Stevens as Chief Engineer, President Roosevelt decided that the time had come to turn the work over to the U. S. Army Engineers. His decision has been abundantly justified by the remarkable results achieved.

advantages decidedly superior to those of the former terminus.

EARLY TRADE OF PANAMA

This interoceanic communication was of the utmost value to the Spanish Crown after the conquest of Peru, and the isthmian territory grew in importance year by year. The vast treasure that was extracted from the mines of the south came to Panama in the first stage of transit to the Royal Treasury. From the Pacific port it was carried to Porto Bello on pack-animals, and thence was shipped to Spain. Upon the arrival of vessels from the mother country, fairs were held at Cartagena and Porto Bello. Thither came merchants from far and near and caravans from Panama. An extensive trade was conducted at these periodical marts and the goods brought from Spain found their way through Panama to South and Central America and even to the mainland and islands of Asia. Thus was demonstrated at an early stage the logical trend of trade and the great advantages of a trans-isthmian route.

A CHECK TO CANAL PROJECTS

The policy of Philip the Second with regard to the American possessions was very different from that of his father. The former was averse to the expansion of his empire in the New World and distinctly antagonistic to the plans for an isthmian canal. He reasoned with astuteness that the existence of a water route through the continent of America would give easy access to his new possessions on the part of other nations and in time of war might be of greater advantage to his enemies than to himself. This policy of Philip was maintained for two centuries after his death by succeeding rulers.

During this period of quiescent policy on the part of Spain the most notable event in the history of the Isthmus was furnished by the disastrous attempt of William Paterson to establish a colony in the province of Darien. In

1695 the Scotch Parliament, with the approval of William the Third, authorized the formation of a company to plant colonies in Asia, Africa and America and to carry on trade.

THE ILL-FATED DARIEN EXPEDITION

Paterson cherished a scheme of stupendous colonial commerce, the Darien Expedition being but the initial step in the enterprise. Toward the close of the year 1698, five vessels, having on board twelve hundred Scottish settlers, anchored in a bight which they called Caledonia Bay, a name it retains at this day. The colonists were received in friendliness by the Indians and purchased from them the land upon which the settlement of New Edinburgh was made. It was Paterson's design, based upon sound enough reasoning and knowledge previously acquired from the buccaneers of the West Indies, to extend his posts to the Pacific Ocean and open up a trade with the countries of the South Sea and Asia, in the manner which had been so profitable to Spain. He had not, however, anticipated the effect of the climate upon his northern-bred emigrants. Before any steps could be taken towards the contemplated extension of the operations, the colony was decimated by disease. The misery of the settlers was increased by the loss of the supply-ship on which they had depended for fresh provisions, and, eight months after the landing, a pitiful remnant of the original expedition abandoned the settlement and returned to Scotland. But before this disaster had become known at home other vessels with additional emigrants were despatched to the new colony. These made an effort to revive and maintain the settlement, but with no better results than those which had befallen their predecessors. The numbers of the later comers had become sadly reduced when they were attacked by the Spaniards. After a feeble resistance they capitulated. So weak were the survivors that they could not reach their ships without the aid of their enemies.

Thus ended the Darien Expedition with the loss of more than two thousand lives and the expenditure of vast sums of money.

In this section of the country the Spaniards completely failed to secure the friendship of the Indians or to effect their subjection. Their amicable reception of the Scotch immigrants and their invariable readiness to assist the buccaneers in their incursions against the Spanish settlements indicated the persistent hatred with which they regarded the first invaders of their land. The Darien region was wild in the extreme and abounded in secret passes and safe retreats. From their fastnesses the Indians made frequent raids upon the Spanish posts and retired by trails which were known only to themselves.

In the latter half of the eighteenth century, during the governorship of Andres de Ariza, a determined effort was made to establish permanent communication between the coasts at this part of the Isthmus. Plans were laid for a line of military posts to be connected by a road which should run from a point on Caledonia Bay to a terminus on the Pacific Ocean. The project was put into operation, but met with such formidable resistance on the part of the inhabitants that the Spanish authorities became convinced of the futility of their endeavors. In 1790 they entered into a treaty with the Indians, agreeing to disband the garrisons and withdraw from the country.

CORTES ESTABLISHES A TRANSCONTINENTAL ROUTE

It will be remembered that in the first quarter of the sixteenth century Cortes received implicit instructions from the Crown to use every resource at his command in a search for the longed-for strait. In pursuit of this object the coast of Mexico was carefully examined and the Coatzacoalcos River explored. Montezuma afforded valuable assistance in this investigation by furnishing descriptions and maps of certain portions of the country. Whilst these efforts failed of their principal object, they had important results. Cortes established a transcontinental route along the course of the Coatzacoalcos, over the divide, and down the Pacific slope to Tehuantepec. This line of communication soon gave birth to an extensive trade between Spain and her provinces on both coasts of America as well as some parts of Asia. The Ead's ship-railway of modern days was planned to follow practically the same line as this early route of Cortes.

Towards the end of the eighteenth century there were discovered at Vera Cruz some cannon of ancient date which bore the mark of the old Manila foundry. This discovery aroused speculation as to how the pieces of artillery had been brought to the Atlantic coast of Mexico. It seemed improbable that they had been transported around the continent, especially when it was remembered that the only commercial intercourse with the Philippines had been through the Pacific port of Tehuantepec and over the route established by Cortes. This trade-way had long since been abandoned, but interest in it was at once revived by the incident which has been recited, and a remembrance of its former importance prompted the viceroy of Mexico to institute an investigation.

By this time it had become an accepted idea that maritime communication between the oceans could only be secured by the creation of artificial waterways. Two engineers were directed to explore the country from the mouth of the Coatzacoalcos to Tehuantepec with a view to ascertaining the practicability of a waterway from ocean to ocean. This was the first canal project entertained for this region.

INVESTIGATION OF THE NICARAGUA ROUTE

The report on this exploration, which included a cursory survey, was not such as to encourage the institution of operations. It had the effect, however, of stimulating the interest in the subject and in 1779 the feasibility of connecting the Nicaragua lakes with the sea was investigated by royal command. Manuel Galisteo, to whom the task had been intrusted, passed an opinion unfavorable to the project. Nevertheless, a company was formed in Spain, with the patronage of the Crown, to carry out the undertaking, but nothing effective ever came of it.

Galisteo's expedition had been accompanied by the British agents at Belize in a private capacity. Upon their return they made highly favorable representations to their Government, stating that the project was entirely feasible and not accompanied by any difficulties that the engineering capabilities of the day need fear to encounter. This report made a deep impression in England and when, in the following year, war broke out between that country and Spain an effort was made to gain possession of the Nicaragua country. In 1780, an invading force was organized at Jamaica. Captain Horatio Nelson was in command of the naval contingent, and in his despatches stated the general purpose of the expedition as follows: "In order to give facility to the great object of the government I intend to possess the Lake of Nicaragua, which, for the present, may be looked upon as the inland Gibraltar of Spanish America. As it commands the only water pass between the oceans, its situation must ever render it a principal post to insure passage to the Southern Ocean, and by our possession of it Spanish America is divided in two." The English were successful in their encounters with the Spaniards, but in the climate they found an irresistible enemy that forced them to abandon the enterprise. Of the crew of Nelson's ship, the *Hinchinbrook*, numbering two hundred, more than eighty fell sick in one night, and only ten survived the return of the expedition to Jamaica. The hero of Trafalgar barely escaped with his life after a long illness.

At the beginning of the nineteenth century Spain retained possession of the entire territory embraced in the question of interocean communication, but she had made no practical progress towards its settlement. Neither had she added materially to the available knowledge of the world on the subject, for the results of Spanish exploration and survey in this direction have never been made public. With the exception of the re-opened communication by way of Tehuantepec, the old Spanish overland routes had all fallen into disuse, and traffic between the mother country and the possessions on the west coast of America and in the Pacific Ocean was maintained by vessels sailing round Cape Horn and the Cape of Good Hope. Humboldt visited Mexico at about this time and recorded the ignorance that prevailed amongst the local authorities regarding the interior of the country. He stated that there was not a single mountain, plain, or city from Granada to Mexico of which the elevation above the sea was known.

DISINTEGRATION OF SPAIN'S AMERICAN COLONIES

Ere this the entire civilized world had become keenly interested in the question of an interoceanic canal, and the investigations of Humboldt commanded wide attention. Amongst other effects, they aroused the Spanish Government to action in the matter. In 1814 the Cortes passed an act authorizing the construction of a canal through the Isthmus and providing for the organization of a company to carry out the enterprise. Before anything of importance had been accomplished under this legislation the revolutions occurred which wrested from Spain her provinces in South and Central America. With the loss of territory went the opportunity for profit and glory by connecting the oceans.

In 1819, the states of New Granada, Ecuador, and Venezuela united in forming the Republic of Colombia, under Simon Bolivar; in 1831 they separated into three independent republics. In 1823 the Federal Republic of the United Provinces of Central America was formed by the union of Guatemala, San Salvador, Honduras, Nicaragua, and Costa Rica. These political changes, in what may be termed the canal region, opened up new possibilities in connection with the much-mooted question of a waterway and claimed the attention of capitalists and statesmen of all the commercial nations. From this time the matter is taken up with definiteness of purpose and never allowed to rest. Plans and negotiations of various kinds involving all the possible routes follow fast upon each other until we arrive at the inception of the work by the United States Government and the assurance of its accomplishment.

CHAPTER II

Canal Exploration

Early in 1825, the Republic of Central America, through its representative at Washington, conveyed to Henry Clay, then Secretary of State, a desire for "the co-operation of the American people in the construction of a canal of communication through Nicaragua, so that they might share, not only in the merit of the enterprise, but also in the great advantages which it would produce." Clay was fully alive to the importance of the project, the execution of which, he said, "will form a great epoch in the commercial affairs of the whole world." He returned a favorable answer to the proposition and promised an investigation on the part of the United States of the claims advanced in favor of the Nicaragua route.

CONCESSION TO AN AMERICAN FROM NICARAGUA

In 1826, the Republic of Central America, having grown impatient of the delay on the part of the United States, entered into a contract with Aaron H. Palmer of New York for the construction of a canal capable of accommodating the largest vessels afloat. The work was to be started within a year from the date of the agreement. The contract was to remain in force as long as might be necessary for the reimbursement of the capitalists engaged, in the amount of the money invested, together with ten per cent per annum, and for seven years after such reimbursement the company was to receive one-half of the net proceeds of the canal. At the expiration of the seven years in question the property was to be transferred to the Republic. It was expressly stipulated in this contract that the passage should at all times be open to the ships of friendly and neutral nations without favor or distinction.

Having secured his concession, Palmer endeavored to organize a construction company with a capital of five million dollars. The utter inadequacy of this amount is illustrative of the lack of explicit information which characterized all similar enterprises until quite recent times. Palmer failed both in America and in England to enlist the necessary financial aid and the contract was never acted upon.*

After an abortive attempt to complete arrangements with a Dutch company, the Central American Republic again addressed the Government of the United States with an offer to grant to it the right to construct a canal. In response to a recommendation of the Senate growing out of these overtures, President Jackson commissioned Charles Biddle to visit Nicaragua and Panama, with instructions to examine the different routes that had been contemplated and to gather all the information and documents procurable bearing upon the matters in interest. No satisfactory results followed this mission. A message was sent to the Senate to the effect that it was not expedient at that time to enter into negotiations with foreign governments with reference to a trans-isthmian connection. The truth is that the Government and its agents were not sufficiently assured as to the stability of the new republics and feared to create relations that might lead to political embroilment.

BAILY'S EXPLORATION OF THE NICARAGUA REGION

Meanwhile the active interest in the canal question was not confined to the United States. In 1826 an English corporation sent John Baily to Nicaragua for the purpose of securing a concession. In this object Baily was forestalled by the American, Palmer, but he remained in the

---

*House Report No. 145, 30th Cong., 2d session.

country, and about ten years later was employed by President Morazin to determine the most favorable location for a cutting.

Baily threw valuable light upon the Nicaragua route and made a very able report. He recommended a route from Greytown to Lake Nicaragua, across the lake to the Lajas, and thence to San Juan del Sur on the Pacific coast. With the termini he expressed himself as well satisfied. He proposed to utilize the entire length of the San Juan, which would necessitate blasting the rocks at the rapids, diverting the Colorado into the San Juan and deepening the latter river. He found the four principal rapids within a stretch of twelve miles, formed by transverse rocks, with a passage on either side affording a depth of from three to six fathoms. The river was navigated at the time by *piraguas*, large flat-bottomed boats of as much as eight tons burden, which passed the rapids without serious hazard.

Baily's line from the mouth of the Lajas, which he proposed to use for three miles of its length, was seventeen miles. This he thought might be reduced to about fifteen and a half miles. His summit level was 487 feet above the lake and the canal was to accommodate ships of twelve hundred tons with a depth of eighteen feet. He offered an alternative plan which would reduce the summit level to 122 feet above the lake but would necessitate the connection of two of his stations by a tunnel over two miles in length. The report frankly estimated the difficulties involved in the undertaking, and closed with the statement that although he could not speak confidently as to the feasibility of the route, which had never been surveyed, he believed that a continuation through the Tipitapa into Lake Managua and thence to the port of Realejo was worthy of serious consideration. Whilst these investigations were proceeding in the north, examination of other probable routes was being made. In 1827 President Bolivar commissioned J. A. Lloyd to survey the Isthmus of Panama with special regard to the possibilities of rail and water communication. Despite the fact that this was the first transcontinental route, the scientific knowledge of the territory was most significant. The geography of the strip was imperfectly known and the relative heights of the oceans or the altitude of the mountains separating them had never been ascertained.

THE FIRST SURVEYS OF THE PANAMA LINE

Lloyd made a careful survey from Panama to a point within a few miles of the mouth of the Chagres. He seems to have considered plans for a canal premature, but said that should the time arrive when such a mode of communication might be favorably entertained the route of the Trinidad River would probably prove the most desirable. He recommended for immediate purposes a combination rail and water route to take the place of the roads then in use from Chagres and Porto Bello to Panama. His plan contemplated a short canal from a point on the Bay of Limon to the Chagres, the use of that river along its tributary, the Trinidad, to a favorable spot for a junction, and thence a railroad to the coast. As to the terminus he was divided in opinion on the relative advantages of Cherrera and Panama. The former had the merit of shortening the distance, whilst the latter was the capital and an already well-established port.

The Republic of Colombia was disrupted in the year 1831 and the Panama region became a part of New Granada. In 1838, that Republic granted a concession to a French company authorizing the construction of highways, railroads, or canals from Panama to any desired point on the Atlantic coast. This company spent several years in making surveys and forming plans. The results were submitted to the French Government with a view to enlisting its aid in carrying out the undertaking. The project was presented in an extremely optimistic light and as one comparatively easy of accomplishment. The concessionnaires claimed to have discovered a depression in the mountain range which would permit of a passage at no greater height above the average level of the Pacific than thirty-seven feet. The company's statements excited extraordinary interest, and in 1843 Guizot, then Minister of Foreign Affairs, instructed Napolean Garella to proceed to Panama, to investigate the company's statements, and to make an independent examination of the entire situation.

Garella's report,* which was an able treatment of the subject, heavily discounted the claims of the Salomon company and led to its failure. An interoceanic canal was recommended as the only means of communication that could adequately meet the future demands of commerce. Garella agreed with Lloyd that the Atlantic terminus should be in the Bay of Limon rather than at the mouth of the Chagres. That river would be met by his canal near its junction with the Gatun. The reported low depression which had raised hopes of the practicability of a sea-level canal at a reasonable cost, could not be found. Garella suggested the passage of the divide by means of a tunnel more than three miles in length. The floor of this tunnel was to be 325 feet below the summit, 134 feet above the ocean, and the water level 158 feet above extreme high tide at Panama. The canal was to have a guard lock at each entrance and the summit level was to be reached by eighteen locks on the Atlantic slope and sixteen on the Pacific. The water supply was to be derived from the Chagres through two feed-canals. The Pacific terminus was placed at Vaca de Monte, about twelve miles south of Panama. Garella estimated the cost of a canal on these lines at about twenty-five million dollars. For an additional three millions he calculated that a cut might be made in place of the tunnel.

DEVELOPMENT OF THE UNITED STATES AS A FACTOR IN THE CANAL QUESTION

"About the middle of the century a succession of great events vastly increased the importance of a maritime con-

---

* Reprinted in House Report No. 322, 25th Cong., 3d session.

nection between the two oceans to the United States. The dispute with Great Britain as to the boundary line west of the Rocky Mountains was settled by the Buchanan-Packenham Treaty in 1846, and in August, 1848, an act of Congress was passed under which Oregon became an organized territory. The war with Mexico was commenced early in 1846, and by the terms of the Guadalupe-Hidalgo Treaty, which closed it in 1848, California was ceded to the United States. Before the treaty had been ratified gold was discovered there, and in a few months many thousands from the eastern part of the country were seeking a way to the mining regions. To avoid the hardships and delays of the journey across the plains or the voyage around the continent, lines of steamers and packets were established from New York to Chagres and San Juan del Norte and from Panama to San Francisco, some of the latter touching at the Pacific ports in Nicaragua. For a while those traveling by these routes had to make arrangements for crossing the isthmus after their arrival there, and were often subjected to serious personal inconveniences and suffering as well as to exorbitant charges.

THE UNITED STATES INSTITUTES NEGOTIATIONS FOR A RIGHT OF WAY

"The requirements of travel and commerce demanded better methods of transportation between the Eastern States and the Pacific coast, but there were other reasons of a more public character for bringing these sections into closer communication. The establishment and maintenance of army posts and naval stations in the newly acquired and settled regions in the Far West, the extension of mail facilities to the inhabitants, and the discharge of other governmental functions, all required a connection in the shortest time and at the least distance that was possible and practicable. The importance of this connection was so manifest that the Government was aroused to action before all the enumerated causes had come into operation, and negotiations were entered into with the Republic of New Granada to secure a right of transit across the Isthmus of Panama."* This object was effected by a treaty that was ratified in June, 1848.

In the following year, Elijah Hise, the representative of the United States in Nicaragua, negotiated a treaty with that republic. By its terms Nicaragua undertook to confer upon the Government of the United States, or a corporation composed of its citizens, the exclusive right to construct and operate roads, railways, or canals, or any other medium of communication by means of ships or vehicles, between the Caribbean Sea and the Pacific Ocean and through the territory of the former state. The concessions made by this treaty were extremely liberal, but in consideration of them it was required that the United States should pledge itself to the protection of Nicaragua and should hold its army and navy and any other effective resources it might be able to command available for the defense of the Latin-American republic against foreign aggression. Nicaragua was prompted in this negotiation by the desire for aid in withstanding the policy of Great Britain, which at that time appeared to be directed toward extending her control of the Mosquito coast to the lower waters of the San Juan.

The United States Government was not prepared to assume the responsibility involved in this treaty, in making which Hise had exceeded his authority, and it was not ratified. Another convention was formulated with the object of furthering the plans of The American, Atlantic and Pacific Ship Canal Company, composed of Cornelius Vanderbilt and others. Although this fell through, its purpose was effected by the Clayton-Bulwer Treaty of 1850.

THE VANDERBILT COMPANY IN NICARAGUA

This agreement required the contracting parties to support such individuals or corporation as should first commence

---

* Report of the Isthmian Canal Commission. Washington, 1899-1901.

a canal through Nicaragua. It practically insured the interests of the company in whose behalf the negotiations of the year before had been conducted. The Republic granted to the Vanderbilt company the exclusive right, for a period of eighty-five years, to make a ship canal from any point of the Atlantic coast to any point on the Pacific coast of Nicaragua, and by any route. The contract also gave to the company the exclusive right to construct rail or carriage roads and bridges and to establish steamboats and other vessels on the rivers and lakes of the territory as accessories to its enterprise. It was also provided that in case the canal or any part of it should be found to be impracticable, then the company should be privileged to substitute a railroad or other means of communication subject to the same conditions. In order to facilitate the operations, the company was incorporated by the Republic of Nicaragua in March, 1850. In the following year the arrangement was modified for the convenience of the company, by the granting of a new charter to enable the subsidiary operations on the inland waters to be separated from those connected with the canal proper. Under this charter the Accessory Transit Company immediately established a transportation line from Greytown up the San Juan and across Lake Nicaragua, by steamboats, to Virgin Bay on the western shore of the lake, and thence by stage coaches, over thirteen miles of good road, to San Juan del Sur. In connection with this route regular steamship communication was maintained with New York on one side and San Francisco on the other. This line proved a boon to the gold-seekers and was traveled by thousands on their way to and from California. It was obliged to close, owing to the disturbed condition created by the Walker expeditions, but at a later date was reopened under a new charter by another company.

The American, Atlantic and Pacific Ship Canal Company did not deem any of the surveys or reports that had previously been made of the Nicaragua country sufficiently reliable to determine their route upon, and Colonel Orville

Childs of Philadelphia was engaged to direct a thorough instrumental survey of the entire region.

AN ABLE SURVEY OF THE NICARAGUA ROUTE

Colonel Childs' report was submitted to President Filmore in March, 1852, and by him to two United States army engineers, by whom the plan was pronounced as entirely practicable, although they recommended some modification of its details. In view of the fact that the British Government was jointly pledged with the United States to protect the enterprise, the plans were subjected to examination by English experts. These concurred in the opinion of the American engineers.

Nothing further was done by the Vanderbilt company towards the construction of a canal, but the Childs' report has always been of great value to later investigators in an examination of the subject. In 1856, Nicaragua declaring that the company had failed in the performance of certain clauses of the contract, revoked the concession, annulled the charter, and abolished the corporation. The company disputed the right of the Republic to take this action and made several futile attempts to re-establish its status.

In 1858, despite the continued protest of the former concessionaries, the Government of Nicaragua considered itself free to enter into a new contract. This it did jointly with Costa Rica. The grantee in this case was Felix Belly, a citizen of France. The rights and privileges accorded to him under this agreement were very similar to those which had been enjoyed by the Vanderbilt company, and the organization which he proposed to create for the purpose of accomplishing the work was to be similarly protected by the terms of the Clayton-Bulwer Treaty. But the contract with Belly contained a clause insuring to the French Government the right to keep two ships of war in Lake Nicaragua as long as the canal remained in operation. This novel feature in the agreement no sooner came to the

RUINS OF ST. ANASTASIUS, OLD PANAMA.

The Cathedral of St. Anastasius was one of the noteworthy of the magnificent buildings of Old Panama. Only the ruins remain as a silent reminder of the glory of a bygone age.

knowledge of the United States than that country lodged an emphatic protest with the Governments of Nicaragua and Costa Rica. The proposed arrangement was characterized as obnoxious. It was pointed out that "the neutrality and security of these interoceanic routes constitute a great portion of their value to the world, and that the exclusive right to any one nation to exercise armed intervention would be just ground for dissatisfaction on the part of all others." No attempt was made to enforce the offensive clause and, as the company failed to put its project into execution, the grant was cancelled. More than once negotiations have been blocked by political obstructions and for many years American statesmen have been averse to the idea of a waterway across the American Isthmus under foreign control.

In the meantime the demand for transcontinental transportation created by the discovery of the gold-fields of California led to the building of the railroad across the Isthmus of Panama. A concession was obtained for the road by three Americans. This concession contained the important proviso that no canal might be constructed there unless the consent of the company be obtained. This line was opened early in 1855 and, whilst it afforded very valuable service, it stimulated rather than satisfied the desire for a ship canal. Exploration and survey were actively prosecuted in the Darien region by the governments and private citizens of the United States, Great Britain and France. By this time precise information was available as to the conditions obtaining along the Nicaragua and Panama routes, but the interior of the eastern section of the Isthmus was still unknown except to the Indians, although it had often been traversed by Spaniards.

EXPLORATIONS IN THE DARIEN REGION

This region had the obvious advantage of short distances between the oceans and there were good harbors available on either coast. So, when the difficulties of the tested routes had been proved, attention turned to the southern extreme of, what may be called, the canal area, in the hope that the physical features of that region might present difficulties of less magnitude than those existing in the sections already surveyed. This hope found justification in the common report that the mountains of the interior offered a low depression which had long been used by the Indians as a portage for their canoes when traveling from one ocean to the other. Indeed, there was a tradition of a long-existing uninterrupted waterway from coast to coast which was said to have been effected by cutting a short canal from the upper reaches of the Atrato to a small stream, the San Juan, emptying into the Pacific.

In the examination of this region three general lines were followed—those of San Blas, Caledonia Bay, and the Atrato River. Each of these names indicates the Atlantic terminus of the route, but there were many variations in the courses followed and the contemplated points of termination at the Pacific ranged over three hundred miles of coast. These investigations, in which the United States freely lent its assistance to private endeavors, had good results in the extension of topographic and geographic knowledge of the country and seemed to warrant further efforts in the same direction.*

AN IMPORTANT SENATE INVESTIGATION

In the year 1866, the Senate, with a view to determining the scope and direction of further investigation of the interoceanic canal question, requested the Secretary of the Navy to furnish all the available information pertaining to the subject and to ascertain whether the Isthmus of Darien had been sufficiently explored.

Secretary Welles responded, in the following year, with a voluminous report† by Admiral Charles H. Davis. This

---

* Details of these expeditions in the Darien district may be found in Senate Ex. Doc. No. 1, 33d Cong., 2d session, and House Ex. Doc. No. 107, 47th Cong., 2d session.
† Senate Ex. Doc. No. 62, 39th Cong., 1st session.

document enumerates nineteen canal and seven railroad projects in the isthmian country extending from Tehuantepec to the Atrato. It excludes from consideration the plans relating to Tehuantepec and Honduras as being infeasible and meritless.

With reference to the eight proposed routes through Nicaragua, Admiral Davis says: "It may safely be asserted that no enterprise, presenting such formidable difficulties, will ever be undertaken with even our present knowledge of the American isthmuses. Still less is it likely to be entered upon while such strong and well-founded hopes are entertained by the promoters of the union of the Atlantic and Pacific oceans of finding elsewhere a very much easier, cheaper, and more practicable route for a canal in every way suited to the present demands of commerce."

He condemns a project that had strong advocates at the time, with these words: "The examination of the headwaters of the Atrato, of the intervening watershed, and of the headwaters of the San Juan, satisfactorily proved that nature forbids us altogether to entertain an idea of a union of the two oceans in this direction." The Admiral gives a general description of the other lines in Panama, Darien, and the Atrato valley. He states that "the Isthmus of Darien* has not been satisfactorily explored," and that "it is to the Isthmus of Darien that we are first to look for the solution of the great problem of an interoceanic canal. For these reasons and because "there does not exist in the libraries of the world the means of determining, even approximately, the most practicable route for a ship canal across the isthmus," he recommends the further investigation of the subject in this region.

ESTABLISHMENT OF THE INTEROCEANIC CANAL COMMISSION

President Grant, in his first message to Congress, recommended an American canal. That body promptly

---

* Until quite recently the words Darien and Panama were used interchangeably with reference to the strip of land now more generally designated as the Isthmus of Panama. It is in this broader sense that Admiral Davis uses the term "Isthmus of Darien."

adopted a joint resolution providing for more extensive exploration by officers of the Navy, and the chief of the Bureau of Navigation was authorized to organize and send out expeditions for this purpose. In 1872 the Interoceanic Canal Commission was established. Its members were General A. A. Humphreys, Chief of Engineers, United States Army; C. P. Patterson, Superintendent of the Coast Survey; and Commodore Daniel Ammen, Chief of the Bureau of Navigation of the Navy. Under the directions of this commission explorations were conducted in various parts of the isthmian territory.

The Tehuantepec route was surveyed by a party of which Captain Shufeldt had charge. It was found that under the most favorable conditions a canal along the Tehuantepec line would be more than one hundred miles in length, with a summit level at least 732 feet above the sea and requiring one hundred and forty locks. This report, confirming as it did the conclusions of Admiral Davis and other experts, put the Tehuantepec route out of the question for all future time.

At about the same time (1872), an expedition under Commander Edward P. Lull, assisted by A. G. Menocal, as chief civil engineer, surveyed the entire Nicaragua route, following the line taken by Childs, except for a slight deviation in the passage of the divide beyond the lake. Commander Lull's report was favorable. It included a detailed plan for a canal at an estimated cost of $65,722,137.

Whilst this work was progressing in the north, Commander Selfridge and other officers of the United States Navy were engaged in surveying the most promising lines in the Darien region. In 1875 the Panama route was minutely surveyed by Lull and Menocal. They reported in favor of a course 41.7 miles from the Bay of Limon to the Chagres, ascending its valley and that of the Obispo to the divide, and descending the Pacific slope by the valley of the Rio Grande to the Bay of Panama. The line as marked out in this report has been followed in general in subsequent plans without deviation except in minor details.

REPORT OF THE INTEROCEANIC CANAL COMMISSION

The Interoceanic Commission now had before it the reports of the expeditions which have been mentioned and, in addition, plans and surveys relating to every route in any degree practicable from one end to the other of the canal country. Its report,* which was unanimous, was returned in February, 1876, and embodied the following conclusion: "That the route known as the Nicaragua route, beginning on the Atlantic side at or near Greytown; running by canal to the San Juan River, thence . . . to . . . Lake Nicaragua; from thence across the lake and through the valleys of the Rio del Medio and the Rio Grande to . . . Brito, on the Pacific coast, possesses, both for the construction and maintenance of a canal, greater advantages and fewer difficulties from engineering, commercial, and economic points of view than any one of the other routes shown to be practicable by surveys sufficient in detail to enable a judgment to be formed of their respective merits."

Meanwhile Lieutenant L. N. B. Wyse, as the representative of a French syndicate, was negotiating with the Colombian Government for a concession, which he secured in 1878. An account of this important contract and of the Panama Canal Company, which operated under it, will be given in a later chapter.

VARIOUS SHIP RAILWAY PROJECTS

Whilst the report of the Interoceanic Commission was generally accepted with regard to the infeasibility of the Tehuantepec route for a ship canal, it appeared to James B. Eads to offer special advantages for a ship railway, and in 1881 he secured a charter from the Mexican Govern-

---
* Senate Ex. Doc. No. 15, 46th Cong., 1st session.

ment conveying to him authority to utilize it for that purpose. Eads' plan was entirely feasible and no doubt would have been carried to a successful conclusion had he lived, but with his death in 1887 the project was abandoned.

In 1860 Sir James Brunless and E. C. Webb proposed to Napoleon the Third a ship railway across the Suez Isthmus instead of the projected canal, but the proposition was rejected by de Lesseps. The same engineers prepared plans for the Government of Honduras, in 1872, for a similar transportation line from Puerto Caballos to Fonseca Bay, to carry ships of twelve hundred tons. The Republic failed to obtain the money necessary to carry out the plans.

The year after Eads' death the celebrated Chignecto Ship-railway was commenced, after years of preparation. It is now in successful operation over seventeen miles between the Bay of Fundy and the Gulf of St. Lawrence. The projected Hurontario Railway, of a similar character, will be sixty-six miles in length. Mere distance, however, whilst it enhances the cost of such an undertaking, does not necessarily increase the difficulty of it.

Eads' proposed line adhered in general to the course mapped for a canal. The length of the railway was to have been 134 miles. The summit of 736 feet is reached by easy grades, the heaviest being less than fifty-three feet in the mile. The railway was designed to carry vessels up to seven thousand tons, and the total cost of the line, lifting-docks, harbors, stations, shops, machinery and all other equipment was estimated at less than fifty millions.

In 1884 a treaty had been negotiated between the United States and Nicaragua for the construction of a canal by the former, to be owned by the two states jointly. Whilst it was under consideration in the Senate the treaty was withdrawn by the President for the reason that it proposed a perpetual alliance with Nicaragua and, like the Hise treaty, imposed obligations on the United States for the protection of the former country which it was inadvisable to assume.

In April, 1887, Nicaragua granted a concession to A. G. Menocal for the construction of a ship canal from Greytown to Brito. Thus far the story has been a recital of plans, projects, and theories. When we take up the thread of it in a later chapter it will be to recount active operations.

CHAPTER III

THE PANAMA RAILROAD

The great migration to the Pacific coast following the discovery of gold in "Forty-nine" acted as a strong incentive to the immediate establishment of an isthmian route by which the long and hazardous journey across the western territories of the United States might be avoided. In the last chapter a brief account was given of the enterprise conducted by the American Atlantic and Pacific Ship Canal Company, which, although it never effected its original purpose of opening a waterway, afforded valuable service to the gold-seekers in the early fifties by maintaining a transportation line across Nicaragua.

At the outset of the gold movement thousands made their way to California by way of the Isthmus of Panama. Steamships carried them from New York to the mouth of the Chagres. The journey thence to the Pacific coast, although no more than fifty miles by the trail, occupied from five to ten days and was accompanied by almost as much hardship and danger as in the days of Balboa. The emigrants were rowed or towed up the river by natives to a point near Cruces. The rest of the way to Panama was covered on foot or on mules. Women, when means would permit, were carried by *selleros*. These were native Indian porters, with a kind of chair strapped to their backs. There was, at that time, no regular steamship line between California and Panama. The travelers were often subjected to long and wearisome waits in the city. The old battery and the adjacent ramparts were favorite resorts of impatient watchers for a vessel from San Francisco, and their names and initials are cut in the stones by hundreds. On

EMPIRE-CHORRERA 16-FOOT MACADAM ROAD.

This road is being built with Zone convict labor and shows the excellent type of highways being constructed by the government.

more than one occasion epidemics made serious inroads among them. General Grant, in his memoirs, tells us that he was with the Seventh United States Infantry at Panama in 1852, en route to California, when cholera broke out. Fifteen per cent of the regiment succumbed to the disease and more than five hundred emigrants died of it. Cholera is not one of the prevalent diseases of the Isthmus. An influx of foreigners to Panama has always been accompanied by an outbreak of yellow fever, to which the natives are immune.

This transflux of travelers determined certain American capitalists to undertake the construction of a railroad across the Isthmus. A grant for the purpose had been made by the Government of New Granada to Mateo Kline on behalf of a French syndicate, in 1847, but it had expired by default in 1848. In the following year, William Henry Aspinwall, John Lloyd Stephens, Henry Chauncy, of New York, and their associates incorporated under the name of the Panama Railroad Company.

THE TERMS OF THE CONCESSION

Having declared all former similar concessions null and void, the Government of New Granada extended to this company the exclusive privilege of building a road and of operating it for a period of forty-nine years from the date of completion, which was to be not later than six years after the signing of the contract.

Subsequently this agreement was modified in important particulars, and in its present form entitles the company to "the use and possession of the railroad, the telegraph between Colon and Panama, the buildings, warehouses, and wharves belonging to the road, and in general all the dependencies and other works now in its possession necessary to the service and development of the enterprise for a period of ninety-nine years from the 16th day of August, 1867. At the expiration of this term the Government is to be substituted in all the rights of the company and is entitled to the immediate possession of the entire property. The Republic is bound to grant no privilege during this term to any other company or person to open any other railroad on the isthmus, nor without the consent of the company to open or work any maritime canal there to the west of a line drawn from Cape Tiburon, on the Atlantic, to Point Garachine, on the Pacific; nor to establish any such communication itself. But the company can not oppose the construction of a canal except directly along the route of its road, and the consent required is only to enable it to exact an equitable price for the privilege and as indemnification for the damages it may suffer by the competition of the canal. It is also stipulated that the company shall forfeit its privilege should it cede or transfer its rights to any foreign government."

THE GREAT DIFFICULTIES OF THE UNDERTAKING

When the Republic of Colombia superseded the Government of New Granada (1867), new requirements were imposed upon the railroad company. It was compelled to pay to Colombia a quarter of a million dollars annually and to "transport free of charge the troops, chiefs, and officers, and their equipage, ammunition, armament, clothing, and all similar effects that may belong to, are or may be destined for the immediate service of the Government of the Republic or the State of Panama, as also their officials in service or in commission, and those individuals who, with their families and baggage, may come to the country in the character of emigrants, and of new settlers with the permanent character of such, for account of the Government up to the number of 2,000 annually." This agreement was worked by the Colombian Government to the utmost, and the tremendous amount of "deadheading" with which the company was forced to put up cut into its profits seriously. Some idea of the extent to which this abuse was carried may be inferred from the fact that during the year 1903 the company carried 4,663 first-class passengers who paid their fares and 11,098 passengers and 6,601 troops free. In addition a considerable amount of freight was transported gratis under the agreement.

The Panama Railroad Company, with characteristic American energy, attacked the difficult undertaking without delay. The engineering staff was on the ground in the autumn of 1849. "Their quarters were on board a sailing ship. They worked by day, waist deep in mud and slime, making surveys and cutting a trail, and slept at night on their floating home. Nothing but the indomitable will and push for which Americans are justly praised could have overcome the terrible difficulties that met them at every step. The country was a howling wilderness, pestilential and death-dealing; the forests teemed with poisonous snakes and other equally unpleasant inhabitants; night was made hideous by the large, broad-chested, active mosquitoes of that part of the coast, who bite through clothing most successfully; the country produced absolutely nothing, and every mouthful of food had to come from New York. Despite these obstacles, that brave little band worked ahead, and kept on with their surveys. At the very outset they encountered the difficulty of finding a suitable location for the line traversing the quicksands and swamps between Colon of to-day and Gatun. It is reported that in some of the swamps the engineers under the late Colonel George M. Totten, and Mr. Trautwine, failed to find bottom at 180 feet. An embankment was created for the road by throwing in hundreds of cords of wood, rock, and more wood. This causeway, as it may be called, cost a fabulous sum of money; but at last it was completed and they floated their tracks, so to speak, over the swamps."*

Despite its ample resources and the unflagging application of its representatives in the field, the company at the end of two years had completed only about one-half of the

---

*Five Years in Panama. Wolfred Nelson, M.D., New York, 1889.

permanent way, or, to be more exact, the twenty-three miles between Colon and Barbacoas. The transportation of passengers and baggage across the Isthmus was, however, in operation. The railway line was used as far as it was completed; canoes were employed upon the Chagres to Gorgona or Cruces; and the remainder of the journey was performed by road.

SOME FEATURES OF THE CONSTRUCTION

At Paraiso, thirty-eight miles from the Atlantic, the line attained its greatest elevation, being 263 feet above the mean level of the ocean. Upon the western side of the divide the maximum grade was one in ninety; upon the Pacific slope it was a little more. Twenty-three miles of the road were level and twenty-five straight, but there were sharp curves in places. There were no fewer than one hundred and thirty-four culverts, drains, and bridges of ten feet and less, and as many as one hundred and seventy bridges from a twelve-foot span to the length of the Barbacoas. The line was still a single one with sidings when it was taken over by the Canal Commission in connection with the construction work on the canal. The railroad was paralleled by a telegraph line. Of this, Pim, in his "Gateway to the Pacific," says: "There are twenty-six posts to the mile, constructed in the following manner: A scantling four inches square, of pitch-pine, is encased in cement, molded in a cylindrical form, tapering toward the top, and sunk four feet in the ground. I was assured that when once dry these posts would last for ages. The cost of each was five dollars. They have the appearance of hewn stone and are quite an ornament along the line."

At the close of the year 1854 the construction had arrived at the divide. The Culebra pass afforded the greatest depression but it was practically two hundred and forty feet above sea level. The rails were carried over at this point and down the Pacific slope to Panama. On the 27th day of January, 1855, Colonel Totten went over the line upon the first locomotive to cross the American continent from ocean to ocean.

The utmost credit is due to the promoters of this great enterprise and to those who executed it. Aside from the important services the road has rendered to commerce during the past fifty years, its efficacy as a pioneer movement has been inestimable. The railroad opened the way over the Isthmus, stimulated the desire for a canal, and afforded indispensable facilities for its consummation.

The cost of the road was considerably in excess of the original estimate. After its opening to through traffic, many improvements were carried out, including the expensive bridge at Barbacoas, and it is probable that the outlay in establishing the route exceeded eight million dollars.

From Colon the road ran almost due south by west for more than seven miles until it met the Chagres at Gatun. Its general direction thereafter was south-easterly, along the valley of the river as far as San Pablo, the half-way point between the oceans.

THE FINE BRIDGE ACROSS THE CHAGRES

Here the Chagres was spanned by the splendid Barbacoas, which word itself, in the native language, signifies a bridge. It was built of iron over six hundred feet long, resting upon stone piers. It cost upwards of half a million dollars. During the dry season the river dwindles to a shallow, almost sluggish, stream, perhaps less than two hundred feet in width, but in the rains it becomes a torrent, sometimes far exceeding its normal bounds. Thus in 1878 the Chagres flooded its valley and rose to a height of fifteen feet over the railway. The earthquake of 1882 threw the bridge slightly out of alignment but apparently without seriously damaging it.

From San Pablo the road hugged the left bank of the river to Obispo, where it turned off suddenly at right angles to the stream. In the vicinity of Obispo is Cerro Gigante, the hill from whose summit Balboa is said to have gained his first view of the Pacific. There is no historic evidence on this point, and it seems more probable that if the exact spot could be ascertained it would be on one or the other of the heights that flank the Culebra pass. At Paraiso, on the Pacific slope, the company's engineers had an experience that is inseparable from excavation works in this part of the world. A cut had been made forty feet in depth and the rails laid along its bottom, when the torrential rain swept the earth back and covered the track at a depth of twenty feet. A similar occurrence befell the Panama Canal Company more than once, affording a warning to the American engineers which they have carefully heeded.

EXTRAORDINARY LABOR DIFFICULTIES

Reference has been made to some of the difficulties which were encountered in what Tomes ("Panama in 1885") characterizes as the "almost superhuman" task of building the railroad across the Isthmus of Panama. Not the least of these were involved in the efforts to secure an adequate supply of labor. It was soon found that the natives could not be counted upon to any extent. The company concluded to import Chinamen and a ship landed eight hundred of them at Panama. They immediately began to fall sick and in a week's time upward of a hundred were prostrated. The interpreters attributed this to the deprivation of their accustomed opium. A quantity of the drug was distributed to them and had a marked effect for the better, but, to quote Tomes, "a Maine opium law was soon promulgated on the score of the immorality of administering to so pernicious a habit, and without regard, it is hoped, to the expense, which, however, was no inconsiderable item, since the daily quota of each Chinese amounted to fifteen grains, at a cost of at least fifteen cents." Deprived of what from long habit had become a necessary stimulant and subjected to the depressing effect of the unaccustomed climate, the coolies lost all vigor and courage. In less than two months after their arrival there was hardly one of the original number fit to wield a pick or shovel. They gave themselves up to despair and sought death by whatever means came nearest to hand. Some sat on the shore and stoically awaited the rising tide, nor did they stir until the sea swallowed them. Some hanged themselves by their queues or used those appendages to strangle themselves. By various methods hundreds put an end to the misery of their existence. The remnant, fewer than two hundred, sick and useless, were shipped to Jamaica.

The next experiment of the railroad company was hardly less disastrous. A number of Irish laborers were imported at considerable expense, but, although the mortality amongst them was not so great as that experienced from the Chinese, it is said that the company failed to secure a single good day's labor from one of them. A great number were buried on the Isthmus and the remainder were sent to New York, where most of them died from the effects of the fever contracted in the south.*

The road was finally completed with the labor of some three thousand men of mixed races, but chiefly negroes from Jamaica and East Indian coolies.

THE CANAL COMPANY SECURES THE RAILROAD

The Panama Canal Company learned at an early stage in its operations that control of the railroad was essential to the success of its project. In the fall of 1879 the stock was offered to de Lesseps for $14,000,000, being at the rate of $200 each for 70,000 shares. This would appear to have been a very fair price when the worth of the line to the canal

---

* It should be stated that the late Colonel George M. Totten, chief engineer of the road, threw discredit upon these statements of excessive mortality which, however, have emanated from several apparently reliable authorities. Colonel Totten repeatedly stated that the number of men employed in the construction of the railroad at no time exceeded 7,000 and that the total deaths among the laborers during the five years of the operation were not in excess of 1,200. If we assume an average of 5,000 laborers per annum, probably an underestimate, we have a mortality of 48 per thousand, an incredibly low figure, when the conditions under which the road was built and the later experiences of the French are considered.

company is considered and the fact that its extremely profitable business, which had returned profits ranging from twelve to twenty-two per cent per annum, was in prospect of practical annihilation on the completion of the waterway. De Lesseps, however, perhaps hoping to secure better terms, declined the proposition. The construction of the canal was commenced early in the following year but the operations were obstructed at every step by the railroad company, which instituted a systematic scheme of delay in the delivery of goods to the canal company. At length it was forced upon de Lesseps that the American corporation commanded the situation, and he decided to buy the company's shares. But in the meanwhile they had been steadily advancing, and when the transfer was effected the price had risen to $250 a share. Six-sevenths of the entire stock was sold to the Panama Canal Company,* the remainder being retained in American hands for the purpose of keeping the charter alive.

With the opening of the railroad a large traffic across the Isthmus sprang into existence and grew rapidly with the advance of time. The products of Asia and the countries upon the Pacific coast of America were carried from Panama to Colon, there to be distributed amongst steamships making the ports of Europe, Canada, the United States and the West Indies. Moving in the reverse direction, goods from these countries reached, by the same transisthmian route, South and Central America and San Francisco. From the last named port reshipment was made to the Pacific islands and points on the Asian mainland. A number of steamship lines made regular calls at the terminal ports of the railroad. The line occupied a commanding position as the essential link in this chain of traffic, and took full advantage of the fact. Its charges were exorbitant and its profits enormous for many years. Its rates were based on, in general, fifty per cent of the through tariff. For instance, of

---

*The company has been generally known in America by this name, but its corporate title was "La Compagnie Universelle du Canal Interoceanique de Panama."

COLUMBUS AND THE INDIAN MAIDEN.

This beautiful bronze statue of the Great Discoverer overlooks the Atlantic entrance to the Canal, beholding at last the "New Route to India."

THE PANAMA RAILROAD

the total cost of shipping goods from New York to Valparaiso, one half represented the charge of the railroad company for its share of the carriage. In some instances this policy of mulcting the shipper excessively resulted in loss of business. For many years the road carried enormous quantities of coffee to Europe. The through rate was about thirty dollars per ton. The railroad company received fifteen dollars and the two steamship companies that handled the goods divided a similar sum. In the early eighties a German line commenced to run to South and Central American ports by way of the Straits of Magellan. In a very short while this line had secured all the coffee shipments and much other freight that had previously been sent across the Isthmus.

However, the railroad company was not seriously affected by these diversions, and in the course of time it entered into an agreement with the Pacific Steamship Company which created a condition in the nature of a monopoly, to which reference will be had again.

THE LONG CALMS ON THE PACIFIC COAST

Tramp steamers often make the ports on either side of the Isthmus, and many sailing vessels put in at Colon. The latter are less frequent visitors at Panama on account of the calm that prevails on that coast. Such craft have been known to leave the latter port and return for fresh supplies after lying in the doldrums for weeks without being able to get away. There was the case of the British bark *Straun*, which cleared from Panama in May of the year 1884. After getting out of the Gulf she beat about between latitudes four and six for months and finally put back to port after being out one hundred and five days.

THE ASSETS OF THE RAILROAD AND THEIR VALUE

When the United States Government purchased the property of the Panama Canal Company it acquired 68,887 of the 70,000 shares of the railroad company and afterward bought up the remainder.

The property of the railroad company transfer ed to the United States Government consisted of about forty eight miles of single track with twenty-six miles of sidings; thirty-five locomotives, thirty passenger cars, more than nine hundred freight cars and a quantity of miscellaneous rolling stock. The equipment, like everything else that came from the hands of the French company, was in a condition of unnecessary deterioration. The railroad company owned repair shops, wharves and buildings at both Panama and Colon, and almost the entire island of Manzanillo, upon which the latter city stands, was its property. It held large parcels of real estate along the line, aside from the land actually occupied by the road, and had with the Pacific Mail Steamship Company, an undivided half interest in the islands of Naos, Culebra, Perico, and Flamenco, all in Panama Bay. It was also the proprietor of three steamships having an average tonnage of about twenty-seven thousand. The entire property, "cost of road, real estate, and equipment," including the steamships, tugs, lighters, etc., was carried on the books at what would seem to be the conservative valuation of a little over twelve millions and a half.

As soon as the Government assumed charge of the railroad, complaints of the traffic monopoly were made by shippers who had been without means of redress under the old conditions. The justice of these complaints was fully recognized by the authorities. General Davis, the first governor of the Canal Zone, severely criticised the management of the road, and Secretary Taft, in the report to which reference has already been made, says: " . . . Whatever may have justified the rates charged by the railroad company, the salaries paid by it, and the character of its corporate organization, and the expenses of the office in New York, certainly for the purposes and under the control of the United States, radical changes must be made."

A contract existed between the railroad company and the Pacific Mail Steamship Company, which secured to the latter concern the exclusive privilege of issuing through bills of lading on freight from San Francisco to New York. Mr. Taft expressed the opinion that this contract was "invalid under the laws of Colombia and the laws of Panama." The Panama Railroad Company ran three cargo steamers on the Atlantic side, between New York and Colon, and would recognize no through bills of lading except those issued from its office in New York. Goods shipped across the Isthmus by any other line were charged the heavy local freight rates in force between Panama and Colon. This arrangement, together with its control of the docking facilities at Colon, most effectually enabled the company to shut out any competition in the Atlantic carrying trade.

SUGGESTED RAILROAD AND STEAMSHIP TRAFFIC REFORMS

Early in 1905, Joseph W. Bristow was commissioned to investigate the situation under consideration. After an examination extending over several months he substantiated the foregoing facts and made the following recommendations: That the road should be continued as a commercial line, that it should be double-tracked, equipped with modern rolling stock, and supplied with additional wharves and other improvements; that the rates for through freight should be made as low as the cost of the service and provision for a fair dividend will permit; that the steamship line maintained by the road between Colon and New York should be continued by the Government; that the exclusive contracts with the Pacific Mail Steamship Company and the two South American west coast lines should be cancelled, "and the ports of Colon and Panama be opened to the use of all steamship lines on equal terms;" that in case a new steamship line be not established within reasonable time by private capital between Colon and the Gulf ports, the railroad company should establish and maintain such a line (it is cheaper and more convenient to move the products of the Mississippi Valley by way of these ports than through New York); that in the event of the Pacific Mail Steamship Company discontinuing its service between San Francisco and Panama some other private corporation should be encouraged to take its place, but failing this, the Panama Railroad Company should run a line of steamers over the route.

It will be seen that the report contemplated a considerable extension of the Government's commercial operations, but only as alternative measures to be resorted to in case the desired objects could not be attained through private enterprise. Mr. Bristow recommended favoring American ships in traffic relations as far as might be consistent with treaty obligations, but, upon the theory that the railroad was performing the functions of a canal, he did not deem it practicable to discriminate to the advantage of American bottoms at the ports of Panama and Colon.

The report met with the approval of the Government, and steps were taken to carry out its general recommendations.

THE RELOCATED PANAMA RAILROAD

A first necessity was to relay the line so that its tracks would at all times be above the level of Gatun Lake after the opening of the canal; a task nearly as costly as building the entire road anew.

The new, or relocated line of the Panama Railroad, is 47.11 miles long, or 739 feet longer than the old line. From Colon to Mindi, 4.17 miles, and from Corozal to Panama, 2.83 miles, the old line is used but the remaining 40 miles are new road. From Mindi to Gatun the railroad runs, in general, parallel to the Canal, and ascends from a few feet above tide water elevation to 95 feet above. At Gatun the road leaves the vicinity of the Canal and turns east along Gatun Ridge to a point about 4½ miles from the center line of the Canal, where it turns southward again and crosses the low Gatun Valley to Monte Lirio, from which point it skirts the east shore of Gatun Lake to the beginning of the Culebra Cut at Bas Obispo. In the Gatun Valley section there are several immense embankments, necessary to place the line above the lake level, which in the 3-mile section, aggregate about 5,000,000 cubic yards. Likewise, near the north end of Culebra Cut, where the line is located so as to furnish waste dumps for spoil from the Canal, there are several very heavy embankments. Originally it was intended to carry the railroad through Culebra Cut on a 40-foot berm along the east side, 10 feet above the water level, but the numerous slides have made this plan impracticable, and a line is now constructed, on a high level around the Cut, known locally as the Gold Hill Line. Leaving the berm of the Canal at Bas Obispo, the Gold Hill Line cuts through a ridge of solid rock, and gradually works into the foot hills, reaching a distance from the center line of the Canal of 2 miles opposite Culebra; thence it runs down the Pedro Miguel Valley to Paraiso, where it is only 800 feet from the center line of the Canal. This section of the line is located on a maximum grade of $1\frac{1}{4}$ per cent, compensated, and has a total length of $9\frac{3}{8}$ miles. The sharpest curve on the whole line is 7°. From the south end of Culebra Cut at Paraiso, the railroad runs practically parallel with the Canal to Panama, with maximum grade of 0.45 per cent. Where the railroad crosses the Gatun River, near Monte Lirio, a steel girder bridge has been erected, the center span of which will be made into a lift span where the Gatun Lake is formed, to permit access to the upper arm of the lake. The Chagres River at Gamboa is crossed on a steel girder bridge, $\frac{1}{4}$-mile long, with one 200-foot through truss channel span. Numerous other rivers and small streams are crossed on reinforced concrete culverts. Near Miraflores, a tunnel 736 feet long has been built through a hill. The total cost of the new line has been $8,866,392.02.

At present the Panama Railroad is relatively the busiest

line in the world. During 1910 the freight movement over its fifty miles of roadbed approximated 300,000,000 tons. Whilst the commercial traffic is considerable, it accounts for but a fractional part of the whole. The great bulk of the material carried consists of spoil from the works, and supplies for the Commission. The engineering department of the Canal operates about 300 miles of construction trackage and the Panama Railroad acts as a clearing house for its traffic. It receives the dirt trains loaded and returns them empty. From 700 to 800 dirt trains a day are handled, each composed of a locomotive and 18 flat cars, the full load being 500 tons.

The passenger traffic on this little railroad is also extraordinarily great. All day long employees are journeying between the many towns that are strung along the line. During the year about 1,500,000 passengers are carried. In the mornings and evenings closely packed laborers' trains of a special type are run.

It is hardly necessary to state that as an adjunct to the canal construction the railroad is of the highest importance —indeed, it is a *sine qua non*. With the completion of the waterway, the road will lapse into the condition of a mere local line between Colon and Panama. It should, nevertheless, continue to be a valuable property in the hands of either the Government or a private corporation. As a means of transporting men and material employed in the operation of the completed canal it will always be of service. It is probable that a considerable amount of freight will be reshipped even after the canal is opened. Many voyagers will leave vessels at the point of entering the canal in order to avoid what will generally be an unpleasant passage and secure the opportunity of spending a few hours in Panama by making the transit by rail. Both the terminal ports, but especially Panama, must grow rapidly under the influences of future traffic and the local business of the railroad will be proportionately increased.

CHAPTER IV

THE ISTHMIAN COUNTRY

During recent years the ribbon of land that joins the continents of North and South America has loomed large in the public eye.

Since the days of Greece's glory no such small strip of soil as the Isthmus of Panama has gained equal distinction. It has been the scene of stirring adventure and the site of the wealthiest city in the world. It has been the subject of epoch-making diplomacy and a sphere for political disturbances. It is the seat of the greatest engineering enterprise in history; an enterprise which is destined to largely revolutionize the commerce of the earth and, more than any other modern factor, to influence the fortunes of nations.

In the second decade of the sixteenth century Angel Saavedra mooted the idea of a canal through this narrow neck of inter-ocean territory. Since that time the thought could not be banished from the minds of men though a King of Spain decreed death to any who should voice it. For two hundred years and more plans and projects for the great waterway have been advanced. The first attempt to construct it ended in a cataclysmal failure. In these early years of the twentieth century the opening of a passage is at length assured, and it will be available to the traffic of the world almost, perhaps exactly, four hundred years from the discovery of the Pacific.

THE ISTHMUS OF PANAMA

The neck of land separating the two great oceans of the globe, which is called the Isthmus of Panama, forms the southern termination of the great American isthmus extending north to Mexico. This strip of land curving about four hundred and seventy miles from west to east has commonly been styled the Isthmus of Darien, but that name is more properly applied to the section of country between the Gulfs of Uraba and San Miguel. The Isthmus of Panama is traversed along its entire length by the Cordillera de Baudo, separated from the Andes by the Valley of the Atrato which marks the northern limit of South America. Erroneous impressions are apt to be created by the usual practice of studying geography with the aid of the ordinary flat maps, which have the effect of exaggerating the size of countries in high latitudes and diminishing the equatorial areas. One thousand miles in latitude 60 degrees occupies upon the ordinary map twice as much space as does one thousand miles along the equator. It is a revelation to many a well-informed person to learn that South America is very nearly as large as North America. For the study of the Panama Canal in its relations to the rest of the world the use of a globe, or a map on the polyconic projection is recommended. Another point worth noticing in this connection is that the most pronounced diversion from the general north and south trend of the Americas is found in the Isthmus of Panama, which takes a lateral direction east and west and throws the southern continent, so to speak, to the east of the northern, so that a line dropped due south from New York would pass through the Pacific Ocean off the coast of Chile.

In looking at a map of the western hemisphere we are accustomed to finding the Atlantic Ocean to the east or on the right hand. For this reason a sectional map of the Canal region is likely to be a little confusing at first glance. It will show the Pacific on the right and the Atlantic on the opposite side of the page. This is due to the fact that the Isthmus makes a northerly loop in the portion containing the Canal Zone, and Panama is actually east of Colon, from which port the Canal will take a south-easterly direction to its Pacific terminus. A line from Buffalo continued south

THE CHURCH OF SAN FRANCISCO, PANAMA.
An excellent example of Spanish architecture.

THE ISTHMIAN COUNTRY 61

would bisect the Canal and leave Panama on the right and Colon on the left.

The writer finds an excuse for these explanations in the knowledge that many intelligent persons have been puzzled by the unfamiliar geographical conditions involved.

POLITICAL CHANGES IN PANAMA AND COLOMBIA

Having secured their independence from Spain, the provinces of Venezuela, Ecuador, Colombia, and Panama formed a republican federation. Subsequently, the two first-named seceded, and Panama with Colombia established the United Sovereign States of New Granada. Although each of the states combined in this political union exercised sovereign powers, the paramount authority in the territory became gradually centralized at Bogota. In 1861, against the wishes of the leading citizens of Panama, the United States of Colombia were organized with a new constitution conferring greater powers on the government at Bogota. Twenty-five years later, after a civil war in which many lives were lost, Colombia succeeded in establishing the republic which took her name. By this measure Panama lapsed to the condition of a mere department with a governor appointed by the Colombian president and vested with little independent authority. The Panamans, whilst forced to submit to this degradation, have always protested against it and have consistently declared their right to the position of a constitutional state. The government of Panama by the corrupt Colombian politicians had always been bad, and the people of the Isthmus had entertained the design of independence for years before America opened negotiations for the Canal and, indeed, had enjoyed it for three years following 1857.

THE REVOLUTION OF PANAMA

Panama threw off the yoke of Colombia at an extremely opportune time as regards the plans of the United States for the construction of the Isthmian Canal. The coincidence of the event was the only basis for the utter nonsense written in this country upon the subject at the time. While the opportunity was seized most promptly by our executive officials, doubtless saving the delays of lengthy and expensive negotiations, there is absolutely no ground for the accusation that the American authorities instigated the *coup* which gave independence to the Isthmus, but, on the contrary, sufficient evidence that, although they may have had some inkling of the attempt before its occurrence, they were entirely free from participation in it. The suspected representatives of our Government have denied that any American official instigated or assisted in the revolt. In this they are borne out by the statements of the leading Panaman revolutionists and by Doctor Herran, the Colombian Minister to Washington at the time.

The Hay-Herran Treaty was negotiated at Washington in 1903 between the representatives of the Governments of the United States and the Republic of Colombia. Its purpose was to secure to the former state the privilege of making a canal through the Isthmus of Panama. Colombia was to authorize the French company to sell out to the United States and to give a strip of land thirty miles wide for a Canal Zone over which Colombia should retain sovereignty but the United States have police control. The United States was to pay ten millions of dollars at once and one hundred thousand yearly after the ninth year. The national legislature of the latter country, moved it is believed by the hope of inducing us to pay a higher price, failed to ratify the treaty.

A COMIC OPERA COUP D'ÉTAT

The Panamans are much more astute than is generally supposed. They had realized fully the enormous advantages that would accrue to their country from the operation of the Canal by America, and when the opportunity seemed to be in danger of destruction by the action of the

THE ISTHMIAN COUNTRY

Colombian politicians, the leading men in Panama who, as has been said, have harbored thoughts of independence for years, determined to take matters into their own hands. No doubt they calculated, as they reasonably might, upon the United States acknowledging them as soon as they had knocked off their shackles. The revolution was bloodless and savored of *opera bouffe* in the absurdity of its details. The Government of Bogota learned of the plot before it was put into execution and despatched several hundreds of the ragamuffins that composed its "army" to Panama under Generals Tobal and Amaya, with orders to arrest the conspirators and carry them to the capital. When the detachment arrived at Colon the generals hurried forward over the railroad with their warrants and were promptly placed in confinement by the revolutionary leaders.

Meanwhile, Colonel Shaler, the Superintendent of the Panama Railroad, unquestionably placed impediments in the way of the further progress of the troops. It must be remembered, however, that Colonel Shaler, although an American, was not an official and acted as the representative of the corporation which was interested in the sale of the canal property to the United States, for the Panama Canal Company owned the railway.

The sympathy of the American Government and people was unquestionably with the Panamans, but they received no official aid from this country.

Marines were landed from an American gunboat and two days later the Colombian troops took ship for Cartagena. Panama immediately declared itself an independent republic and was recognized by the United States without delay.

THE AMERICAN PART IN THE AFFAIR

There is reason to believe that the Colombian soldiers were bribed—at the rate of about five dollars apiece—by friends of Panama, but the statement that the money was distributed or handled by an officer of the American Navy is a gross and stupid libel. The presence of the marines was without a doubt a decisive factor in the accomplishment of the revolution, but that it was not premeditated and had no other purpose than the protection of American lives is proved by the following official report of the officer commanding the *Nashville:*

"U. S. S. *Nashville*, Third Rate.
"Colon, U. S. Colombia, November 5, 1903.
"Sir: Pending a complete report of the occurrences of the last three days in Colon, Colombia, I most respectfully invite the Department's attention to those of the date of Wednesday, November 4, which amounted to practically the making of war against the United States by the officer in command of the Colombian troops in Colon. At 1 o'clock p. m. on that date I was summoned on shore by a preconcerted signal, and on landing met the United States consul, vice-consul, and Colonel Shaler, the general superintendent of the Panama Railroad.

"The consul informed me that he had received notice from the officer commanding the Colombian troops, Colonel Torres, through the prefect of Colon, to the effect that if the Colombian officers, Generals Tobal and Amaya, who had been seized in Panama on the evening of November 3, by the independents, and held as prisoners, were not released by 2 o'clock P. M., he, Torres, would open fire on the town of Colon and kill every United States citizen in the place, and my advice and action were requested. I advised that all the United States citizens should take refuge in the shed of the Panama Railroad Company, a stone building susceptible of being put into good state of defense, and that I would immediately land such body of men, with extra arms for arming the citizens, as the complement of the ship would permit.

UNITED STATES MARINES ARE LANDED

"This was agreed to, and I immediately returned on board, arriving at 1.15 P. M. The order for landing was immediately given, and at 1.30 P. M. the boats left the ship with a party of forty-two men under the command of Lieutenant-Commander H. M. Witzel, with Midshipman J. P. Jackson as second in command. Time being pressing, I gave verbal orders to Mr. Witzel to take the building referred to above, to put it into the best state of defense possible, and protect the lives of the citizens assembled there—not firing unless fired upon. The women and children took refuge on the German steamer *Marcomania* and the Panama Railroad steamer *City of Washington*, both ready to haul out from dock if necessary.

"The *Nashville* got under way and patrolled along the water-front, close in and ready to use either small arm or shrapnel fire. The Colombians surrounded the building of the railroad company almost immediately after we had taken possession, and for about one and a half hours their attitude was most threatening, it being seemingly their purpose to provoke an attack. Happily our men were cool and steady, and while the tension was very great no shot was fired.

"At about 3.15 P. M. Colonel Torres came into the building for an interview and expressed himself as most friendly to the Americans, claiming that the whole affair was a misapprehension, and that he would like to send the *alcalde* of Colon to Panama to see General Tobal and have him direct the discontinuance of the show of force. A special train was furnished and safe conduct guaranteed. At about 5.30 P. M. Colonel Torres made the proposition of withdrawing his troops to Monkey Hill if I would withdraw the *Nashville's* force and leave the town in possession of the police until the return of the *alcalde* on the morning of the 5th.

THE NERVE OF AMERICAN MARINES PREVENTS A CONFLICT WITH COLOMBIA

"After an interview with the United States consul and Colonel Shaler as to the probability of good faith in the matter, I decided to accept the proposition and brought my men on board, the disparity in numbers between my force and that of the Colombians—nearly ten to one—making me desirous of avoiding a conflict so long as the object in view—the protection of American citizens—was not imperiled.

"I am positive that the determined attitude of our men, their coolness and evident intention of standing their ground, had a most salutary and decisive effect on the immediate situation, and was the initial step in the ultimate abandoning of Colon by these troops and their return to Cartagena the following day. Lieutenant-Commander Witzel is entitled to much praise for his admirable work in command on the spot.

"I feel that I can not sufficiently represent to the Department the grossness of this outrage and the insult to our dignity, even apart from the savagery of the threat.

"Very respectfully,
"JOHN HUBBARD,
"Commander, United States Navy, Commanding.
"The Secretary of the Navy,
    Navy Department, Washington, D. C."

In his more detailed report Commander Hubbard stated: "I beg to assure the Department that I had no part whatever in the negotiations that were carried on between Colonel Torres and the representatives of the provisional government; that I landed an armed force only when the lives of American citizens were threatened, and withdrew this force as soon as there seemed to be no grounds for further apprehension of injury to American lives or property; that I relanded an armed force because of the failure of Colonel Torres to carry out his agreement to withdraw and announced intention of returning; and that my attitude throughout was strictly neutral as between the two parties, my only purpose being to protect the lives and property of American citizens and to preserve the free and uninterrupted transit of the isthmus."

THE ISTHMIAN COUNTRY

THE PRESIDENT'S DENIAL OF OFFICIAL COMPLICITY

President Roosevelt, referring to the foregoing reports, says: "This plain official account of the occurrences of November 4 shows that instead of there having been too much prevision by the American Government for the maintenance of order and the protection of life and property on the isthmus, the orders for the movement of the American warships had been too long delayed: so long, in fact, that there were but forty-two marines and sailors available to land and protect the lives of American men and women. . . . At Panama, when the revolution broke out, there was no American man-of-war and no American troops or sailors. At Colon Commander Hubbard acted with entire impartiality toward both sides, preventing any movement, whether by the Colombians or the Panamanians, which would tend to produce bloodshed. On November 9 he prevented a body of the revolutionists from landing at Colon."

In his message to Congress the President made the following reference to the treaty and the complications which grew out of it: "During all the years of negotiation and discussion that preceded the conclusion of the Hay-Herran treaty, Colombia never intimated that the requirement by the United States of control over the canal strip would render unattainable the construction of a canal by way of the Isthmus of Panama; nor were we advised, during the months when legislation of 1902 was pending before the Congress, that the terms which it embodied would render negotiations with Colombia impracticable. It is plain that no nation could construct and guarantee the neutrality of the canal with a less degree of control than was stipulated for in the Hay-Herran treaty. A refusal to grant such degree of control was necessarily a refusal to make any practicable treaty at all. Such refusal therefore squarely raised the question whether Colombia was entitled to bar the transit of the world's traffic across the isthmus. . . . Colombia, after having rejected the treaty in spite of our protests and warnings when it was in her power to accept it, has since shown the utmost eagerness to accept the same treaty if only the *status quo* could be restored. One of the men standing highest in the official circles of Colombia on November 6 addressed the American minister at Bogota, saying that if the Government of the United States would land troops to preserve Colombian sovereignty and the transit, the Colombian Government would 'declare martial law, and, by virtue of vested constitutional authority, when public order is disturbed, (would) approve by decree the ratification of the canal treaty as signed; or, if the Government of the United States prefers, (would) call an extra session of the Congress—with new and friendly members—next May to approve the treaty.'

"Having these facts in view, there is no shadow of a question that the Government of the United States proposed a treaty that was not only just, but generous to Colombia, which our people regarded as erring, if at all, on the side of overgenerosity, which was hailed with delight by the people of the immediate locality through which the canal was to pass, who were most concerned as to the new order of things, and which the Colombian authorities now recognize as being so good that they are willing to promise its unconditional ratification if only we will desert those who have shown themselves our friends and restore to those who have shown themselves unfriendly the power to undo what they did. I pass by the question as to what assurance we have that they would now keep their pledge and not again refuse to ratify the treaty if they had the power; for, of course, I will not for one moment discuss the possibility of the United States committing an act of such baseness as to abandon the new Republic of Panama."

DESCRIPTION OF THE ISTHMUS OF PANAMA

The recognition of the independence of Panama by the United States was followed by a treaty between the two countries which will be referred to in a succeeding chapter.

STEAM SHOVEL LOADING ROCK.

These great machines which are able to dig out and load several tons of material at each operation have made the rapid progress in digging the Canal possible.

The physical features of the Isthmus of Panama are very diversified. The center of the country is occupied by mountains and hills. In some parts these elevations extend to the coast, but usually they are flanked by alluvial plains or gently rolling country. This again is fringed by a strip of coastal swamp covered with mangroves. Heavy forest and dense jungle clothe the mountain districts. The growth is so strong and rapid that the railroad company has to maintain a constant fight against its inroads. If not checked it would in six months bury the line. The Chagres is the principal river in every respect, but there are a number of smaller streams.

The territory of the Republic of Panama is divided into provinces and these into municipal districts. The canal route traverses two of these provinces—those of Colon and Panama. Their prosperity is assured by the American enterprise now in process of development.

THE INHOSPITABLE SAN BLAS COUNTRY

The province of Darien is not a promising region. It is largely made up of mountainous wilderness and impassable swamps. Rumor has persistently credited the San Blas district with rich gold deposits, but verification is rendered difficult by the unfriendly attitude of the Indians there, who have always displayed an unconquerable objection to the presence of white men. The San Blas Indians occasionally visit Panama on trading or marketing excursions, but they are reticent about their country and their affairs and decidedly averse to any but the most temporary relations with foreigners. The provinces of Chiriqui and Veragua support industries of considerable importance and appear to be capable of much greater development under favorable conditions. David, the capital of Chiriqui, occupies an extremely picturesque site upon a well-wooded coast. Behind the town stretches a fertile savanna backed by a range of mountains from two to three thousand feet in height. It is one of those quaint old settlements with which the traveler in Spanish-America becomes familiar, but he never tires of the air of restful simplicity that pervades them. The houses, generally one story in height, are square whitewashed structures with roofs of red tile and front verandas. The inhabitants are hospitable, contented and inclined to take life easily. Several of them are well-to-do and not a few highly cultured.

THE ANCIENT GRAVES OF CHIRIQUI

Chiriqui became suddenly famous several years ago on account of the interesting relics that were unearthed there from the *guacas*, or graves, of the ancient inhabitants. A great number of these treasures were found in the district of David. "History is silent about the people who are buried in thousands there. The discovery of these old cemeteries came about in this wise: Many, many years ago in cutting a trench through a peaceful forest to drain off water, the Indian diggers came across an image of gold. Great was their surprise and the *execrable sedd'ore*, or 'the cursed thirst of gold,' settled upon that primitive people like a nightmare. They kept on digging, and unearthed quantities of golden ornaments and images of various kinds. Soon hundreds were digging in the forest, and it has been estimated that gold ornaments were uncovered to a value exceeding $400,000 in a space of five or six years. They were sold for weight, or value in coin, and went into the melting pot. Later, some archæologists took an interest in the matter, and some systematic work was done, they directing and the natives doing the digging. It would seem that in the majority of cases the graves first were dug, their sides lined with pieces of stone, and then cross pieces were laid over these. Inside, the pottery was placed, together with ornaments of gold, cooking utensils, etc. The graves of the poorer class contained nothing but cooking utensils and no gold ornaments were found in them.

"A native locates a grave by tapping the earth as he walks along. As soon as he gets a hollow sound familiar to his expert ear he commences digging and digs down. The contents are stone implements, pottery implements, ornaments and pure gold, and ornaments of gold gilt, a species of pinchbeck, called by the natives here *tumbago*. There are also ornaments in copper, and a few bone instruments.

"There are a number of small idols in stone, varying from nine to eighteen inches high. There is also a species of grinding stone, on which they evidently ground their corn, or its equivalent. The better class of these grinding stones were from eighteen to twenty-four inches in length, and from twelve to fifteen inches in width. I am now speaking of some of the largest. They were concave on top, and in the graves were found stone rollers fitting the upper surface. Generally they were made to represent some animal.

CURIOUS IMPLEMENTS OF A BY-GONE RACE

"There were some with tiger-shaped heads and four legs. The tail generally folded around and rested on the left hind leg. A commoner type of grinding stone resembled a low stool of stone without any ornamentation. In the graves were found an endless variety of stone chisels and stone hatchets. Some of these chisels and hatchets were beautifully proportioned, presenting various planes and surfaces for examination, and their edges in many instances were sharp even after having been exposed for long centuries to the effects of that humid soil. These were the implements with which the people did all their carving.

"In the pottery implements the variety was almost endless, not only suggesting considerable ingenuity, but also some knowledge of the anatomy of the human body. Between many of these pieces of pottery and the male angels on the doors of La Merced, at Panama, there was a striking analogy. . . . Roughly classifying the pottery utensils, they were of two kinds, glazed and unglazed, and many of the markings on them had been made in black and red pigments. Many of the borders, while crude, were very suggestive. There was a series of gods, little squat figures with triangular faces; nearly all of which had been glazed and were ornamental. Their pectoral development was remarkable. It is supposed that they were a kind of idol. . . . Then there were rattles of ingenious construction, with which they soothed the gentle baby in early days. There was a series of whistles (it is supposed that they were bird calls) producing all sorts of notes, from a full rich sound to a gentle twitter. . . .

THE MYSTIC FROG OF THE EARLY INDIANS

"Among the gold ornaments found in the *guacas* at Chiriqui were many frogs. The frog seems to have been a favorite type of ornament with those early races. The largest frog of pure gold uncovered there weighed eighteen ounces. . . . Another thing that seemed very strange to me was a kind of bell. It was of gold, and an exact counterpart of the oldtime sleigh-bells, or those with a slot. It had a handle and within were little pieces of metal, and these little bells, when shaken, emitted quite a musical sound. . . . Among the *tumbago* ornaments the majority represented birds or frogs. From a careful examination of a number of them the body seemed to be made of copper covered with a film of gold. How it was put on I am unable to say, but certainly gold it was. . . . I saw another specimen which caused me a deal of speculation. It evidently was intended for the figure of a king. It was in bronze, and that surprised me greatly, because the art of casting in bronze is deemed an art to this day."*

By classifying these discoveries it is shown that the Isthmian Indians were about on the same level of civilization

---
* Wolfred Nelson.

as the Indians of Mexico and Peru. They were in a later stage than the stone and bronze age.

THE MINERAL RESOURCES OF PANAMA

It is very probable that with the exploitation that is likely to follow the opening of the Canal, the Isthmus will prove to have rich and extensive mineral resources. Gold, copper, manganese, and coal are known to exist in different parts, but the greater portion of the country is yet to be subjected to geological surveys. When the waterway comes into use a great market for coal will be established at Panama and the demand will doubtless lead to the operation of local mines. The island of Muerto, near David, is said to be almost a solid mass of coal covered with a stratum of clay. As early as 1851 the geologists, Whiting and Schuman, made a report on this deposit which was published in London. Here would seem to be a favorable opportunity for American capital and enterprise.

There are large areas of good grazing ground in the western provinces, and the industry has been pursued to some extent. When the Canal is in use there will be a ready and profitable market for meat at Panama and cattle raising should become one of the chief industries of this section.

The country about the Chiriqui Bay already has a large and flourishing fruit trade. The entire region in the neighborhood of the Costa Rica border is exceeding rich—as rich as any in the tropics, perhaps. It might be developed with comparative ease. It has a pleasant and salubrious climate. The people are genial and hospitable; well disposed towards Americans and eager for improvement.

THE FAMOUS PEARL ISLANDS OF PANAMA BAY

The famous Pearl Islands lie in the Gulf about forty miles off the city of Panama. By the Spaniards they were called the King's Archipelago. The pearl fisheries are of very ancient origin. Balboa secured a number of the gems from the Indians, and was told by them that the pearl oyster had been sought in these waters during uncountable ages. At one time these fisheries were probably as rich as any in the world, but reckless methods injured them, and whilst they are still worked in a desultory fashion, it may be said that the old beds are practically exhausted.

The pearls of Panama have always been noted for their size. It is said that specimens as large as filberts have been found. They are very lustrous and have a silvery sheen, differing from the creamy shade of the pearl of Ceylon.

The native Panamans are a more attractive people than one would be led to suppose from the accounts of travelers who have only come in contact with the lower classes in the city of Panama who are a mixed and far from representative lot.

It has long been a practice with the well-to-do creole families to send their children of both sexes to the best colleges of Europe and America. Consequently the upper class is distinguished by refinement and culture as well as many natural qualities of an admirable character. They entertain the strongest feelings of admiration and respect for the American people, and, if we may judge from recent experiences, our relations to the Panamans will continue without difficulty or friction.

The disbandment of the army by President Amador was effected with little trouble because of the kindly intervention of the American minister, whose advice was accepted by both sides in a friendly spirit. It is doubtful if any other South American Republic could attempt the retirement of the entire military force, no matter how weak, without precipitating a revolution.

The *rancheros* of the country districts are peacefully inclined and contented with their simple pastoral life. They live in huts of the simplest construction and till a few acres of ground. Their wants are very few and easily supplied. The condition of the peon will be improved with the general prosperity that is in store for the Isthmus.

Except upon the coasts the climate of the Isthmus is not worse than that of the average tropical region and in some parts of the territory it is quite healthful and pleasant. Hundreds of Americans have been employed by the railroad and many of them have enjoyed excellent health during residences extending from ten to twenty years. The average temperature is about eighty degrees and there is generally a refreshing breeze from the north. The humidity in the rainy season is great and its effect very enervating to natives of higher latitudes. There are two seasons. The wet season commences about the middle of April and lasts for eight months. The dry season from the middle of December is generally considered healthy even in the canal region. During this period the sky is a cloudless blue by day and at night the moon and stars are sublime.

CHAPTER V

Colon and Panama

In the days when Spain maintained a great trade route across the Isthmus, the Atlantic terminus was Porto Bello, about twenty miles east of the mouth of the Canal. A cluster of Indian shacks upon a low beach now marks the place where the Spanish galleons were wont to land their cargoes of merchandise and take on board the pearls and precious metals consigned to the king's treasury. The ruins of the old city are shut in by heavy woods and lost in a tangle of dense undergrowth.

The construction of the railway gave birth to the modern port. The Americans called it Aspinwall, after one of the chief promoters. By the French it was named Colon. The city is built upon the Island of Manzanillo, a sand-covered coraline formation, three-quarters of a mile in length and not more than six hundred yards broad. It stands a very few feet above the ocean at high tide and is connected with the mainland by the railway embankment. The original town was anything but a pleasant or healthy place of residence. The railroad buildings, dwellings, laborers' quarters, and shops, mostly of wood, were scattered about without any particular system or order. The center of the island was occupied by an almost stagnant lagoon, creating a most undesirable condition from a sanitary point of view.

During the disturbances incident to the revolution of 1885, Colon was completely destroyed by fire. It was reconstructed with somewhat more regard for convenience and sanitation, but still leaving much to be desired in both respects.

STEAM SHOVEL BURIED UNDER FALL OF ROCK.

Slides and rock falls have been serious problems for the Canal engineers. The soil is particularly liable to slide, but it is expected that the pressure of the water in the Canal will counteract this tendency. This shovel was working on the bottom of Canal when destroyed.

COLON AND PANAMA

COLON AN UNATTRACTIVE CITY

The Colon of to-day is a straggling, unattractive city with some redeeming features, however, and a promise of more in the near future. The railroad company occupies the greater part of the water-front with its various buildings, including wharves and docks. Parallel with these is the main street, composed almost entirely of frame buildings. There are some good shops and a number of conscienceless dealers in spurious curios who, together with the enterprising money changers, reap a royal harvest from unsophisticated travelers. From the moment of landing the stranger is beset by a howling crowd of nondescripts who contend with one another for the privilege of fleecing him. His baggage is distributed amongst as many different individuals as possible, and upon his arrival at the hotel he is called upon to pay each one an exorbitant fee for his service, although it may have consisted in carrying a newspaper only. Before the American advent there was no escape from this imposition. If a victim refused to be mulcted he was haled before a magistrate who invariably supported the extortioners. In those days a man dared not ask a native the name of a street unless he was prepared to pay for the information. This system of bleeding the helpless foreigner is now confined within the bounds of semi-decency and an American, at least, is treated with a show of honesty.

COLON WAS AN UNSANITARY TOWN

Along the beach to the east of the town is the foreign quarter, containing some comfortable residences, an Episcopal church built of stone, and a tolerable hotel. On the west side, fronting the ocean, stand the handsome houses of the old French officials. They are grouped in a park beautifully laid out and convey the impression that our predecessors of the Canal did not neglect their personal comfort. The residence of de Lesseps is a particularly attractive structure of two stories surrounded by a double pier of verandas. Back of the city upon the mainland is Mount Hope, or Monkey Hill, whose cemetery has a population greatly in excess of that of Colon.

A COMPARATIVELY HEALTHY TOWN

Despite its known disadvantages and extremely forbidding aspect Colon has a record in the matters of health and mortality that compares favorably with that of Panama and belies the apparent conditions. Yellow fever has rarely appeared at Colon and malaria is seldom contracted there. Perhaps the city owes its comparative healthfulness to its situation on an island and the fact that a considerable portion of its surface is washed by sea water in which, it is said, mosquitoes will not breed.

Time was when the word Panama suggested untold wealth and voluptuous luxury. That was in the halcyon days when the old city, designated the Key to the Pacific and the Gate of the Universe, was the receiving point for the gold of Darien, the pearls of the Gulf islands, and the silver from the mines of South America. Fabulous treasure was often stored in "Panama, the Golden," awaiting a favorable opportunity for carriage by the king's horses over that splendid engineering achievement, the paved way that crossed the Isthmus to Porto Bello.

THE DEPARTED GLORY OF PANAMA VIEJO

Panama Viejo was a beautiful city. On either side stretched a picturesque tree-lined coast. In the background the mountains reared their rugged heads and between them and the city rolled a noble savanna laid out in fertile fields and lovely drives. The city contained twelve thousand or more buildings. Many of the grand mansions were built of stone and others of aromatic cedar. There were palatial public buildings; a handsome stable for the king's horses, and a castellated depository for the king's treasure. The churches were gorgeous and their plate and fittings world-famous. There were no fewer than eight monasteries and a magnificent hospital. The viceroy maintained a regal splendor; his suite and the many other wealthy inhabitants lived in the greatest luxury. The natives were their slaves. Money poured into their coffers without any exertion on their part. They merely took their ease and collected toll of the minerals going to the east and of the merchandise passing through Panama on its way to Asia and the Pacific islands.

THE PIRATES OF THE SPANISH MAIN

No account of the early days of the Isthmus can be complete without mentioning the English pirates or buccaneers who menaced the rich trade of Spain with her western possessions. Though England was not technically at war with Spain yet a practical state of war existed between the two nations for many years. Spain resented the visits of traders of other nations who came on peaceful visits. This resentment soon grew into open hostility, for the English were particularly quick to take up the challenge. The result was the rise of a horde of brilliant adventurers who preyed on the Spanish commerce for nearly a hundred years. England winked at their depredations in spite of the insistent protests of Spain. Among the most notable of these buccaneers may be mentioned Sir Francis Drake, Morgan, Parker, Ringrose, Sharp, Dampier and Wafer. Though their ethical standards may be questioned in these days the conditions largely justified their methods. The cruelty and rapacity of the Spaniards in their acquisition of treasure, their monopolistic attitude toward trade and the methods adopted by them to insure this monopoly to a great extent offset the tactics of the rovers. That the English achieved special distinction in this semi-warfare was probably due to the long strife between England and Spain and to the fact that English traders came in greater numbers to the Spanish main. It is related that Sir Francis Drake while on a peaceful trading expedition with Sir John Hawkins was treacherously set upon by a Spanish fleet and barely escaped with his life. From that day he vowed vengeance on the Spaniards and for a quarter of a century he harried the Spanish main and was a terror to every Spanish town from Trinidad to Campêche. In 1572 Drake set out with two ships and seventy-three men upon one of the boldest enterprises in history, namely, the sack of Nombre de Dios and the capture of the rich treasure convoy which he knew through spies was due to go across the Isthmus. In these objects Drake was entirely successful, securing considerable loot from the city and a great amount of gold, silver and jewels from the treasure caravan, probably amounting to not less than a hundred thousand dollars' worth. He again sacked and burned the town of Nombre de Dios in 1595 and sacked Porto Bello just afterward but here contracted the disease of which he afterward died. The success of Drake's raids and the enormous profit secured opened the eyes of other adventurous Englishmen to the rich field for their enterprises and for a century afterward preying upon Spanish commerce was a recognized occupation. The transportation of treasure across the Isthmus became so dangerous that the route around the Horn was adopted until Drake by his adventurous voyage through the Straits of Magellan captured so much booty and created such havoc among the Spanish treasure ships that trade once more returned to the Isthmus.

After Drake, perhaps the most noted of the freebooters was Henry Morgan, because of the greatness of the devastation he wrought in the Spanish trade and of the very interesting and minute account of his adventures written by Esquemeling. Morgan was a Welshman who gained considerable note on the Spanish main by his association with a Dutch pirate named Mansvelt in a project to create a buccaneer stronghold on the island of Santa Catalina. Mansvelt died and the island fell into the hands of the

Spanish. Morgan however was in Jamaica when the island was taken and consequently was safe, as Jamaica had been seized by the English in 1655, some ten years before. Soon afterward Morgan, having gathered a fleet of nine ships and nearly five hundred men, set out to capture and sack Porto Bello. In this daring enterprise Morgan was entirely successful. Anchoring his ships some nine leagues from the city the pirates entered small boats and landed shortly after midnight and attacked a castle near the city. After considerable difficulty they captured this and blew up the garrison. This attack alarmed the city however and for the rest of the day a desperate fight raged about one of the defending castles. The buccaneers were repeatedly repulsed until they hit upon the scheme of placing ladders against the battlements and driving nuns and priests ahead of them up these ladders. The garrison fired upon these religious people, but though they died painful deaths the plan worked and with the ladders so placed the capture of the castle and fall of the city soon followed. For two weeks the rioting and sack of the city continued, then having extorted a ransom of $125,000 from the citizens Morgan departed, returning to the West Indies. The money did not last long however and Morgan was soon planning a new raid. With the reputation gained on his Porto Bello expedition he had no trouble in gathering a force and having decided to attack Old Panama he set sail with thirty-seven ships and two thousand men. Stopping at Santa Catalina he captured the island after a faint resistance and holding the main body of the expedition there he sent one of his captains named Brodley ahead to take the fortress at the mouth of the Chagres river, called Fort San Lorenzo. It was a tremendous undertaking with so small a force (four ships and four hundred men) but Brodley succeeded in his endeavor after an heroic attack in the face of desperate resistance. In a few days the main force under Morgan appeared and leaving a garrison at Fort San Lorenzo began his famous march across the

Isthmus with twelve hundred men. The crossing occupied ten days of hunger, thirst and terrible hardships, but at last they arrived before the city of Panama, garrisoned by four hundred cavalry, twenty-four hundred infantry and heavy artillery. Fortunately for the tired buccaneers, the Spanish instead of awaiting their attack elected to charge them. On they came across a swampy field in the face of a tremendous fire from the pirates. It was too much and soon the charge broke and turned to a rout, the Spaniards taking refuge in the jungle. This left the way to the city opened and Morgan was not slow to pursue his advantage. After a brief resistance he found the city at his mercy and marching in ordered a round-up of the citizens in a systematic scheme for extracting all the wealth the city contained. For three weeks the pirates robbed and pillaged, though without many of the excesses which had marked the capture of Porto Bello. During this time a large portion of the city was burned though the origin of the fire is not known. Satisfied that they had obtained all possible loot from the city Morgan's men began the march back across the Isthmus to Fort San Lorenzo. Here the spoil was divided and great dissatisfaction ensued when it was found that each man's share amounted to only about one hundred dollars. It seemed a poor return for the hardships and privations endured. Morgan was blamed for an unfair division of the spoils and so bitter were the denunciations that he thought it wise to depart without the formality of a leave-taking, followed by a few only of his ships. The balance of the pirates were left to get away as best they could. Morgan sailed to Jamaica, made his peace with the governor by dividing his share of the loot. It is somewhat remarkable to relate that he abandoned buccaneering and soon succeeded to the governorship. In that office he was notably diligent in the suppression of piracy!

After Morgan's great raid on Panama buccaneering began to die out on the Spanish main. The ports were not entirely neglected however and Hawkins, Sharp and others continued operations for some years. The greatest exploit of these later pirates was the attack upon the rebuilt city of Panama. With a force of about three hundred and fifty men they sailed for Panama and fought a great naval battle in the Bay of Panama with five Spanish men-of-war. Though victorious in this they did not attempt a landing, but after a ten day stay in the harbor sailed for the coast of South America where the expedition split into two sections. One party under the pirate leaders Dampier and Wafer, referred to earlier in this chapter, made the perilous journey across the Isthmus. Surrounded by hostile Indians, at the mercy of the swollen streams and tropical jungle they at last managed to reach the Atlantic and Dampier's ship.

Today one must look for the ruins of Panama Viejo amidst a rank growth of tropical vegetation, above which rears the sturdy tower of St. Anastasius, at whose altar Pizarro made votive supplication before setting out upon his momentous voyage to the south. The sudden and tragic fall of the old city, in the pride of its beauty and strength, had a depressing effect upon the Spaniards and left them with no heart to resurrect it. They transferred the capital to a site about six miles to the west, but the glory of "Panama the Golden" was never revived in its adumbrant successor.

NEW PANAMA BUILT WITH REGARD TO DEFENSE

In building the new Pacific port the Spaniards were not unmindful of the lesson taught by the buccaneer raid. The city was laid out upon a rocky peninsula, the whole of which is occupied by it. A wall, thirty to forty feet in height and of solid masonry, in places sixty feet broad, skirted the entire shore. Along the bay-front the outer wall was reinforced by another, and the intervening space formed a moat. This wall and its accessories cost more than eleven millions of dollars, despite the fact that the natives were forced to render almost gratuitous service in its construction. Much of the wall still remains in a good condition of preservation. It is used as a promenade by the citizens and as a playground by their children. The moat has long been dry and some of the poorer dwellings have been raised within it. There is a story of a king of Spain who was noticed one day to be looking out toward the west from a high window of his palace. A minister, who remarked the strained expression of the monarch's eyes, ventured to enquire what might be the object of his anxiety. "I am looking," said the king, "for those costly walls of Panama. They ought to be discernible even at this distance."

THE HOUSES AND CHURCHES CONVERTIBLE INTO FORTS

All the old buildings of Panama were designed for use as forts in case of need. The houses have walls of stone, three feet thick, with heavy doors, often iron-clad, and windows only in the second story. Similar precautions were observed in the construction of the churches. Their sides were made to resist the heaviest artillery of the day, and their windows stand sixteen or twenty feet above the ground. These defensive measures were justified by after events, for, although the later Panama never fell into the hands of an enemy during the Spanish dominion, its strength alone saved it from attack on more than one occasion. Shortly after its foundation an unsuccessful attempt to take it was made by a force of buccaneers. That extraordinary man, Captain Dampier, took part in this enterprise.

The substantial houses of Panama are much like those of the old Spanish colonies in other parts of the world—solid, heavy, forbidding structures, the upper story of which alone is occupied by the owners. In Panama, as in San Juan and Manila, the best families are to be found living over a herd of natives, or negroes, unless the ground floor is given up to a store, or workshop. The lower portions of the houses seldom have any windows in front, and if any

PRESIDENT ROOSEVELT ON A GIANT STEAM SHOVEL.

During his visit to the Isthmus, while President, Mr. Roosevelt dispensed with ceremony, went among the men, talking and eating with them. In this way he obtained a very intimate knowledge of the great enterprise. His visit marked the first occasion upon which a President of the United States left the country during his term of office.

exist, they are strongly barred. A veranda, overhanging the sidewalk, is the evening resort of the occupants of the upper half of the dwelling.

The streets, formerly paved with cobble-stones, are tortuous and often very narrow. There is too much congestion for health, or convenience, and the improvements in this direction will be a boon to the inhabitants. It is gratifying that, unlike the people of other Spanish-American cities which have been treated to a clean-up by us, the Panamans are immediately appreciative of our efforts in their behalf.

THE INTERESTING CHURCHES OF MODERN PANAMA

The churches and ecclesiastical ruins of Panama present a rich field for the research of the antiquarian and the architect, and a capable writer might find material for a highly interesting volume in them. "The oldest church is that of San Felipe Neri, in the long past the parish church of the city within the walls. Its side is on a narrow street, and over the sole entrance one reads, 'San Felipe Neri, 1688,' cut in a shield." The early Spaniards were famous for making cements, both colored and uncolored. So hard were they that they have stood the effects of the heat and moisture of that destructive climate without damage. This old-time cement to-day is as hard as stone. Over the entrance to public buildings and churches they made their inscriptions in these cements, in many instances filling in odd spaces with ornamental work made of the large pearl shells from the famous *Islas de Perlas*, or Pearl Islands, in the Gulf of Panama. Such designs when new must have been chaste and beautiful, as the smooth mother-of-pearl surfaces of the large shells on a background of reddish cement must have made a beautiful contrast, the shells reflecting the sun rays in a thousand directions. "This quaint and most substantial old edifice faces on a small street. At one time it made the corner of the Plaza San Francisco. The large door is reached by a few stone steps on either side of which are plain columns, while there are a few lancet shaped windows above. Its front is very plain. The whole is surmounted by a quaint old tower of the true Moorish type. It is built wholly of stone with a rounded cupola of the same material. Lashed to cross-pieces are the old-time bells. The door is a huge affair of most substantial make, studded with huge brazen heads or knobs. When closed from within, persons in the church could stand a siege very successfully. The side windows of the church are fully twenty-five feet above the street, and they were purposely so made in case of attack. The walls of San Felipe Neri are nearly five feet thick, and the windows are so deeply recessed as to remind one of an ancient fortress or prison." A larger, and not less interesting church is that of San Francisco, facing upon the square of the same name. It was built early in the eighteenth century. The interior is very imposing with its gracefully arched roof and fine supporting columns, dividing the entire length of the edifice. The altar is an exceedingly large and beautiful structure of carved hardwood.

THE FAMOUS FLAT ARCH OF ST. DOMINIC

A strange story attaches to the ruins of St. Dominic. When intact it must have been an extremely handsome edifice, but its noble towers and grand facade are things of the past, and the massive remains of the old church are now overrun by vegetation. The most striking portion of the building has survived the attacks of fire and the shocks of earthquake. It is one of the most peculiar arches in the world. It stands complete near what was the main entrance. It is a single span of about sixty feet, its chord so flattened as to be almost horizontal. Architects are puzzled to account for this arch standing without further support than the terminal columns. Legend has it that this curious structure was erected three times and each time fell. A fourth time it was set up, and the monk who designed it stood beneath the arch and declared that if it should not fall upon his head the work was good and would endure.

The churches of La Merced, San Juan de Dios, St. Ana, and the Cathedral, deserve description if space permitted. Nelson makes an interesting statement with regard to the origin of the last-named building: "The cathedral of Panama was built at the sole expense of one of the bishops of Panama, and was completed about 128 years ago. The bishop's father was a Panamanian by birth—a colored man. He made charcoal near La Boca de la Rio Grande, or the mouth of the Grand River, a stream entering the Bay of Panama some two miles from the Panama City of today. This colored man made his charcoal and brought it on his back from house to house to sell— a custom that obtains to this day. He gave his son, the future bishop, as good an education as was possible. In due time he became a deacon, priest, and finally bishop of Panama—a bishop of proud Panama, for in those days it was a wealthy city. He was the first colored bishop of Panama. This son of a charcoal burner developed into a grand man, and in time crowned a life of usefulness by building the cathedral from his private means." Much of the stone used in its construction is from the highlands of the interior, and was brought many leagues on the backs of men. After long years the building was completed in 1760.

The churches of Panama are both numerous and noisy, facts that are impressed upon the stranger by the almost incessant clanging of their bells. Panama has been the scene of three or four great fires, in which several ecclesiastical buildings were damaged or destroyed.

THE DEAD ARE TEMPORARY TENANTS OF THEIR GRAVES

The city has several cemeteries, but the system of temporary tenancy forbids any calculation of the number of past occupants. When a graveyard becomes crowded the coffins are taken up, the bones shaken out in a heap, and the empty receptacles offered for sale, or hire. The same system of leasing space is in force in the *boveda* enclosures. A *boveda* is a niche just large enough to accommodate the coffin of an adult. The cemetery is formed of a quadrangle surrounded by three tiers of *bovedas*. These are rented for a term of eighteen months, and after a coffin is deposited in one, the opening is closed with a slab, or bricked up. Where the space has been permanently secured, a memorial tablet often seals the aperture. When the rent of one of these sepulchers is overdue its contents are thrown out in just as business-like a manner as that in which a harsh landlord might evict a delinquent tenant. Perhaps the foregoing statements ought to have been made in the past tense, for the Canal Commission, in the exercise of its right of control in sanitary matters, has vigorously moderated all similar practices There has been an abatement of the evil in recent years as a result of the protests of foreigners. This disgraceful custom of disturbing the dead was confined to the natives. In the Chinese cemetery and in that of the Jews, corpses have been permitted to rest in peace, and it goes without saying that such has been the case in the burial grounds controlled by the railroad and canal companies.

IN SPANISH-AMERICA GRAFT EXTENDS TO THE GRAVE

One would naturally infer from the conditions, that the Panamans entertained no respect for the memory, or bones, of their deceased relatives, but such is not the case. The truth is that the system of renting graves is an exhibition of the "graft" that has for ages pervaded every rood of territory under Spanish rule. The right to conduct a cemetery, like the privilege of running a gambling establishment, was farmed out to the highest bidder, and the *concesionero* might regulate his business in almost any manner he pleased. The price of a permanent grave was placed so high that the poorer classes could afford no more than a temporary lease, and when that had expired often found themselves unable to renew it. The fact that they did not dispense with consecrated ground, as they might have been excused for doing under the circumstances, is sufficient evidence of their regard for the welfare of their dead.

Panama was once a most disorderly city, filled with low grog-shops, and reminding one of Port Said in the seventies. Robberies, murders and hold-ups were every day affairs, but to-day it is a quiet and orderly place, with a well-equipped and efficient police force.

AMERICAN AUTHORITY IN THE PANAMAN REPUBLIC

The treaty with the Republic of Panama gave to the United States jurisdiction in the matter of sanitation and order, beyond the limits of the Canal Zone, into the cities of Colon and Panama and over the adjacent waters. The Commission determined to make Panama a clean and, at least, moderately healthy city. The task was a stupendous one, and the difficulties involved by it were fully appreciated, but it has been successfully attacked and plans for a thorough transformation of the capital realized. Panama existed without a water supply, or a sewerage system, for more than three centuries, and a magazine writer once remarked that it would not seem to matter greatly if it were left in the same condition for another decade or so. That, however, was not the way in which the Commission viewed the matter. These defects have been considerably remedied and a great deal toward their complete removal has been accomplished.

PANAMA ENJOYS THE BOON OF GOOD WATER

By the enlargement of a dam, which the Panama Canal Company had constructed at the headwaters of the Rio Grande, an extensive reservoir has been formed. The water has been piped from this to another reservoir, on the summit of a small hill at Ancon, having a capacity of one million gallons. Thence it flows by gravity to the city. The system is designed to furnish sixty gallons a day per head to a population of thirty thousand. At points on the streets, or other public places, where portions of the population may not have sufficient means to make house connections, hydrants have been placed, so that an unlimited supply of good water may be obtained without cost or difficulty. Before deciding upon the source of the supply, the Commission submitted samples of the water from the upper, or Rio Grande, reservoir to expert bacteriologists and chemical analyzers. After thorough tests the water was pronounced satisfactory before even the banks and bed of the reservoir had been cleaned of vegetation.

A system of sewerage has been installed which cares for sixty gallons per head of the population per day and, in addition, one inch of rainfall per hour. This does not provide for the disposal of the maximum precipitation in the rainy season, but any excess over the capacity of the sewers will be carried through surface channels. The sewerage system, with a total length of nearly eighteen miles, serves every portion of the city, and may be readily extended to outlying districts.

CHAPTER VI

THE FRENCH PANAMA CANAL COMPANY

Whilst the American Interoceanic Canal Commission was investigating the comparative merits of the various isthmian routes, a project for a waterway through the Isthmus of Panama was set on foot in France at the suggestion of Count Ferdinand de Lesseps.

In 1875 the subject was discussed at length by the Congrès des Sciences Géographiques at Paris, which strongly recommended the immediate prosecution of surveys with a view to decisive action. Following the session of the Congress a provisional company was formed by General Türr and other individuals for the purpose of securing a concession from the Republic of Colombia. This syndicate was composed of speculators whose sole motives were of a commercial nature. They despatched to the Isthmus Lieutenant L. N. B. Wyse, an officer of the French Navy and a brother-in-law of General Türr, with instructions to select a route and negotiate with the Colombian Government for a concession. In making his selection the Lieutenant was to be guided by a consideration for the prime object of the syndicate, which was to make as large a profit as possible from the sale of whatever interests it might acquire. Wyse and his employers were not actuated by any utilitarian sentiments, but merely by a desire to make money out of the scheme regardless of ultimate consequences. The spirit that moved them in the promotion was exhibited by their successors in the conduct of the enterprise, the management of which was "characterized by a degree of extravagance and corruption that have had few, if any, equals in the history of the world."

COLOMBIA'S CONCESSION TO THE FRENCH PROMOTERS

Lieutenant Wyse made a perfunctory survey, commencing at Panama and extending only about two-thirds of the way to the Atlantic coast. Nevertheless, he calculated the cost in detail and claimed that his estimate might be depended upon to come within ten per cent of the actual figures. The Colombian Government entered into a contract with the Lieutenant which in its final form was signed two years later. It gave to the promoters the exclusive privilege of constructing and operating a canal through the territory of the Republic without any restrictive conditions, excepting that, if the route adopted traversed any portion of the land embraced in the concession to the Panama Railroad, the promoters should arrive at an amicable arrangement with that corporation before proceeding with their operations. On the part of the concessionaires it was agreed that the course of the canal should be determined by an international congress of engineers.

The concession was transferred to La Compagnie Universelle du Canal Interoceanique de Panama, generally known as the "Panama Canal Company," and on the fifteenth day of May, 1879, the International Conference met to determine the route. It was composed of one hundred and sixty-four members, of whom more than half were French and the remainder of various nationalities. Forty-two of the members only were engineers. The proceedings were pre-arranged and those who knew most about the subject in hand found that their opinions were least in demand. The following conclusion was put to the vote and carried by a small margin, the engineers who voted affirmatively being in a minority:

CONCLUSION OF THE INTERNATIONAL CONFERENCE

"The conference deems that the construction of an interoceanic canal, so desirable in the interests of commerce and navigation, is possible and, in order to have the indis-

CULEBRA CUT LOOKING NORTH FROM LAS CASCADAS.
All trains are standing on the bottom of cut, elevation +40.

THE FRENCH PANAMA CANAL COMPANY 93

pensable facilities and ease of access and of use, which a work of this kind should offer above all others, it should be built from the Gulf of Limon (Colon) to the Bay of Panama; and it particularly recommends the construction of a ship canal on a level in that direction."

It was at this meeting that Ferdinand de Lesseps made his first public appearance in connection with the enterprise. He took the chair and dominated the sessions of the Conference, and there is no doubt that his will was the most potent influence in bringing about its decision. Several members, who were radically opposed to the conclusions, rather than declare their difference from the opinions of a man of the great distinction and high reputation that de Lesseps enjoyed at the time, absented themselves when the final vote was taken.

FERDINAND DE LESSEPS, DIPLOMATIST AND PROMOTER

Ferdinand de Lesseps was born in France in 1805. At an early age he entered the consular service of his country and on more than one occasion distinguished himself in critical emergencies. In 1854, he visited Egypt and conceived the idea of the Suez Canal. For several years the opposition of the British Government obstructed his efforts to carry out the great undertaking which was eventually brought to a successful conclusion by him. He also promoted the construction of the Corinth Canal.

De Lesseps was at the height of his reputation when he assumed the direction of the ill-fated Panama venture. His great intellect may have been on the wane, but it is certain that his self-confidence and boundless belief in his own abilities were never greater than when he made the declaration, that "the Panama Canal will be more easily begun, finished and maintained than the Suez Canal." The disgraceful failure that resulted must be attributed largely to de Lesseps himself. He publicly assumed the responsibility for the enterprise and its management from the outset. Although he was not an engineer and had but a very limited knowledge of the science of engineering, he considered himself better informed than men who had the advantage of technical training and experience. He laid out the work, acting upon data which a professional engineer would have deemed insufficient or unreliable. With fatuous disregard for the opinions of experts, he altered plans and estimates to conform with his own unsupported ideas and, in short, exercised an arbitrary and unwise control over every feature of the undertaking. Almost to the last he cherished the belief that he enjoyed the unbounded confidence of the French people and that their purses would never be closed to his demands. Although his plans were fatally faulty and largely impracticable, there is no reason to doubt de Lesseps's good faith in the earlier stages of the enterprise. As it advanced and the errors of his basic calculations were forced upon him, he resorted to deception and, with the constantly increasing difficulties of the situation, his words and actions took an ever increasing divergence from the direction of truth and honesty.

Notwithstanding that the project was essentially a French one, and the money absorbed in it was subscribed in France, the interest in it was universal, and the collapse of the Company caused widespread excitement. Not the least serious of the results was the discredit cast upon the whole question of interoceanic communication and especially upon the Panaman phase of it. Exaggerated pessimism succeeded to the optimistic hopes which attended the launching of the venture, and even after this lapse of time doubts of its practicability are extensively entertained. Such doubts, however, can not find a logical basis in the fiasco produced by the Panama Canal Company. Its entire enterprise was built upon an unstable foundation. The plans were conceived in error and in ignorance of some of the most potent factors in the problem to be solved. Important circumstances were overlooked or inadequately pro-

THE FRENCH PANAMA CANAL COMPANY 95

vided for. Available knowledge was neglected and past experience disregarded. One man's preconceived ideas were applied to the situation in substitution of a scientific study of the conditions. The original miscalculations were followed by a series of avoidable mistakes, the inevitable consequence of which was the final disaster.

The mismanagement of the undertaking amply sufficed to insure its failure, but the catastrophe that ensued was rendered greater by the insane extravagance and the unbounded corruption which characterized the conduct of the Company. Froude, in his book on the West Indies, says:

FROUDE'S CHARACTERIZATION OF THE FRENCH MISMANAGEMENT

"In all the world there is not, perhaps, now concentrated in any single spot so much swindling and villainy, so much foul disease, such a hideous dung heap of moral and physical abomination, as in the scene of this far-famed undertaking of nineteenth century engineering. By the scheme, as it was first propounded,* six and twenty millions of English money were to unite the Atlantic and Pacific oceans, to form a highway for the commerce of the globe and enrich, with untold wealth, the happy owners of original shares. The thrifty French peasantry were tempted by the golden bait and poured their savings into M. de Lesseps's money box."

Commenting upon the causes that contributed to the failure, a writer in the *Forum* stated that "following his acknowledged principles of being sole arbiter of the companies which he founded, M. de Lesseps has directed every step without counsel, control or, it may be added, knowledge of what was required. His eye has been bent steadily upon the Bourse. He has never put forward a single estimate that has not been falsified by the event. For the

---
* The noted author meant to say, the equivalent of "six and twenty millions, etc." Very little English money was invested in the scheme.

work of a responsible engineer he has substituted the action of what he called consultative committees, superior councils, and the like, which have been, for the most part, little more than picnic parties at public cost, and with the recommendations of which he has dealt as he thought fit."

RUINOUS FINANCING FROM THE OUTSET

The first and a continuous drain upon the financial resources of the Company was in the form of "founders' profits." At the initial meeting of the shareholders, when they all fondly imagined that the venture was a bonanza, they were informed that they had to pay the following claims, and accepted the statement without a murmur:

ESTABLISHMENT EXPENSES OF THE PANAMA CANAL COMPANY

For the Concession	$2,000,000
Preliminary Expenses	2,160,000
Profit on Preliminary Expenses	2,360,000
American Financial Group	2,400,000
Total	$8,920,000

The greater part of this sum was taken by the founders out of the first $20,000,000 paid in. It is doubtful if any of the outside shareholders knew precisely, or even approximately, what these figures represented. They were too absorbed in visions of vast prospective profits to concern themselves overmuch with present expenditures.

In addition to the immediate cash benefits the founders were to receive fifteen per cent of the net profits of the Company. These prospective payments were capitalized under the name of *parts de fondateur* in "parts" of $1000 each. There were originally five hundred and later nine hundred of these "parts," which attained a price of $16,000 each. De Lesseps is authority for the statement that in November, 1880, they sold at $76,000 each.

In 1883 the promoters netted $716,900 and the directors

THE FRENCH PANAMA CANAL COMPANY

and staff, $186,900, out of the "profits" of the undertaking. The directors were allowed a further three per cent of the profits, which contingent benefit they commuted into a present payment of $48,000.

RECKLESS EXTRAVAGANCE ON THE ISTHMUS

Dr. Nelson, who was upon the ground whilst the Panama Company's operations were in progress, makes the following statement: "The famous Bureau System is what has obtained in the Isthmus up to the present time, with changes and amplifications without number. There is enough bureaucratic work, and there are enough officers on the Isthmus to furnish at least one dozen first-class republics with officials for all their departments. The expenditure has been something simply colossal. One Director General lived in a mansion that cost over $100,000; his pay was $50,000 a year; and every time he went out on the line he had his *deplacement*, which gave him the liberal sum of fifty dollars a day additional. He traveled in a handsome Pullman car, especially constructed, which was reported to have cost some $42,000. Later, wishing a summer residence, a most expensive building was put up near La Boca. The preparation of the grounds, the building, and the roads thereto, cost upwards of $150,000. . . . Another man had built a large bath-house on the most approved principles. This cost $40,000. Thousands and tens of thousands have been frittered away in ornamental grounds, for all had to be *beau*, utility being a secondary consideration."

THE ORGANIZATION OF THE PANAMA CANAL COMPANY

We will now resume the history of the Panama Canal Company. It was capitalized at $80,000,000, in shares of $100 each, which were opened to public subscription in Europe and America in August, 1879. Less than one-tenth of the amount was taken up and the organization of the corporation was indefinitely postponed. In the criminal trial that followed the failure of the Company, Charles de Lesseps stated that after the abortive effort to float the Company his father placed the financial arrangements connected with the disposal of the shares in the hands of an influential group of financiers and journalists, who undertook to mould public opinion to a favorable form Here we find the explanation of three of the enormous items of preliminary expense which are given above. Early in 1880 M. de Lesseps arrived at Colon, accompanied by an international technical commission which was charged with the work of making the final surveys and marking the precise line to be followed by the Canal. This highly important task, like all the other preliminary steps of the undertaking, was performed in haste and the party left the Isthmus before the close of February.

RECKLESS ESTIMATES OF THE COST OF CONSTRUCTION

The Paris Congress had estimated the cost of constructing the Canal at $214,000,000, and the time necessary for its completion at twelve years. The technical commission expressed the opinion that the entire operation might be finished in eight years at a cost of $168,600,000. In view of the fact that several of the engineer-members of the congress considered the former estimate too low, it is difficult to understand how the commission arrived at its figures. The reduction was not, however, sufficiently great to satisfy the purpose of de Lesseps, which was to present to the public a proposition so attractive as to be irresistible. In order to promote this object, he took upon himself to alter the sum fixed by the commission to $131,600,000, which he declared would be sufficient to provide for the entire expenses of the operation. The first year's traffic was estimated at 6,000,000 tons, assuring a revenue of $18,000,000, and this was claimed to be a very conservative assumption, whereas, it was in reality almost beyond the possibility of realization. The limit of fanciful prediction had not, however, been reached. In May, 1880, Mr. A. Couvreux, Jr., a member of a large contracting firm, publicly stated that his house was prepared to undertake the entire work at a cost of only $102,400,000. In the light of our present knowledge the absurdity of these statements is patent, but we must remember that at the time the whole proposition rested upon a basis of theory. The fact should have been an incentive to conservatism, and, although there may not be sufficient ground at this stage of the enterprise to impugn the honesty of the promoters, the recklessness with which M. de Lesseps submitted his inexpert calculations to the public was little short of criminal.

THE STOCK IS OVERSUBSCRIBED BY THE PUBLIC

Having prepared his new financial prospectus on the alluring lines indicated, M. de Lesseps made a tour of the United States, England, Belgium, Holland, and France, delivering speeches in which the enormous profits to accrue to the fortunate investors in the Panama Canal project were depicted in the seductive rhetoric that was always at his command. Following this campaign of words, $60,000,000 in shares of $100 denomination were offered to the public and doubly subscribed for.

It was agreed that the first two years should be a period of organization to be devoted largely to surveying and ascertaining from actual experience something of the cost of excavation and other features of the operation. In other words, the public having invested its money upon the strength of certain wild guesses advanced with all the assurance of conviction, it was now proposed to investigate the facts. Later developments proved that even the surveys of the line were unreliable. Three years after the engineering force had been at work upon the ground it was discovered that what they supposed to be an almost fathomless swamp was composed of solid rock a few feet below the surface, and this was only one of a number of similar misapprehensions. The second period, of six years, was to be occupied with the actual work of construction under contract.

THE COMPANY COMMENCES THE WORK OF CONSTRUCTION

In February, 1883, the latter stage was entered upon with Mr. Dingler as engineer in chief. His plan for a sea level canal made the following provisions: The canal, which had its origin at Colon, in Limon Bay, was to follow the bottom of the Chagres Valley for a distance of about 28 miles, to Obispo; it was then to cross the Cordilleras, the passage accounting for about 7 further miles of its length; continuing thence, the line traversed the Valley of the Rio Grande and terminated in deep water near the Island of Naos, in the Bay of Panama. The full length of the proposed cut was 46 miles. The depth of the canal was to be 30 feet and its width at bottom 72 feet.

For the regulation of the waters of the Chagres, which vary from 26 cubic yards at low water to 2,620 cubic yards in flood, it was proposed to construct a large storage reservoir at Gamboa by damming the river and deflecting its affluents to the sea on either side of the Isthmus.

The cube of the excavations provided for by this plan was a minimum of 157,200,000 yards, being 59,000 more than had been estimated by the commission and 98,250,000 more than the congress had indicated.

This plan was accepted and, despite the enormous increase of work entailed by it, de Lesseps adhered for a year longer to his original estimate of cost and time of construction. It was not until a meeting of the shareholders in 1885, that he increased the former to $120,000,000, and extended the latter to July, 1889.

A SIMPLE UNDERTAKING ACCORDING TO DE LESSEPS

At the inception of the enterprise M. de Lesseps established a Bulletin which became the medium for the dissemination among the shareholders and the general public of

VIEW IN THE TOWN OF CULEBRA, CANAL ZONE.

This shows the type of buildings used for bachelor quarters and employees' clubhouses. The high hill back of the clubhouse is "Gold Hill." The Canal runs between the clubhouse and Gold Hill.

THE FRENCH PANAMA CANAL COMPANY

the most exaggerated reports and the most reckless misstatements. In March, 1881, de Lesseps stated in this publication: "But two things need be done: to remove a mass of earth and stones, and to control the river Chagres. . . . The canal is, therefore, an exact mathematical operation." This statement alone betrays the promoter's ignorance of the great engineering problems inseparably connected with the undertaking; for the control of the Chagres involves the most intricate and difficult calculations and engineering works imaginable. In addition were the thousand and one obstacles: disease, labor problems, inadequate machinery, public distrust of the project and financial difficulties to be encountered and which de Lesseps entirely ignored or made light of.

By the middle of 1885, hardly one-tenth of the estimated minimum excavation had been done, and it became evident, even to the non-professional observer, that the program could not be carried out in accordance with the assurances repeatedly given by de Lesseps. The enterprise began to be severely criticised and passionately discussed in the press of France. The credit of the Company was seriously affected by these assaults and it became necessary to adopt drastic measures for the restoration of public confidence in order to secure the additional funds that were already needed. At this critical juncture, the promoter, for M. de Lesseps had long since taken the whole affair into his own hands, sought the aid of the Government, which had been extended to him during the Suez Canal operation. He applied for permission to issue lottery bonds, but the desired authority was not granted at that time.

By this time it was widely recognized that, de Lesseps's declaration to the contrary notwithstanding, the Panama project involved immeasurably greater difficulties than those encountered in the Suez undertaking. In fact, the two operations were so dissimilar in every essential respect that the latter afforded no criteria by which to judge the former. At Suez, the entire line lay along low ground and most of the way traversed lakes, marshes, and swamps. One of the chief difficulties rose from the softness and instability of the material to be dealt with. In Panama the main problems are the passage of a chain of mountains and the disposition of a number of streams. At Suez, the tides are the same at each end of the Canal; at Panama there is a difference of twenty feet between the Atlantic and Pacific extreme oscillations. In the earlier enterprise neither climate nor labor entailed unfavorable conditions, whereas in all the operations upon the American Isthmus they have been among the most vexatious factors entering into the situation. The constructors of the Suez Canal had the support of the French Government and of the Khedive of Egypt, and the encouragement of the whole world. In his later venture de Lesseps started with well-founded opposition against his plans and which steadily increased as the attempted execution of them betrayed their futility. The comparison admits of extension were that necessary.

In his letter of August the first, 1885, to the Minister of the Interior, praying for authority to raise a loan of $120,000,000 on lottery bonds, Ferdinand de Lesseps stated:

"The organization of the working camps, the installation along the whole line of twenty-seven contractors piercing the isthmus at their own risk and peril, an immense stock on working footing, is such as to allow the canal to be completed and inaugurated in 1888."

THE SEA-LEVEL PROJECT INVESTIGATED BY THREE PROMINENT ENGINEERS

The Chamber of Deputies recommended that the desired permission should be granted to the Company without delay, but the Government decided before complying to send a competent engineer to the Isthmus with instructions to investigate and report upon the situation. At the time that this official was conducting his examination, two other engineers were similarly engaged. Each proceeded independently of the others, but all arrived at one conclusion, which is the more remarkable since two of them were in the employ of the Company. In the forepart of 1886 the reports were submitted to the respective principals.

Armand Rousseau, the Government commissioner, found that the completion of the Canal with the resources available and in prospect was practically impossible unless the plan was changed to one involving the use of locks.

M. Jacquet declared that, after a thorough investigation of the work in all its details, he was convinced of the necessity of abandoning the original design, and he recommended the construction of a lock canal along the precise line adopted for the sea level project. Leon Boyer, who held the position of Director of Works upon the Isthmus, stated that the completion of a canal on a level was impossible with the money at command and in the time stipulated. He suggested a *temporary* waterway, to be operated by locks and to be replaced by a sea level canal as soon as possible.

This weight of expert opinion, which it must be remembered was in corroboration of similar expressions voiced by eminent engineers on previous occasions, de Lesseps discarded in his usual high-handed manner. He would not listen to a word against the sea level project, but declared in the most emphatic terms his intention to pursue it to the end. He had "promised the world a canal at the level of the oceans," and he proposed to keep his word despite all opposition. At this stage of the proceedings the "Great Undertaker," as he began to be dubbed, assumed the role of the persecuted philanthropist.

The shareholders of the Company were frequently informed henceforth that all kinds of powerful interests were in league against their enterprise, but at the same time they were assured that he, de Lesseps, might be depended upon to circumvent the machinations of these wicked plotters.

Lest the reader should fall into misapprehension as to

the true significance of the recommendations of the engineers which have been cited, it may be well to remind him that the undertaking of the Panama Canal Company was a purely commercial enterprise, and that the reports and suggestions of the experts in question were made with that fact constantly in mind. None of them expresses the opinion that a sea level canal is impracticable, nor is the question taken into consideration by either of them directly. The point of their decision was whether a sea level canal could be constructed at a cost and in such time as to make its after operation a profitable business for the shareholders. Time, of course, is a great factor in the cost of an operation involving hundreds of millions. Interest increases at an enormous rate during the later years. Therefore, considerations which would preclude the pursuit of a project solely contemplating commercial results might not be of sufficient weight to deter a government from following the same lines. The United States, observing business principles to the utmost reasonable extent, might justifiably construct a sea level canal at an expense that would entail the ruin of a private corporation. Even though the operation of the canal should fail to return any interest upon the money invested, the Government might well consider itself fully compensated for the outlay by the political advantages secured, the great savings in the movements of warships, and other desiderata which will be noticed in detail in later chapters.

FURTHER EFFORTS TO RESTORE THE WANTING CONFIDENCE OF THE PUBLIC

Whilst the engineer reports to which reference has been made above were in course of preparation, de Lesseps visited the Isthmus with a large party of individuals, many of whom were influential in the commercial and financial circles of France. Few of them had any technical knowledge, but the majority seem to have been susceptible to the

THE FRENCH PANAMA CANAL COMPANY

persuasive eloquence of the great promoter, for upon their return the enterprise received the endorsements of various chambers of commerce and general boards. In July, 1886, the Government declared its intention of postponing for several months the decision in the matter of the lottery bonds. De Lesseps took umbrage at this action and, relying upon the effect of the moral support of the powerful commercial bodies, withdrew his request. He received from the stockholders permission to issue a new series of bonds, and did so with success, but the enterprise had passed beyond the stage of possible salvation.

AN AMERICAN OFFICER INSPECTS THE OPERATION

In March, 1887, Lieutenant C. C. Rogers, U. S. N., was ordered by the Navy Department to inspect the canal work. He took three weeks to the task and went thoroughly over the line. He found the hospitals and quarters for officers and laborers clean, well-ventilated frame buildings, admirably suited to the climate. The canteens were kept by Chinamen, who boarded laborers at reasonable rates. There were upwards of 10,000 workmen, employed by contractors, who, with the number of the Company's employees, made up a total of 11,566. The laborers were chiefly importations from the West Indies, with a few negroes from the Southern States of America. The standard wage was $1.50 in silver a day. The laborers were paid every Saturday. Sunday was spent in drinking; Monday in recuperation; and on Tuesday they returned to work; "hence," says the lieutenant, "the number of working days in a month seldom exceed twenty or twenty-two." The Company endeavored to put 20,000 laborers upon the ground and, as they could not be had from the West Indies, tried to get them from Western Africa and Southern China, but without success.

The hospital records of the Company showed a death rate of seven per cent of those employed on the work from its inception to July, 1887, but this did not include the great number who contracted disease on the Isthmus and died elsewhere.

SIGNS OF COLLAPSE BEGIN TO BE EVIDENT

By this time the work had become seriously disorganized. There had been changes of contractors. Some had thrown up their contracts, others had brought suits against the Company. There had been frequent alterations in the working plans and there was a general feeling of uncertainty as to the character of the future operations.

In the meanwhile de Lesseps had found his attitude on the sea level question untenable and, after a considerable amount of beating about the bush, he consented to what he called "a provisional lock canal."

The new plans were hurriedly prepared and adopted. The estimates of the expenditure of money and time that would be necessary to carry them out were made low enough to create some hope that the public would advance further financial assistance to the scheme. The new route was to follow the existing line of the Company's work. The surface of the canal at its summit was to be forty-nine meters above the level of the oceans. For the sake of economy the depth of the cut was so far reduced that, had the work been carried to a conclusion, it must have prohibited the passage of a large proportion of ocean-going vessels. The summit was to be reached by the use of hydraulic elevating machinery.

THE FRENCH PUBLIC REFUSES TO SUBSCRIBE FURTHER FUNDS

The next step was to procure the necessary funds. Application was again made to the Government for authority to issue lottery bonds and the Company was granted permission to raise $160,000,000 in this manner. The bonds of $80 denomination were offered at $72 each. They were to bear four per cent interest and to be redeemed by a civil amortization association and to share in semimonthly drawings. The proposition, backed by better security, would have been an extremely attractive one, but to so low an ebb had the Company's credit fallen that only 800,000 bonds were subscribed for. A second attempt to float the bonds, with extra inducements to subscribers, only proved the futility of the effort.

The Company had already issued shares and obligations approximating the immense sum of $350,000,000 for an undertaking which it had promised to complete at a cost of $120,000,000. It now asked for an additional amount of upwards of $133,000,000 for the purpose of constructing a "temporary" waterway with a very limited capacity. Of the vast sums which the Company had expended, $105,000,000 went for interest, administration expenses, bankers' commissions, etc., and less than half was made available for the actual work. The annual interest charge was running in excess of $16,000,000 and at this time the Company had in hand barely sufficient cash to cover one month's current expenses.

Before the close of 1887 a general belief prevailed in England and America, and, perhaps everywhere but in France, that de Lesseps would never complete the Panama Canal. The failure to place the lottery bonds in the following year showed plainly that at length the French public had lost all confidence in the scheme and its chief promoter, whose statements and estimates had been so greatly, and so often, changed. Bankers could not be induced to handle the loan issues on any terms. The Government was not disposed to advance money to the Company and was itself so involved financially as to put the question of its finishing the canal beyond consideration. It was universally doubted whether the Company could complete the waterway, even though it received the money asked for, and it was shown that, in the event that it did succeed, its fixed charges would be in the neighborhood of $30,000,000, a sum far in excess of the maximum traffic returns of a sea level canal according to de Lesseps's largest estimate. So that upon his own showing the project under the most favorable circumstances would be a financial failure.

A RECEIVER TAKES OVER THE PANAMA CANAL COMPANY

On the fourth day of February, 1889, the civil court of the Seine appointed Joseph Brunet judicial receiver of *La Universelle Compagnie du Canal Interoceanique de Panama.*

We will give a brief statement of the receipts and expenditures of the Panama Canal Company from the date of its organization until the end of the year 1889.*

RECEIPTS.

Proceeds from the Capital Stock, various loans and bond issues..	†$254,336,547
Other receipts from sundry sources	7,933,317
Expenses incurred but not paid..........................	3,668,770
Total amount collected and due by the Company........	$265,938,634

EXPENDITURES.

(Outlay on the Isthmus.)

Salaries and expenses of management......................	$16,540,883
Rents and maintenance of leased property.................	3,301,070
Purchase of articles and material for consumption............	5,847,920
Purchase and transportation of machinery, etc...............	23,874,935
Surveys and preparatory work.............................	270,946
Central workshops and management........................	5,989,577
Various constructions, buildings, and general installation.....	9,407,705
Work of excavation and works of construction...............	89,434,224
Purchase of lands...	950,655
Sanitary and religious service.............................	1,836,768
Total expenditures on the Isthmus.....................	$156,654,687

(Outlay at Paris.)

Paid for the Concession..................................	$2,000,000
Paid to the Colombian Government........................	150,000
Various expenses incurred before organization...............	4,612,244

* A few comparatively small sums should strictly come within the account of 1890, but, for the present purpose, may without impropriety be included in the above statement.
† Fractions have been discarded throughout.

DINING ROOM IN THE MARRIED QUARTERS AT CULEBRA.

The Isthmian Canal Commission has provided comfortable quarters for its employees, carefully designed to meet the requirements of life in the tropics. All buildings are carefully screened to keep out the deadly mosquito.

Paid to American Financial Group................................ $2,400,000
Interest on various obligations.................................. 43,124,272
Amortization transactions....................................... 4,505,617
Expenses of floating bonds, loans, etc., commission, advertising,
    printing, etc... 16,616,840
Paid to agents of the Colombian Government..................... 42,760
Boards of management and direction............................. 1,242,458
Salaries of employees... 1,023,444
Sundries... 742,238
Home Office and furniture...................................... 417,479
Compensation to contractors on cancellation of contracts...... 240,000

    Total expenditures at Paris................................ $78,140,329

SUMMARY.

Receipts from all sources....................................... $265,938,600
Expenditures—
    At Panama.................................. $156,654,687
    At Paris................................... 78,140,329
    Paid for Railroad shares................... 18,653,637
    In connection with Lottery bonds........... 6,452,936
    Advance to the Colombian Government....... 491,015
    Various debtor accounts.................... 2,291,160
    Cash and negotiable paper in hand.......... 3,254,847

    Total equal to receipts.................................... $265,938,600

CHAPTER VII

THE NEW PANAMA CANAL COMPANY

The task entrusted to the receiver of the Panama Canal Company was an extremely difficult one. If the affairs of the Company should be wound up it would be impossible to save the shareholders from total, or almost total, loss of their investments, for the property and work which was estimated as worth $90,000,000 depended for its value upon a continuation of the operation.

The gravity of the situation, in which two hundred thousand persons, the majority of them in moderate circumstances, were involved, was fully appreciated by the Government, and special legislation was effected for the purpose of affording the Company temporary relief from the pressure of its liabilities.

Several circumstances militated against the endeavors of the receiver to reorganize the enterprise. The most serious of these was the public scepticism which had followed the failure of de Lesseps to make even a respectable approach towards the achievement of his undertaking. The shareholders had learned at last that systematic deception had been practised upon them for years, and they felt that they had no reliable knowledge as to the state of affairs at the Isthmus.

AN EFFORT TO RESTORE PUBLIC CONFIDENCE

The first step in the process of restoring public confidence was the investigation of the commission to which reference was made in the preceding chapter. In addition to the statement of the amount of work done and the value

THE NEW PANAMA CANAL COMPANY 111

of the plant, the commission gave an opinion that a lock canal might be completed in eight years at a further cost of $100,000,000.

Any hope that might have been derived from this report was, however, dependent upon the success of the receiver in negotiating new concessions with the Colombian Government, for the time limit, under the contract, for the completion of the canal, neared its termination. Lieutenant Wyse, who had secured the original grant, was sent to Bogota immediately following the commission's report. After *pourparlers* that extended over four months, a new agreement was signed December the tenth, 1890, providing for an extension of ten years.

In the meanwhile Joseph Brunet had died and was succeeded by Achille Monchicourt. The new receiver applied himself with remarkable energy and acumen to the organization of an active company. He had contrived to keep the work going upon the Isthmus, although the scale of operations was greatly reduced. During the years 1891–93, he settled, by a series of compromises, most of the lawsuits existing with the old company and successfully resisted certain creditors and bondholders who would otherwise have ruined the interests of all concerned.

STEPS TOWARDS THE REORGANIZATION OF THE COMPANY

In April, 1893, Colombia made a further concession to the receiver, by granting an extension until October 31, 1894, for the organization of a new company and ten years from that date for the completion of a canal. A few months later "a special law for the liquidation of the Interoceanic Canal Company" was passed and had the effect of suspending the most obstructive actions before the courts. Early in the following year, death relieved Achille Monchicourt and his place was filled by M. Gautron. There remained but a few months in which to effect the organization of the new company and, with the co-operation of the attorney for the bondholders, the receiver bent his energies to the task. They secured the co-operation of the managers of the old company, the contractors, and certain other interested persons, in the new enterprise, in the form of abatements of their claims, and subscriptions to the capital of the reorganization. The amount necessary to complete the full sum was to be asked of the old bondholders and shareholders.

The by-laws of the New Panama Canal Company were filed towards the close of June, 1894. The capital of the company consisted of 650,000 shares of $20 each, 600,000 of which were to be subscribed for, whilst 50,000, absolutely unencumbered, were to be given to the Colombian Government in consideration of the contracts granting extensions. Thus, five years after the appointment of a receiver for the Interoceanic Canal Company, what was generally known as the "New Panama Canal Company" was definitely established.

The new company, like its predecessor, was a commercial concern, pure and simple. Although the French Government, by the exercise of extraordinary legislation, had been largely instrumental in the creation of the company, neither governmental patronage nor responsibility was extended to it.

The directors of the new company appointed a *Comité Technique* to thoroughly examine the whole problem of the canal. This was a wise determination, for the surveys made under the direction of the old company had been of such a cursory character that little reliance could be placed upon them.

WELL-CALCULATED ACTION BY THE NEW COMPANY

The *Comité Technique* was composed of seven French engineers and an equal number of foreign experts, including several who had the special advantage of experience in canal work. Whilst making careful surveys and maturing plans for the ultimate operations, the committee directed the continuance of excavations in places where they were certain to come within the specifications of any plan that might eventually be adopted. In addition to its original investigations, the *Comité Technique* verified and rectified the surveys and measurements of the old company. In short the technical committee performed the most valuable scientific work that had yet been done in connection with the Isthmus and handed over to the Isthmian Canal Com-

declared to be worth at least a million dollars.

REPORT OF THE COMMITTEE OF INTERNATIONAL ENGINEERS

The final report of the *Comité Technique* was submitted at the close of the year 1898. It estimated the cost of a canal, which could be completed in ten years, and would be equal to all the demands of commerce, at one hundred million dollars. Aside from the question of health, the *Comité* recognized two principal difficulties to be overcome—the cut through the divide and the control of the Chagres. The former, whilst a stupendous task, was merely a matter of excavation and involved no serious engineering problem; the latter, on the contrary, presented features sufficiently intricate and perplexing to tax to the utmost the available technical ingenuity of the world. The solution appeared to be susceptible of achievement by several different methods, and numerous plans emanated from sources that commanded respectful attention.

"The studies of the New Company were based on three fundamental principles: (1) To reject any plan that did not, independently of considerations of time and expense, offer every guarantee of a serviceable canal. (2) To reject any fanciful scheme depending on the application of new and untried devices not justified by experience; and (3) to give due weight to the peculiar tropical conditions under which the work must be executed. These must compel the employment of a class of laborers inferior to those available in better climates, and the work will be exhausting to those supervising the constructions. No technical details should therefore be admitted involving operations of exceptional difficulty."*

THE PLAN OF THE NEW PANAMA CANAL COMPANY

The report of the *Comité* included two plans contemplating two summit levels, of which the bottom of the canal was respectively sixty-eight and thirty-two feet above mean tide. The relative costs of construction were nearly the same, but the fact that a canal at the higher level could be completed in much less time decided the *Comité* to recommend that plan.

General Abbott intimated that but for this consideration it is certain that the conclusion of the *Comité* would have been different. He declared that in the hands of the American Government, with expense a minor condition, "there can be no question that the low level variant should be preferred." Since the controversy has already been settled for all time and the canal completed at an eighty-five foot level, it is useless to consider the details of the *Comité's projet*, to which the plan recommended by the first Isthmian Canal Commission closely conformed. The line follows closely that adopted by the old company, which, with slight variations has been accepted by all subsequent technical surveys. More than half the distance follows straight lines, and in the remainder of the route the highly important feature of curvature leaves nothing to be desired This is a detail of the utmost consequence as affecting safety of transit and speed of passage. "Experience on the Suez Canal has compelled, since the route was opened to traffic, a costly increase from the original minimum radius of 700 metres (2,300 feet) to 1,800 metres (5,905 feet). On the Panama *projet* the ruling radius is 3,000 metres (9,842 feet),

---

* Problems of the Panama Canal. Brig.-Gen. Henry L. Abbott, U. S. Army (retired). Late Member of the Comité Technique. New York, 1905.

falling occasionally to 2,500 metres (8,202 feet), the minimum being 1,700 metres (5,577 feet), and this latter only for about half a mile in approaching Obispo, where the width is sufficiently increased to justify the reduction."

The scientific information accumulated by the *Comité Technique* is amongst the most valuable data relating to the Panama Canal extant and is valued at $1,000,000.

CRYSTALLIZATION OF AMERICAN INTERESTS

By the time the *Comité Technique* had made its report, public sentiment in this country had become strongly impressed with the desirability of a trans-isthmian canal under American control, and a majority in Congress favored immediate action to that end. The Nicaragua route appeared to be the best available at the time and general opinion favored it. The situation thus created caused extreme anxiety to those interested in the welfare of the New Panama Canal Company. It had reached precisely the stage where the directors proposed to appeal to the financiers of the world, when its prospects were thus suddenly overshadowed. Although firmly convinced that the Nicaragua route was greatly inferior to their own, the company realized that should the United States construct a waterway there, or elsewhere, commercial competition would be impossible. This and other considerations would surely deter investors from backing the private enterprise. Furthermore, with the American Government in the field, the completion of the Panama Canal would be retarded, if not prevented, by the difficulty in securing labor under competitive conditions.

In this dilemma the directors decided upon a course calculated to bring the comparative merits of the Nicaragua and Panama routes squarely before the American Government. Since the report of the *Comité* had not been made public, the directors were satisfied that the United States authorities could not possibly have anything like adequate knowledge or appreciation of the superior advantages of their proposition.

The full report of the *Comité Technique*, including details of the *projet* recommended by it, was accordingly placed in the hands of President McKinley during the first week of December, 1898. On the twenty-first day of that month the Senate, by a large majority, passed a bill providing for government support of the Maritime Canal Company in its Nicaraguan enterprise, but the House adjourned without taking action upon the measure. On the reassembling of Congress the French Company secured a hearing before the Rivers and Harbors Committee of the lower house, to whom the Senate bill had been referred on an amendment. The Company's representatives frankly explained their project and expressed the willingness of the Company to re-incorporate under American laws in case the Panama route should be decided upon. The Senate amendment was defeated and, in March, 1899, Congress authorized the President to make an exhaustive investigation as to the most practicable and feasible Isthmian route for a canal that should be under the complete control of the United States and the absolute property of the nation.

APPOINTMENT OF THE FIRST ISTHMIAN CANAL COMMISSION

In accordance with these instructions President McKinley placed the work of investigation in the hands of a body which was officially styled "The Isthmian Canal Commission," and which was composed of the following members: Rear-Admiral John C. Walker, U. S. N. (retired); Hon. Samuel Pasco; George S. Morison; Lieutenant-Colonel Oswald H. Ernst, Corps of Engineers, U. S. A.; Lewis M. Haupt, C. E.; Alfred Noble, C. E.; Colonel P. C. Hains, Corps of Engineers, U. S. A.; Wm. H. Burr, C. E.; Prof. Emory R. Johnson. The Commission made an examination of the New Panama Canal Company's project, both in Paris and on the Isthmus, and then proceeded to ascertain

OLD FRENCH MACHINERY RUSTING IN THE JUNGLE.

A pathetic reminder of the gigantic failure of De Lesseps.

upon what terms and conditions the property and rights of the Company might be transferred to the United States, for the law under which the Commission was acting forbade the consideration of government support to a private enterprise. The Republic of Colombia having signified its willingness to consent to the alienation of the concession, it only remained for the Commission to learn the purchase price in order to make its report to the President. There was considerable delay and some misunderstanding about this last detail. The Company was naturally reluctant to submit a definite figure to a body which "had no authority to accept or reject any terms," but proposed instead to make a tentative offer subject to an itemized valuation and arbitration where necessary. To this the Commission would not listen, but insisted upon a statement of the Company's price in a lump sum without reservation.

THE REPORT OF THE COMMISSION FAVORS THE NICARAGUA ROUTE

The report of the Isthmian Canal Commission was presented to the President in November, 1901. It discarded altogether the detailed memorandum of valuations submitted by the Company and briefly declared that the "total amount for which the Company offers to sell and transfer its canal property to the United States" is $109,141,500. The value set upon it by the Commission was $40,000,000. It needs no extensive calculation to determine that this was an underestimate, even when due allowance is made for the usual depreciation of second-hand property. It will be remembered that the receiver of the old company valued the assets that passed into his hands at about $90,000,000, and several millions had been expended in a judicious manner by the new company.

The report closed with the following recommendation: "After considering all the facts developed by the investigations made by the Commission and the actual situation as it now stands, and having in view the terms offered by the New Panama Canal Company, this Commission is of the opinion that 'the most practicable and feasible route' for an Isthmian canal, to be 'under the control, management, and ownership of the United States' is that known as the Nicaragua route."

THE FRENCH COMPANY MEETS OUR BID

When this finding became known at Paris the directors of the New Panama Canal Company immediately resigned, and at a general meeting of stockholders held in the last days of the year it was decided to meet the terms of the Commission's estimate. Accordingly an offer to sell out all assets, rights, and interests for the sum of $40,000,000 was telegraphed, the owners realizing that with only one possible purchaser and the certainty of the property becoming practically valueless unless taken by that purchaser, no alternative existed. The Company's change of base impelled the Commission to make a supplementary report, in which it stated that "the unreasonable sum asked for the property and rights of the New Panama Canal Company when the Commission reached its former conclusion overbalanced that route, and now that the estimates by the two routes had been nearly equalized, the Commission can form its judgment by weighing the advantages of each and determining which is the more practicable and feasible. . . . After considering the changed conditions that now exist, the Commission is of the opinion that 'the most practicable and feasible route' for an Isthmian canal to be 'under the control, management, and ownership of the United States' is that known as the Panama route."

THE SENATE INVESTIGATES THE QUESTION OF ROUTE

In the meanwhile, and before the Isthmian Canal Commission had filed its report, an ill-considered bill had been passed by the House, authorizing the President to secure a concession from Nicaragua and to proceed at once to the construction of a waterway by that route. Fortunately the Hepburn Bill was not hastily disposed of in the Senate. The matter was thoroughly investigated in committee and extensively debated in the chamber. The weight of engineering opinion was overwhelmingly in favor of the Panama route, but, perhaps, the most effective statement in its favor was delivered by Senator Hanna, who had made a close personal investigation of the question. A series of practical inquiries submitted by him to eighty shipowners, shipmasters, officers and pilots engaged in operating the most important intercontinental steamship lines and sailing vessels elicited replies which were without exception strongly in favor of the Panama route. More than ten per cent of these emanated from persons interested in sailing ships and familiar with the navigation of them, a result especially significant in view of the fact that one of the very strongest objections advanced against the more southerly location is its assumed disadvantage to sailing craft.* The debate in the Senate was followed by the passage in both branches of Congress of the Spooner Bill. This measure authorized the President to acquire the rights and property of the New Panama Canal Company for a sum not to exceed $40,000,-000 and to secure by treaty with the Republic of Colombia the perpetual control of the territory needful for operating the canal; it also provided for the prosecution of the work by an Isthmian Canal Commission consisting of seven members to be appointed by the President.

We have already recited briefly the incidents of the imbroglio that followed the failure of the Colombian Legislature to ratify the Hay-Herran Treaty and culminated in the independence of Panama. Sufficient has been said to show how nearly the American people came to being committed to the Nicaragua route. What, in such an event, would have been the actual outcome it is impossible

---

* Full details of this interesting information will be found in the Congressional Record, June 9, 1902.

to conjecture, but there is ample ground for the belief that the undertaking would have proved more hazardous, more difficult, and less satisfactory when completed, than the Panama project.

It will be convenient at this point to consider briefly the most important features of difference between the two routes. In the first place, the verified data upon which to work was very much greater in the case of Panama, not to mention the fact that a considerable proportion of the task had already been accomplished at that point. In fact the Nicaragua project is still a mass of theory which application might prove to be infinitely erroneous, whilst at Panama the stage of uncertainty had been virtually passed and the operation presented definite and calculable tasks.

THE NICARAGUAN ROUTE COMPARED WITH THAT OF PANAMA

The American Isthmus does not contain a single natural harbor on the Nicaraguan coast A satisfactory approach to a canal might be excavated upon the Pacific side, but the Atlantic littoral offers no such facility. The harbor of Greytown, which was once a good one, has long since been closed by the formation of banks whose material is constantly carried down by the San Carlos and Serapiqui Rivers. These obstructions could be cleared, but only at great expense and the maintenance of the necessary channel would involve incessant dredging. At Panama, an excellent entrance was available at either end of the Canal.

Whilst both routes lie within the zone of seismic disturbances, there was no recorded convulsion, nor any physical evidence of one, in the Isthmus of sufficient force to have seriously damaged a lock level canal, much less one upon the sea level. Nicaragua, on the other hand, presents volcanic features, including Lake Nicaragua itself, which betoken tremendous upheavals in the past. The earth-

THE NEW PANAMA CANAL COMPANY 121

quake that occurred in that region in 1844 must have caused great destruction to a canal had one been in existence at the time, as well as to the shipping on it. The proposed line passes close to the active volcano Ometepe, which was in violent eruption as late as 1883. The great volcano, Momotombo, on the edge of Lake Managua, after fifty years of inactivity, burst out with great violence in the month of February, 1905. This eruption was preceded by earthquakes.

NICARAGUAN ROUTE PRESENTS MANY EXTRAORDINARY DIFFICULTIES

The region traversed by the Nicaraguan route is subject to strong winds and heavy rainfall, which would militate against the safe navigation of a canal. The latter preventing clear observation would tend to delay or prevent passage at night. It is true that Panama is also subject to heavy rainfall, but it is neither so continuous nor so great as upon the Atlantic coast of Nicaragua, which has no definite dry season. Moreover, any delays occasioned from this cause would be of shorter duration and of less consequence in Panama owing to the difference in length of passage.

Serious difficulties in the case of the Nicaragua construction would be created by the San Juan River, which may be considered as at least equal to those involved in the regulation of the Chagres. The course of the former stream is extremely tortuous, and expert opinion holds that it would be impossible to reduce it to a safe curvature. General Abbott says: "This long river route, exceeding in length the entire distance from ocean to ocean by the Panama line, must remain subject to the combined effects of strong winds, sharp curvature, and longitudinal and cross currents, to say nothing of the obscuration due to heavy rainfall. It may well be doubted whether any system of artificial lighting could render night transit safe for large ships, and without it delays and possible congestion could hardly be avoided." A popular idea prevails that the Nicaragua route offers a great advantage in the seventy miles of lake section, but this is fallacy. Something like one half of the distance is over bottom that presents a similar problem to that encountered at Lake Menzeleh in the construction of the Suez Canal, to wit, the opening and maintenance of a channel through soft mud. The Isthmian Canal Commission estimated the cost of this portion of the operation at $8,000,000. Even when made, this expensive and difficult channel would be a source of frequent danger, for Lake Nicaragua is subject to violent storms, during which there would be serious liability of vessels grounding. To quote General Abbott: "It remains to refer to what from an engineering point of view would be perhaps the most serious objection to the Nicaragua route if completed and opened to traffic. This would be the risk of longer or shorter interruptions liable to result from the complicated systems of water supply in seasons of drought of long duration; and the lake lies in a district where they are far from uncommon. It has been claimed that a vast lake about 3,000 square miles in extent must furnish an ideal source of supply, but the matter will bear a little examination.

CONTROL OF LAKE NICARAGUA A SERIOUS PROBLEM

"By the dam on the lower San Juan river the channel of the present stream would be transformed into an arm of the lake, maintained sensibly at the same level, and through this arm all shipping must pass, the depth of water depending wholly on the stand of the lake. This stand is now subject to a natural oscillation of about 13 feet. Under the projected conditions the entire outflow must pass over the dam at a distance of 50 miles from the main lake, and if the level is allowed to rise above the present high water stand, valuable lands under cultivation on the west shore of the lake would be flooded and claims for damages would result. On the other hand, the bed of the river is crossed by many ledges of rock, and the cost of excavation fixes a limit to the depth economically practicable. . . . The level of the lake must be held approximately between 111 feet and 104 feet above tide and the bed of the present river must be excavated sufficiently to afford a sailing depth of 35 feet at all times. But the records establish that years of high lake and years of low lake follow in no regular succession. As it is impossible to provide a reserve sufficient to control the level of an immense body of water 3,000 square miles in extent, the regulation of this vital element must be left to the foresight and good judgment of the operator controlling the outflow of the dam. . . . Carelessness or bad judgment on the part of the operator at the dam, or an abnormal season, might therefore involve the stoppage of traffic for an indefinite period. A really desirable canal should be subject to no such contingency."

The Nicaragua route shows some savings in distances between important shipping points as measured upon the map, but these would almost certainly be made up for by the much shorter time of passage through the Panama Canal.

It must be borne in mind that the decision of the Isthmian Canal Commission in favor of Nicaragua was prompted by the price asked by the Company for its interests in the Panama enterprise and that decision was promptly reversed as soon as the Commission's estimate was accepted. As the cost of constructing and maintaining the respective waterways was practically equal in the Commission's opinion, it is evident that the alacrity with which they turned to the Panama proposition when the terms were favorable was due to a conviction of the superior merits of that project.

CHAPTER VIII

The American Enterprise

The Hay——Bunau-Varilla Treaty was negotiated between the respective representatives of the United States and Panama in the autumn of 1903 and fully ratified February, 1904. The most important features of this convention are as follows:

Article 1. "The United States guarantees and will maintain the independence of the Republic of Panama."

Article 2. "The Republic of Panama grants to the United States in perpetuity the use, occupation and control of a zone of land, and land under water for the construction, maintenance, operation, sanitation and protection of said Canal, of the width of ten miles, extending to the distance of five miles on each side of the center line of the Canal to be constructed; the said zone beginning in the Caribbean Sea three marine miles from mean low-water mark and extending to and across the Isthmus of Panama into the Pacific Ocean to a distance of three marine miles from mean low-water mark, with the proviso that the cities of Panama and Colon and the harbors adjacent to said cities, which are included within the boundaries of the zone above described, shall not be included within this grant. . . . The Republic of Panama further grants in like manner to the United States in perpetuity all islands within the limits of the Zone above described and, in addition thereto, the group of small islands in the Bay of Panama, named Perico, Naos, Culebra and Flamenco."

Article 3. "The Republic of Panama grants to the United States all the rights, power, and authority within the Zone mentioned and described in Article 2 of this agree-

Photograph, Underwood & Underwood, N. Y.

THE INTERSECTION OF THE AMERICAN CANAL WITH THE OLD FRENCH CANAL AT MINDI.

This picture also shows the dredges operating in the Atlantic Entrance to the Canal.

ment . . . which the United States would possess and exercise if it were the sovereign of the territory within which said lands and waters are located, to the entire exclusion of the exercise by the Republic of Panama of any such sovereign rights, power or authority."

Article 6 provides for compensation to private property owners, by the United States, for any damage to private property occasioned by the canal operations and for the assessment of such compensation by arbitration.

UNITED STATES AUTHORITY IN COLON AND PANAMA

Article 7. ". . . The Republic of Panama agrees that the cities of Panama and Colon shall comply in perpetuity with the sanitary ordinances, whether of a preventive or curative character, prescribed by the United States and, in case the Government of Panama is unable, or fails in its duty, to enforce this compliance by the cities of Panama and Colon with the sanitary ordinances of the United States, the Republic of Panama grants to the United States the right and authority to enforce the same.

"The same right and authority are granted to the United States for the maintenance of public order in the cities of Panama and Colon and the territories and harbors adjacent thereto in case the Republic of Panama should not be, in the judgment of the United States, able to maintain such order."

Provision is made in this article for the reimbursement of the United States for any outlay it may make, under the discretionary authority referred to above, in "works of sanitation, collection and disposition of sewage, and distribution of water, in the cities of Panama and Colon."

Article 9. "The United States agrees that the ports at either entrance of the canal and the waters thereof, and the Republic of Panama agrees that the towns of Panama and Colon shall be free for all time, so that there shall not be imposed, or collected, custom-house tolls, tonnage, anchorage, light-house, wharf, pilot, or quarantine dues, or any other charges, or taxes of any kind upon any vessel using, or passing through the Canal, or belonging to, or employed by, the United States, directly or indirectly, in connection with the construction, maintenance, operation, sanitation and protection of the main Canal, or auxiliary works, or upon the cargo, officers, crew, or passengers, of any such vessels, except such tolls and charges as may be imposed by the United States for the use of the Canal and other works, and except tolls and charges imposed by the Republic of Panama upon merchandise destined to be introduced for the consumption of the rest of the Republic of Panama, and upon vessels touching at the ports of Panama and Colon and which do not cross the Canal."

THE PRICE OF THE CONCESSION

Article 14. "As the price of compensation for the rights, powers, and privileges granted in this convention by the Republic of Panama to the United States, the Government of the United States agrees to pay to the Republic of Panama the sum of ten million dollars ($10,000,000) in gold coin of the United States on the exchange of the ratification of this convention and also an annual payment, during the life of this convention, of two hundred and fifty thousand dollars ($250,000) in like gold coin, beginning nine years after the date aforesaid. . . ."

THE CANAL TO BE NEUTRAL FOREVER

Article 18. "The Canal, when constructed, and the entrances thereto, shall be neutral in perpetuity, and shall be open upon the terms provided for by section 1 of article three of, and in conformity with all the stipulations of, the treaty entered into by the Governments of the United States and Great Britain on November 18, 1901."*

---

*The reference is to the Hay-Pauncefote Treaty, which was designed to facilitate the construction of the Panama Canal.

In accordance with the provisions of the Spooner Bill, the President appointed a commission of seven members to prosecute the canal operations. They were: Rear-Admiral John G. Walker, U. S. N. (retired), Chairman; Major-General George W. Davis, U. S. A. (retired), Governor of the Canal Zone; William Barclay Parsons, C. E.; William H. Burr, C. E.; Benjamin M. Harrod, C. E.; Carl E. Grunsky, C. E.; Frank J. Hecker. John F. Wallace, an engineer of experience and ability, was appointed Engineer-in-Chief, and Surgeon-Colonel W. C. Gorgas, of the United States Army, whose splendid record in Cuba marked him as pre-eminently fitted for the task, was placed in charge of the Sanitary Department.

In a letter dated May the ninth, 1904, the President directed the Honorable William H. Taft, Secretary of War, to assume supervision of the work of the Isthmian Canal Commission. The same document defines the duties of the Commission, which are, in general, to make all needful regulations for the government of the Zone; and "to make or cause to be made, all needful surveys, borings, designs, plans, and specifications of the engineering, hydraulic, and sanitary works required and to supervise and execute the same."

INSTRUCTIONS REGARDING THE INHABITANTS OF THE ZONE

This letter goes on to instruct the Secretary that "the inhabitants of the Isthmian Canal Zone are entitled to security in their persons, property, and religion, and in all their private rights and relations. They should be so informed by public proclamation. The people should be disturbed as little as possible in their customs and avocations that are in harmony with principles of well-ordered and decent living.

"The municipal laws of the Zone are to be administered by the ordinary tribunals substantially as they were before the change. Police magistrates and justices of the peace and other officers discharging duties usually devolving upon these officers of the law, will be continued in office if they are suitable persons. . . . The laws of the land, with which the inhabitants are familiar, and which were in force on February 26, 1904, will continue in force in the Canal Zone and in other places on the Isthmus over which the United States has jurisdiction until altered or annulled by the said Commission," but the principles of government set forth in the Constitution of the United States are to be observed in the administration of the Zone.

In a later letter to the Secretary, the President makes an important declaration of the broader policy of the United States towards the Republic of Panama as follows:

ATTITUDE OF THE UNITED STATES TOWARDS PANAMA

"The United States is about to confer on the people of the State of Panama a great benefit by the expenditure of millions of dollars in the construction of the canal: but this fact must not blind us to the importance of so exercising the authority given us under the treaty with Panama as to avoid creating any suspicion, however unfounded, of our intentions as to the future. We have not the slightest intention of establishing an independent colony in the middle of the State of Panama, or of exercising any greater governmental functions than are necessary to enable us conveniently and safely to construct, maintain, and operate the canal under the rights given us by the treaty. Least of all do we wish to interfere with the business and prosperity of the people of Panama. However far a just construction of the treaty might enable us to go, did the exigencies of the case require it, in asserting the equivalent of sovereignty over the Canal Strip,* it is our full intention that the rights which we exercise shall be exercised with all proper care for the honor and interests of the people of Panama. The exercise of such powers as are given us by the treaty within

---

* See Article 3, of the treaty quoted above.

the geographical boundaries of the Republic of Panama may easily, if a real sympathy for both the present and future welfare of the people of Panama, is not shown, create distrust of the American government."

It is not our purpose to enter into a discussion of the political aspects of the treaty, but a careful reading of the portions which have been reproduced will give an idea of the great scope of this convention. To draw attention to but one direction in which its potency extends, the provision for the maintenance of order by the United States in the cities of Colon and Panama is a practical preventive of future revolution in the Republic.

At the close of the year Secretary Taft visited the Isthmus and entered into an agreement with President Amador, covering several supplementary matters of importance. A tariff adjustment, satisfactory to the Panamans, was effected. It was arranged that only supplies for the canal, and goods in transit, were in future to be entered at the Zone ports, thus assuring the Government of Panama of all customs receipts and port dues. The Republic agreed to reduce its tariff from fifteen to ten per cent, except upon wines and alcohol, and to place its postal rates upon the two-cent basis. Panama also agreed to adopt the gold standard, a very necessary measure for the welfare of that republic, as well as for the facility of transactions between the two nations. At the time this understanding was arrived at, the Colombian currency had become so debased that a five-dollar bill was exchangeable for an American nickel, and there was one cent change due at that.

A FUTILE REVOLUTIONARY MOVEMENT

Just before the arrival of Secretary Taft, General Huertas had planned one of the puny revolutions which have furnished librettists with inexhaustible material. He had mobilized the army of 182 half-clad men and boys, with the design of subverting the Amador government. The threat of calling upon half a dozen American marines who happened to be in the city with their side-arms on, induced him to give up the idea. He was placed upon the retired list and the army of the Republic was disbanded.

At a banquet given in his honor by the Panaman President the Secretary delivered a timely homily on the subject of revolutions and urged upon his auditors the necessity of the government preserving the rights of the minority. The speech, which was in the nature of a friendly warning and an intimation that the United States expected the Republic to refrain from any revolutionary disturbances in the future, was well received by the representatives of both political parties, and doubtless had a salutary effect.

THE COMMISSION VISITS THE ISTHMUS

The Canal Commission arrived at the Isthmus in April, 1904. The only work in progress at the time was the excavation of the Culebra Cut, where a few French machines were employed with a force of about seven hundred men. Owing to the long lapse of time since the New Panama Canal Company ceased operations, a chaotic condition prevailed along the entire line of the canal and the plant and equipment transferred by that Company was in such a deteriorated and scattered state as to require months for its collection and repair. Whilst the task of straightening up was being carried out Engineer Wallace tested some American steam excavators and established important data as to units of cost and expenditure of time. Meanwhile the Commission proceeded, by means of new surveys and examinations, to gain such information as might afford a satisfactory basis for the ultimate plans. As has been stated, the French companies performed a great deal of accurate scientific work along the same lines, but much of the data secured from them needed to be modified in order to bring it into harmony with the more extensive scheme of the American project. The Commission was not restricted by the limitations which governed the plans of the purely commercial enterprises, and whilst its work was entirely of a tentative nature, a waterway much larger than any contemplated by the French companies was a foregone conclusion.

THE PLAN OF THE WALKER COMMISSION

The Commission formulated a plan for a lock canal at an 85-foot level with a dam at Bohio and a lake 38.5 square miles extending from that point to Obispo. The Commission rejected the sea-level plan, prefacing its conclusion with the following statement: "If a sea-level canal be constructed, either the canal itself must be made of such dimensions that maximum floods, modified to some extent by a reservoir in the Upper Chagres, could pass down its channel without injury, or independent channels must be provided to carry off these floods. As the canal lies in the lowest part of the valley, the construction of such channels would be a matter of serious difficulty, and the simplest solution would be to make the canal prism large enough to take the full discharge. This would have the advantage, also, of furnishing a very large canal, in which navigation under ordinary circumstances would be exceptionally easy. It would involve a cross section from Obispo to the Atlantic, having an area of a least 15,000 square feet below the water line, which would give a bottom width of at least 400 feet. The quantity of excavation required for such a canal has been roughly computed, and is found to be about 266,228,000 cubic yards. The cost of such a canal, including a dam at Alhajuela and a tide lock at Miraflores, near the Pacific end, is estimated at not less than $240,000,000. Its construction would probably take at least twenty years."

The investigations of the Commission were necessarily directed chiefly to the various suggestions for the control of the Chagres. The question had to be considered from the point of view of a sea level canal as well as that of a waterway with locks. In the former case the flood waters of the river, if admitted into the canal, would create dangerous currents and carry in heavy deposits, necessitating extensive dredging. The various dam projects were examined by the Commission as well as the plans of the French companies for diverting the river through a tunnel to the Pacific Ocean.

Before the Commission closed the first year of its existence the question of its efficiency and adaptability to the work in hand was widely raised. Secretary Taft, upon his return from the Isthmus in December, 1904, had expressed to the President an opinion that the Commission, whilst it had "made as much progress in the necessary preparations for the buildings of the canal as could be expected in the short time since its appointment," was unwieldy and so constituted as to render difficult the apportionment of specific work and responsibility among its members. Chief Engineer Wallace complained that his plans were repeatedly changed and that he was hampered in the effort to carry them out.

THE OBJECTIONS TO THE COMMISSION

In a message sent to Congress on the 13th of January, 1905, President Roosevelt plainly expressed his objections to the existing arrangement. He asked for "greater discretion in the organization of the personnel" to be employed in the management of the enterprise.

"Actual experience has convinced me," he said "that it will be impossible to obtain the best and most effective service under the limitations prescribed by law. The general plans for the work must be agreed upon with the aid of the best engineers of the country, who should act as an advisory or consulting body. The consulting engineers should not be put upon the Commission, which should be used only as an executive instrument for the executive and adminis-

MANDINGO STOCKADE FOR ZONE CONVICTS ENGAGED IN ROAD BUILDING.

A tropical prison. Zone convicts are profitably employed in building government roads.

trative work. The actual work of executing the general plans agreed upon by the Commission, after receiving the conclusions of the advising engineers, must be done by an engineer in charge; and we now have an excellent engineer." The President went on to state that the Commission should consist at most of five members and preferably of three.

In response to this message, the House passed a bill to abolish the Commission and place the government of the Zone and the construction of the Canal entirely in the hands of the President, but the measure was defeated in the Senate. Failing Congressional relief the President determined, in his characteristic way, to deal with the situation himself. He secured the resignation of the entire Isthmian Canal Commission and reformed that body, placing the control of affairs definitely in the hands of an Executive Committee composed of three of the seven members required by law to constitute the whole. Each of the executive members had distinct duties assigned to him. Chairman Shonts was placed in charge of the entire enterprise, with powers resembling those of a railroad president. Engineer Wallace was made field manager, with full control of the construction. Judge Magoon was created Governor of the Canal Zone and United States Minister to Panama. The other four members of the Commission were: Mordecai T. Endicott, Peter C. Hains, Oswald H. Ernst and Benjamin M. Harrod.

WALLACE RESIGNS AND STEVENS STEPS IN

The new arrangement had been in force less than sixty days when the Chief Engineer, for some cause which has never been fully explained, resigned his position. The resignation, coming as it did without warning or adequate explanation, naturally aroused resentment on the part of Secretary Taft, and Mr. Wallace retired from the service under a cloud. The place thus made vacant was promptly and satisfactorily filled by the selection of John F. Stevens, who had been engaged by the War Department to supervise the construction of the new railroads in the Philippines. Mr. Stevens assumed charge of the canal operations in August, 1905.

On the first day of the following month the International Board of Consulting Engineers met in Washington. This body had been formed with the co-operation of several foreign governments for the purpose mainly of examining the principal problems involved in the construction of the Canal.

THE PRESIDENT'S ADDRESS TO THE CONSULTING ENGINEERS

The President addressed the assembled Board at length, explaining that his remarks were to be taken as suggestions rather than as instructions. "I hope," he said, "that ultimately it will prove possible to build a sea-level canal. Such a canal would undoubtedly be best in the end, if feasible, and I feel that one of the chief advantages of the Panama Route is that ultimately a sea-level canal will be a possibility. But, while paying due heed to the ideal perfectibility of the scheme from an engineer's standpoint, remember the need of having a plan which shall provide for the immediate building of the canal on the safest terms and in the shortest possible time.

"If to build a sea-level canal will but slightly increase the risk, then, of course, it is preferable. But if to adopt a plan of a sea-level canal means to incur hazard, and to insure indefinite delay, then it is not preferable. If the advantages and disadvantages are closely balanced I expect you to say so.

"I desire also to know whether, if you recommend a high-level multi-lock canal, it will be possible after it is completed to turn it into, or substitute for it, in time, a sea-level canal, without interrupting the traffic upon it. Two of the prime considerations to be kept steadily in mind are: 1. The utmost practicable speed of construction.

2. Practical certainty that the plan proposed will be feasible; that it can be carried out with the minimum risk."

After a thorough study of the maps and documents in the possession of the Isthmian Canal Commission, the Board of Consulting Engineers spent three weeks on the Isthmus, and on February 19, 1906, presented their report to Congress through the President, advocating a sea-level canal. A dissentient minority of five members, all Americans, made however a detailed report advocating a lock canal eighty-five feet above mean sea-level.

THE MILITARY BOARD

In April, 1907, Mr. John F. Stevens resigned from the position of Chief Engineer. President Roosevelt, with the hearty approval of Mr. Taft, who was then Secretary of War, immediately installed a military organization, in accordance with an idea that had been entertained for some time previous. A new Commission was created, with Colonel George W. Goethals, Corps of Engineers, U. S. A., as Chairman and Chief Engineer. The other members were Lieutenant-Colonel H. F. Hodges, U. S. A.; Lieutenant-Colonel William L. Sibert, U. S. A.; Lieutenant-Colonel D. D. Gaillard, U. S. A.; Civil Engineer H. H. Rousseau, U. S. N.; Colonel W. C. Gorgas, U. S. A.; and Honorable J. C. S. Blackburn. Mr. J. B. Bishop was retained in the position of Secretary to the Commission and Editor of the weekly "Canal Record." The only change in the composition of the membership was occasioned by the retirement of Senator Blackburn at the close of his third year's service. The vacancy was filled by the appointment of Mr. M. H. Thatcher, on April 12, 1910, to the head of the Department of Administration.

When Colonel Goethals and his aides came into control of the Canal, the lock plan, as advocated by the minority of the Board of Consulting Engineers, had been authorized by Congress and accepted by the people of the United States as representing the form which the waterway would ultimately take.

The opportunity of still further strengthening the position of the Chairman of the Commission was not neglected by the President. Colonel Goethals was also made the chief executive of the Canal Zone, exercising the power formerly vested in the Governor, and President of the Panama Railroad Company, thus centering in him the absolute authority upon the work and making him superior to all save the President and the Secretary of War.

THE INVESTIGATING BOARD

In February, 1909, the President ordered Secretary Taft and a board of experts, especially appointed for the purpose, to make an inspection of the work upon the Canal, with particular reference to the Gatun Dam. In the resultant report the Commissioners expressed the opinion that the site of the structure met all the requirements of safety and that excess of precaution characterized the design and measures for its execution. They recommended a reduction in the height of the dam and also suggested some modifications of other parts of the Canal plan.

The changes which were adopted in 1909, and a few that had been previously determined upon, were the last of any consequence to be effected.

The chief departures from the plan as previously described were the removal of the terminal locks at the Pacific end from Sosa to Miraflores, and the consequent elimination of the proposed lake between the divide and the Pacific Ocean, certain increases in the dimensions of the channel; enlargement of the lock capacities; decrease in the height of the Gatun Dam, and the construction of breakwaters at Colon and Panama.

CHAPTER IX

THE HEALTH PROBLEM

The question of sanitation, closely allied as it is to that of labor, has always been an important factor in operations conducted upon the Isthmus of Panama, but fortunately, with the advance of time, the difficulties presented by it have become ever more susceptible to scientific treatment. The Panama railroad was built at an appalling sacrifice of life. At that time a blind contest was waged with disease, but no serious effort was made to mitigate the conditions that produced it. The French companies adopted some preventive measures and their provision for the care of the sick was admirable, but it remained for American administration to attack the problem in the determined and radical manner that minimized effects by reducing causes.

It was recognized at the outset that the Panama Canal could not be built by Americans unless the Canal Zone was first made healthy in order that Americans could live here with reasonable safety. So long as health conditions were bad it would be impossible to recruit a stable labor force, not only on account of actual conditions, but also because the Isthmus of Panama had been given a world-wide reputation for unhealthfulness during the construction of the Panama railroad and the work of the French on the Canal.

A knowledge of conditions as they existed on the Isthmus at the time of the American occupation is necessary to a realization of the truly marvelous results which have been accomplished.

The Isthmus itself was truly a valley of death, in which

malaria, yellow fever and smallpox ran riot. The terminal cities of Colon and Panama were the chief breeding places for these diseases, and their reputation as the worst pestholes in the world was more than justified. Imagine cities whose sidewalks and streets were entirely unpaved, and which during the rainy season (which lasts during nine months of the year) became practically impassable, without any sewage system or system of plumbing, lacking all facilities for the collection of garbage and refuse, so that the only method used by the natives to get rid of such matter was to dump it into the streets, resulting in a condition of almost inconceivable filth and an ideal breeding place for disease!

SANITATION IN PANAMA AND COLON

The American authorities realized that any movement to make the Isthmus healthy must begin with the cleaning up of Colon and Panama. With this idea in mind we were wise enough to specify in our treaty with the Republic of Panama that our Government should have sanitary jurisdiction over these two cities. Thus was the foundation laid for the wonderful transformation which has converted this land of pestilence and death into an abode for Americans which is as healthy as the average city in the United States.

Marvelous as the results have been it must be admitted that they are chiefly due to the brilliant discovery made by the United States army surgeons in Cuba in 1900 that yellow fever, the scourge of the tropics, was transmitted from one person to another solely by a mosquito of a particular type, known as the *stegomyia*. It should be said here in all justice to the surgeons and soldiers of the United States army who risked their lives in the making of this discovery, and particularly to that brave man who sacrificed his life in its pursuit, that it is doubtful if the Canal enterprise could have been brought to a successful termination without their sacrifice and the knowledge which was obtained through it. The four years which had elapsed between the original demonstration of this theory and the arrival of the Americans in Panama gave ample time in which to prove its accuracy. With this information, and the supplementary knowledge supplied by the discovery in 1898 that malaria, which ranks second only in importance to yellow fever as one of the scourges of the tropics, was transmitted in similar fashion from one person to another by a type of mosquito known as the *anopheles*, the work of making the Isthmus a safe habitation for Americans became practically a matter of administration. The dangers were understood; likewise the precautions. Smallpox could be controlled by vaccination, and the plague guarded against by proper quarantine regulations such as are in effect in every American port, so that the sanitary officers of the commission had their work laid out for them clearly and accurately before beginning their task.

MOSQUITOES CARRY DISEASE

The history of the epoch-making discovery of the mosquito transmission of yellow fever is so interesting and remarkable that some mention must be made of it. The theory that yellow fever was transmissible in this way dates back as early as 1847, and was again stated in a paper on the subject by Dr. Carlos J. Finlay of Havana in 1881.

It was not until 1900, however, during the occupation of Cuba by the United States army, that an opportunity arose to make a thorough test of the mosquito theory. In that year yellow fever was epidemic in Havana, and there were an appalling number of cases in the United States army in spite of the use of all known methods of fighting the disease. It did not seem possible to check its spread in the light of knowledge then extant. Many theories were advanced, and at last a board of army surgeons was appointed to investigate the matter of the disease, its causes and method of treatment, consisting of the four army surgeons, Jesse W. Lazear, Walter Reed, James Carroll and Aristides Agramonte. After various experiments they decided to test the theory of transmission by mosquitoes. To do this it was necessary to secure human subjects for experiment, and they decided to make the first experiments on themselves. The mosquitoes were to be secured, allowed to infect themselves with the disease by biting a yellow fever patient, and then in turn to bite them.

One of these officers, Dr. Agramonte, was immune to the disease through previous attacks; another, Dr. Reed, was recalled from the island before undergoing the experiment. Doctors Carroll and Lazear were bitten by infected mosquitoes, with the result that Dr. Carroll suffered a very severe attack of yellow fever from which he barely escaped with his life. Dr. Lazear was not so fortunate. He contracted the disease in its most severe form and died of it. It must be understood that these surgeons fully realized the great danger which they ran in making these experiments, in order to realize their extreme bravery and high devotion to duty. No appreciation of the marvelous achievement of the Canal itself can be complete without a full measure of praise being given to the high courage of these men who made the discovery through which the execution of the work was made possible.

To further demonstrate the truth of this theory a call for volunteers to undergo mosquito infection was made, and it is a high tribute to the bravery of the American soldier to note that there were instant and abundant responses.

It had been demonstrated by the tests of Doctors Lazear and Carroll that considerable time must elapse between the infection of the mosquito and the time at which it could infect another person. One of the soldiers chosen for the test was submitted to the ordeal of being bitten by infected mosquitoes, and it was discovered that the dangerous period began about twelve days after the infection of the mosquito. Experiments made by soldiers to determine whether or not yellow fever was a contagious disease, by wearing

A ROOM IN BACHELOR QUARTERS AT CULEBRA.

This shows a typical room such as is provided for bachelor Americans. The government has taken great pains to provide good food, clothing and living conditions, including amusements, for its employees.

clothes of a yellow fever patient, and sleeping in a bed previously occupied by a patient who had died of yellow fever, amply proved that it was not possible to transmit the disease in this way. Thus it was fully demonstrated that the *stegomyia* mosquito was the sole means of transmitting this dread disease.

MALARIA TRANSMISSION

The discovery that malaria was transmitted not by poisonous air or water, but by the *anopheles* mosquito solely, was made by a British army surgeon, Major Ronald Ross, who, after studying the problem of transmission of malaria, was successful in infecting birds with this disease by means of mosquito bites. This principle was afterwards applied to human beings successfully, and the theory proven that this was at least one of the methods of transmitting malaria. Later on, by means of further experiments, it was demonstrated that it was not possible to infect beings with malaria by means of either air or water from places in which the disease was epidemic.

Armed with this knowledge the surgeons drew up a new set of regulations for the government of Havana during the American occupation. These regulations were put into effect immediately, and consisted mainly of the segregation of all those attacked by the yellow fever in wire-screened houses so that the mosquitoes could not bite them and make themselves the means of carrying the disease. The infected houses were carefully fumigated, swamps, stagnant water and all likely places for the breeding of mosquitoes drained, with the result that within ninety days the disease was entirely stamped out; and with very few exceptions there has not been a recurrence of it in Havana since 1901.

Similar tactics were carried out in the case of the malaria-carrying mosquito, and with signal success, bringing the death rate from malaria down to about forty-five per year or about one-sixth of the previous rate.

The work in Havana was under the direction of Surgeon Major W. C. Gorgas, and the marvelous success achieved there was largely due to his painstaking work and administrative ability. The work accomplished there, of course, pointed the way directly to the sanitation of the Isthmus. President Roosevelt, realizing the value of the work which had been done, and the necessity for a similar but much greater task on the Isthmus, instructed the first commission to pay particular attention to the problem of sanitation. Colonel Gorgas, as the organizer and director of the campaign in Havana, was unanimously chosen as the best man for the leadership in the work on the Isthmus.

The first Isthmian Canal Commission to take charge of the work of constructing the Canal was appointed by the President on February 29, 1904, and confirmed by the Senate on March 3. The Commission arrived on the Isthmus on April 5 on a visit of inspection, accompanied by Col. W. C. Gorgas, Medical Corps, U. S. A., John W. Ross, Medical Director, U. S. N., Capt. C. E. Gillette, Corps of Engineers, U. S. A., and Maj. Louis A. LaGarde, Medical Corps, U. S. A., as experts on sanitation. After a thorough examination of conditions on the Isthmus these experts returned to Washington and reported a plan for the sanitation of the Canal Zone and the cities of Panama and Colon, and on May 8, 1904, Col. Gorgas, as Chief Sanitary Officer, was authorized to proceed with the work. He returned to the Isthmus, arriving on June 28. Between May 19, 1904, and June 30, 1904, Dr. L. W. Spratling, U. S. N., was acting health officer. As the representative of the Commission on the Isthmus, Gen. George W. Davis, Governor of the Canal Zone, issued an order on June 30, 1904, announcing the organization of the Sanitary Department, with Colonel Gorgas as its head.

IDEAL CONDITIONS FOR SPREADING DISEASE

At the beginning of the American occupation the Isthmus of Panama was afflicted with a plague of mosquitoes. The high temperature, which varies little during the year, allowed constant breeding and the pools of water left by the almost continuous rains during the rainy season, which lasts for nine months out of the year, open tanks and water barrels, which formed the water supply system, were ideal breeding places. The interior of the Isthmus was a tropical jungle, another condition likewise ideal for mosquito propagation. Practically all of the inhabitants were subject to malaria, and the mosquitoes had a constant source of infection from which to draw. Somewhat similar conditions prevailed with regard to yellow fever.

The methods to be adopted in the war on the disease were clearly defined, and were resolved into a war on mosquitoes, a campaign for cleanliness, and the education of the natives looking to the suppression of the dangerous practices which had before been in operation. The cities of Panama and Colon must have a sewage and water system which would be strictly sanitary. All houses would be carefully screened and their inhabitants protected from mosquito bites in order to limit the spread of the disease. The extermination of the mosquitoes must be accomplished by the draining of all stagnant pools and the elimination of all standing water in every case possible, and where this could not be accomplished spraying with crude oil must be resorted to in order to kill the mosquito larvæ. The brushwood of jungle growth had to be cut and burned, and a general cleaning up process adopted along the whole of the route of the Canal wherever occupied by Canal forces. These portions were cleared of undergrowth of all kinds for a distance of two hundred yards around all habitations.

No deaths from yellow fever had occurred among the employees of the French Company since 1897, although a few cases had been treated on the Isthmus in the year preceding the arrival of the Americans. A large part of the population of Panama was immune, and it was among the new arrivals that the disease first showed itself. In July, 1904, Charles Cunningham, a white employee of the Police Department, was taken ill with it and died. No other cases were reported for about a month. On November 21, a case developed in Santo Tomas Hospital in the city of Panama, and in December, 1904, seven cases developed in that city.

In the month of January, 1905, the disease broke out in Colon, and in the two cities 19 cases were recorded that month. In February, 14 cases developed; March, 11; April, 8; May, 33. The maximum was reached in June, when 62 cases were reported, and from that month there was a steady decrease, the number of cases that developed in July being 42; August, 27; September, 7, and October, 3. The last case in the city of Panama developed on November 11, and, the last in Colon, on December 11, 1905. In all there were 246 cases in 1904 and 1905, and 84 deaths. Of this number 134 of the cases and 34 of the deaths were among Commission employees.

The disease had been confined to the cities of Panama and Colon. It was fought by preventing the introduction of more cases from the fever ports of nearby countries, keeping patients in screened rooms where mosquitoes could not gain access to them, and by an energetic campaign for the extermination of mosquitoes. The work was carried on at first without the cooperation of the people, but within a year they had been taught to assist in the destruction of the mosquito.

The first work against malaria was undertaken in Empire, Culebra, and Ancon in July, 1904, and by September it had been extended to Gorgona, Paraiso, and Balboa. The situation with regard to malaria in July, 1904, is accurately illustrated by the conditions at Ancon Hospital, and in the various villages. *Anopheles* and *stegomyia* mosquitoes were found in large numbers in the buildings and wards. Mosquito breeding took place within a few yards of the wards and none of the buildings were screened. The decorative plants and shrubs in the grounds were surrounded with clay vessels containing water and vegetation in which mosquitoes were breeding, and all ditches in the grounds were producing mosquito life. There is no doubt that many cases of malaria and yellow fever had been contracted in the hospital itself previous to this time. Examinations of blood taken from the inhabitants of one town in the Canal Zone showed that 80 per cent of the people were infected with the malaria organism, and that Ancon was not an isolated instance was proved by the large percentage of cases from all the villages. In Colon one-sixth of the entire population was suffering from malarial attacks during each week, this deduction being based on the number of cases treated in the hospitals.

The permanent work for the prevention of malaria has been practically accomplished, although certain measures such as grass and brush cutting, oiling pools, and similar routine work must necessarily be continued indefinitely.

Only two cases of bubonic plague have developed on the Isthmus since American occupation. On June 15, 1905, a negro longshoreman, at Balboa (formerly La Boca), was taken ill, and a microscopic examination showed that he was suffering with bubonic. He died eight days later. The village was cleaned and disinfected, and a crusade against rats, the common carriers of bubonic, was begun. On July 9, a "rat brigade" was set at work in Panama, and a systematic effort to exterminate the rats around the docks and throughout the city was made. Rat traps were issued free to all persons who wished them. Later a bounty was placed on each rat delivered to the health department, and this bounty is still in effect.

In January, 1904, Dr. C. C. Pierce, of the Public Health and Marine Hospital Service, took up the work on the Isthmus of despatching ships bound to San Francisco and also of making a sanitary survey of the Canal region. In May, by an arrangement between the State Department in Washington and the Government of Panama, he took charge of the quarantine work for the port of Panama, and since that time the quarantine on the Isthmus has been under American control. In spite of the fact that ports on both the Atlantic and Pacific sides of the Isthmus, north and south, have been infected with bubonic, smallpox, cholera, and yellow fever, the quarantine has been successfully maintained. In both of the stations, Panama and Colon, screened rooms are set aside for yellow fever suspects, and every precaution is taken to guard them from the bite of mosquitoes.

PRESENT HEALTH CONDITIONS

The Canal Zone is at the present day more healthful to the white man than many parts of the United States. There has been an absence of yellow fever during the past nine years and it is safe to say that no epidemic of that disease will ever again occur upon the Isthmus. Malaria is being rapidly reduced and its source eradicated by the persistent labors of the Sanitary Department. The general health of Canal employees, both white and colored, is better than that of the several communities from which they were drawn, but, with regard to the former, it must be considered that they are picked men in the prime of life, and that those among them who succumb to climate or disease are quickly weeded out and sent home.

A total of about $20,000,000 has been spent upon the Canal Zone for sanitation, but in spite of this fact the Isthmus cannot be regarded as a health resort. It is a reasonably healthy place to live, but it must be remembered that this condition can only be maintained so long as the stringent methods of health precaution are enforced.

The fact that medical services are entirely free, and that removal to a hospital is compulsory on the part of the attending physician, has much to do with the excellent conditions of health maintained there. It must be confessed, however, that in spite of all these precautions malaria still exists upon the Isthmus and must be regarded as a serious problem, the only solution of which is the entire extermination of the *anopheles* mosquito. The Canal operating forces must continue to live in screened houses, take quinine in large quantities, remain indoors at night and continue the various precautions which have been adopted.

Considering the nature of the work, the living conditions and the length of time occupied by the enterprise, the death roll has been comparatively small, and to the date of the opening of the Canal there have been in the neighborhood of 6,000 deaths, of which less than 300 were Americans. Of the total number somewhat over 1,000 died from accidents. This really compares very favorably with that of the French, who lost in the nine years of their occupation about 16,000, or nearly three times as many.

CHAPTER X

The Labor Problem

Each of the enterprises that preceded the American occupation of the canal territory found the difficulty in securing satisfactory labor one of the greatest deterrents to success.

The health conditions were so forbidding, the problem so apparently hopeless that even the most adventurous spirits of the races of the world looked askance at Panama. When the Americans took charge, however, all this was changed. The Canal Zone was made healthy and the completion of the work assured by the ample credit of the United States. High pay was offered and many other inducements which soon brought the adventurous of all lands flocking to the Isthmus. Hardly a nation is lacking in representatives on the construction force and the census of the Canal Zone taken in 1912 showed forty nationalities from eighty-six different geographical subdivisions, so that the world at large can justly feel proud in the achievement so truly international in its scope.

RECRUITING A FORCE

The number of men upon the rolls of the Commission has varied greatly. When Wallace took charge in 1904 there were 746 men employed upon the Canal. Immediately recruiting stations were opened in the United States, the West Indies and Europe, with the result that about 45,000 men were imported under contract up to 1912. The force has been anything but permanent, especially during the early days of the enterprise, when many of those employed

CULEBRA CUT LOOKING NORTH FROM CUNETTE.

The two steam shovels shown in the foreground are working on the bottom, elevation +40. The water standing in the outer drainage channel is about six feet below the bottom, elevation +34.

THE LABOR PROBLEM

departed on the same ship that brought them after one look at the conditions. These were improved, however, and the promise of high pay, free lodging, good and cheap food and all the other inducements offered by the Commission kept a steady stream of labor flowing to the Isthmus.

The high water mark of employees on the Isthmus was reached in 1910 when there were 38,676 men upon the rolls. Of these 5,573 were Americans who usually compose from one-sixth to one-seventh of the total working force. Since 1910 the gradual reduction in the force has been permitted by the completion of various parts of the project and at the time of the opening of the Canal only a small operating and maintenance force will be kept there in addition to the military garrison.

The Americans employed on the Isthmus are in positions of supervision or skilled labor in the various trades, steam engineers, steam shovel men, railroad brakemen, conductors, firemen, policemen and in the higher offices.

Few women came to the Canal Zone in the early days, but according to the census of 1912 there were over four thousand women and children of American employees on the Isthmus. Most of the laborers are colored and come from the islands of the West Indies, Barbadoes, Martinique, Jamaica, Trinidad, etc., to the number of about 30,000. Europe has supplied about half as many. Of the Europeans employed over eight thousand were Spaniards and they proved the most satisfactory of all the common laborers employed by the Canal Commission.

The suggested employment of Chinese coolies to dig the canal met with such opposition in the United States that no move was made to put it into effect. Furthermore, little difficulty was experienced after the work was under way in obtaining all the common labor desired.

THE GOLD AND SILVER ROLLS

Some distinction had to be made between skilled and unskilled labor and this was accomplished by dividing the employees into "gold" and "silver" men. The gold roll included all the Americans and those drawing over $75.00 per month who are paid in gold. The silver roll includes all the common and unskilled laborers and these men are paid in the silver money of the Republic of Panama. This distinction is useful in many ways but chiefly in allowing the Commission to draw the color line as it could not do directly, because of the United States Constitution and for other reasons. The distinction, however, is not a hard and fast one, and, consequently, is not open to criticism from that standpoint. In uniformity with this there are separate facilities provided everywhere for the two grades of employees. There are second-class railway cars, special commissary clerks and separate eating-houses.

QUARTERS

The types of quarters furnished for the gold and silver employees of course differ radically, although in both cases living accommodations, together with food, light and water, are supplied by the Government without charge. The gold employees live in two types of quarters, known as *bachelor quarters* and *married quarters*, and assignments to these are made by district quartermasters according to a code of rules, which takes in the date of the applicant's entry into the service, the rate of salary, etc. The quarters for both bachelors and married men are provided with modern plumbing and all necessary furniture. The types of houses differ somewhat according to the salary of the employee, but all are constructed from ingenious designs which adapt them both for convenience and comfort to a tropical climate.

The bachelor employees on the gold roll are housed in quarters like dormitories, and take their meals at hotels established and maintained by the Government.

The silver bachelor employees live in barracks, each of which accommodates seventy-two men. They sleep in a triple tier of bunks, which are fitted with laced canvas

THE LABOR PROBLEM

bottoms. These barracks are cleaned daily by janitors and are kept in good order, no baggage or effects of any kind being allowed on the floor.

AMUSEMENTS

One of the most difficult problems about the labor situation on the Isthmus has been the amusement of the employees after working hours. The cities of Panama and Colon do not supply many forms of amusement, besides the fact that they are inaccessible to those employed inland. To meet this difficulty the Commission has gone to great pains and expense to provide club houses, which are operated by the Young Men's Christian Association, and of which there are seven, located at Cristobal, Gatun, Gorgona, Empire, Culebra, Corozal and Porto Bello. These club houses have facilities for billiards, pool, bowling, gymnasium, reading rooms, and also facilities for social, church and lodge functions. Moving pictures are given in the club houses about once a week. There is also the Isthmian Canal Commission band, an excellent organization which gives regular concerts at the towns throughout the Canal Zone.

In spite of the efforts which have been made, however, it is extremely difficult to maintain a steady force on the Isthmus. For instance in 1911, the force of employees on the gold roll changed to the extent of sixty per cent, and statistics show that the average length of stay of mechanics on the Isthmus is one year. There are very few of the original employees who went to the Isthmus in 1904 who remained to the end of the work. Another reason for this constant change of workmen is that the men who compose the force are to a large extent adventurous spirits, who go to the Canal largely to see the big enterprise and be able to say afterward that they had a hand in its completion.

AN AMERICAN MANUFACTURING COMMUNITY

Few people realize how many different classes of work enter into this great enterprise. The great distance between

Panama and this country has necessitated the establishment of an American manufacturing community with all the facilities of an American community of the same sort, including houses, schools, churches, club houses, municipal improvements, such as waterworks, electric light plants, etc. From a labor standpoint the great machine shops at Gorgona and Empire are very interesting. These shops are equipped to build, assemble and repair all of the machinery used in the construction of the Canal. The raw material is purchased in the United States and made into the finished product. Locomotives, trains, dredges, etc., are purchased in the United States, knocked down and shipped to the Isthmus in sections, to be assembled and put into working condition after arrival there. In many cases it is cheaper to manufacture small articles on the Isthmus than to transport them from the United States.

The item of repairs is a serious one, for the reason that the Canal machinery is driven at a very high speed in the effort to obtain phenomenal results. This results in frequent breakage, so that the shops are ever busy with this class of work. One plant alone, that at Gorgona, covers twenty-two acres of ground, and has a railroad trackage of seven miles. These shops have had to be entirely removed before the opening of the Canal, since the rising waters of Gatun Lake will entirely cover their location before the eighty-five foot level is reached.

The old adage that "Necessity is the mother of invention" has been largely demonstrated during the construction of the Canal. Gigantic obstacles have arisen, only to be met and conquered by the ingenuity of the engineers in charge of the work. Many clever devices have been invented and put to practical use. Among these may be mentioned the lock gate operating device, of which a cut and full description will be found in the chapter on "The Plan and Operation of the Canal." Another extremely clever device, which has resulted in a tremendous saving of time, money and labor, is that known as the *track shifter*,

THE LABOR PROBLEM

invented by W. G. Bierd. This consists of a huge crane with a long boom, which is run out upon the section of track to be moved. Chains are attached to the rails which are spiked to the ties, and the boom is lifted and drawn to one side, shifting the track some three or four feet. The machine is then moved forward and a new grip is taken on the track farther on and the operation repeated. In this way large sections of track may be shifted to one side in a short space of time. The device has proved of great value, especially on the dumps and fills where the excavated material is deposited.

Another clever device is the unloading plow. A long train of cars filled with earth is run to the proper unloading point, and the plow operated by wire ropes is drawn over the beds of the cars, pushing all the material off to the side desired, and effecting a great saving in time and labor.

Strikes upon the Isthmus have not had great success, for the reason that the Government considered that the main object was to complete the Canal in the least possible time and with the least possible trouble, holding that the good of the nation was above any small private grievance. To this end the Commission was given the authority to expel anyone from the Canal Zone who was not necessary to the work, or who became objectionable for any reason. This was upheld by the Supreme Court, which ruled that the Canal Zone was not a part of the United States, and therefore not subject to the Constitution, but could be treated as a military reservation. Men who stirred up trouble in the work by threatening strikes or making themselves objectionable in any way have been promptly deported and their places filled. The Canal Commission has directed the work with a strong hand, as the only method of pushing it forward to a profitable and successful conclusion.

As a matter of fact, there has been no occasion for a strike on the Isthmus, as the sole grounds have been a desire for more money. When it is considered that these men are working under conditions which have been modified to an almost unreasonable extent for their ease and well being, it is hard to see any just grounds for a strike. The men work on an eight-hour day schedule, with an intermission of two hours at noon. They get their food cheaper than they could buy it in the United States, free light, water, fuel, quarters, medical services, low railroad rates, and their wages and salaries average from thirty to eighty per cent more than for similar positions in the United States. It would be hard to find a better treated body of men from any standpoint. They are allowed an annual vacation of forty-two days for gold employees, and should they desire they may save up this leave from year to year and take the accumulated vacation in any one year. They are allowed sick leave also on pay.

The net result of all this is that the work has gone forward practically without any serious interruption from labor troubles.

COMMISSARY

The problem of supplying quarters, food, clothing and the necessaries and luxuries of life for the enormous army of workmen at Panama has been a very considerable one. It has, however, been worked out by the Quartermaster's and Subsistence Departments, which respectively have charge of the buildings and physical property of the Commission, together with the recruiting of labor, storage of the material and supplies, and operation of the commissary store system, which sells merchandise to canal employees at prices but little higher than those at which the articles are bought in quantities. In addition the Subsistence Department has charge of operating the hotels, kitchens and messes in which the gold and silver employees are fed. Central stations have been established for this purpose, with huge bakeries, refrigerating plants and storehouses.

The commissary system consists of twenty-two general stores in as many Canal Zone villages and camps along the relocated line of the Panama Railroad. It is estimated

THE LABOR PROBLEM

that with employees and their dependents there are about 65,000 people supplied daily with food, clothing and other necessaries. The main supply station of this system is located at Cristobal, from which a supply train of twenty-one cars is dispatched every morning, consisting of refrigerator cars containing ice, meats and other perishable articles, and ten cars containing other supplies. These are delivered at stations along the line, and distributed to the houses of employees by the Quartermaster's Department. Some idea of the volume of this business may be gained from the fact that the purchases of this department in the United States amount to about $12,000,000 worth of supplies annually, which require a discharge of one steamer each day.

The hotel branch maintains the well known Hotel Tivoli at Ancon, together with eighteen hotels along the line for white and gold employees, at which meals are served at thirty cents each. At these hotels there are served monthly about 200,000 meals. There are seventeen messes for European laborers, who pay forty cents per ration of three meals. There are also operated for the West Indian laborers sixteen kitchens in which they are served by ration of three meals for twenty-seven cents per ration. The supplies for one month for the line hotels, messes and kitchens cost about $85,000; labor and other expenses, $16,500. The monthly receipts, exclusive of the revenue of the Hotel Tivoli, amout to about $105,000.

The commissary stores have on sale a very large variety of articles which are purchased in large quantities under the contract system in the United States, and this business is managed by the Government on a profit just large enough to make both ends meet, including the costs of transportation, handling and delivering.

The commissary stores are run entirely on a charge basis. Enployees are issued coupon books of varying face values with which they purchase supplies. At the end of the month the value of the coupons used is deducted from the employee's salary. The net result of this great system is that the employees and the Canal Commission are not troubled by the prevailing high prices in the United States, and are a well satisfied and contented body of men.

Photograph, Underwood & Underwood, N. Y. GENERAL VIEW OF THE CITY OF PANAMA.

In the foreground is one of the reservoirs built by the United States Government to supply the city with clean water.

THE GREAT CULEBRA CUT.

At this point the Canal is cut through what is practically a mountain range. The material excavated consisted largely of rock and formed one of the hugest engineering problems in the world's history. The cut is 9 miles long, 300 feet wide, 272 feet greatest depth and required the excavation of 100,000,000 cubic yards of material.

CHAPTER XI

Plan and Operation of the Canal

During the past twenty years a wondrous transformation has taken place in the narrow strip across the Isthmus over which the United States holds dominion, but most of this change has been wrought since the American occupation began. The French did a great deal of work, but it was mainly of the pioneer sort that makes little appeal to the eye and is fully appreciated only by the technician. Their surveys were of incalculable value to our engineers. The buildings and machinery which they left saved us much trouble and expense. They dug a ditch for a few miles inland from the Atlantic and took an enormous mass of material out of Culebra, but the one was as a scratch in the ground, and the other as a notch in the hill, compared with the full extent of the necessary excavation.

The earlier period of the American tenancy was wisely devoted to preliminary measures of the utmost importance, but unimpressive in their immediate results. Plans were carefully considered in detail. Organization was effected. The railroad was reconstructed, machinery and methods were tested. Civil government was installed. And, most important of all, the field of action was made sanitary and the task thereby rendered possible.

When the army engineers assumed charge of the operation, the period of preparation had just closed. The type of the waterway and its main features had been finally decided upon. The labor supply was assured and life on the Isthmus involved no unusual menace to the health of the white man. In short, the period of construction had begun, the plans were drawn, the tools provided, the foun-

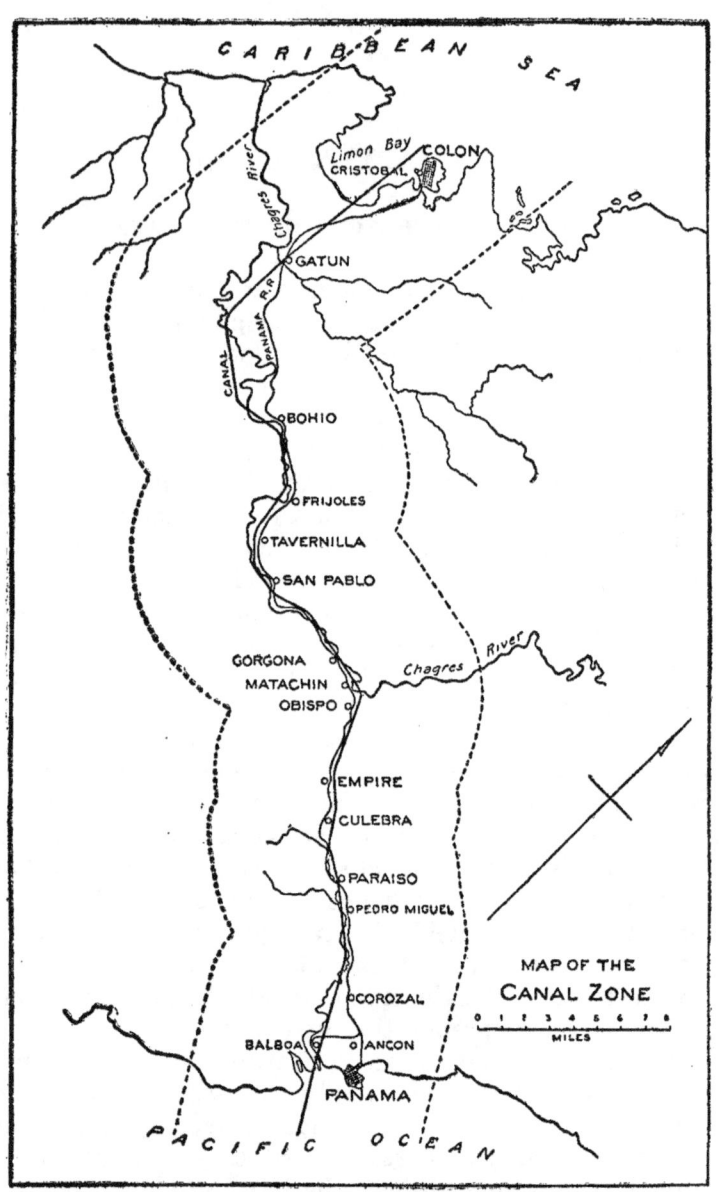

MAP OF THE CANAL ZONE

PLAN AND OPERATION OF THE CANAL

dations laid for the magnificent superstructure which has been built under Colonel Goethals. For this great canal is as impressive as Niagara with its wonderful artificial canyon at Culebra, its great locks, dams and lakes. The thing is stupendous in its entirety, so let us examine it in greater detail.

The total length of the Canal, along the channel extending into the ocean at either end, is fifty and one-half miles; the land length is ten miles less.

Approaching from the Atlantic, a vessel enters Limon Bay by a channel 500 feet wide at bottom, and follows this for about seven miles to Gatun. Here a flight of three locks raises it to the summit level at an elevation of 85 feet. The vessel may traverse the twenty-four mile stretch of Gatun Lake at high speed in a channel varying from 1,000 to 500 feet in width. Culebra Cut is entered at Bas Obispo and the passage of nine miles made through a channel having a bottom width of 300 feet. At Pedro Miguel, where the summit level ends, a lock lowers the vessel to a small lake, with surface at about 55 feet above the level of the sea. At a distance of about one and one-half miles beyond, the two-flight locks of Miraflores are encountered. Through them the vessel descends to tide-water and continues its way to the Pacific by way of a channel eight and one-half miles in length and 500 feet in bottom width. The depth of the Canal throughout is forty-five feet at least, except for the approach channel on the Atlantic side, where the bottom will lie forty-one feet under water at mean tide.

GATUN DAM

The approximate measurements of the Gatun Dam are: one and one-half miles in length along the crest; one-half mile wide at the base; 400 feet wide at the water surface; 100 feet wide at the top, and its crest at an elevation of 115 feet, or 30 feet above the normal level of the lake. The dam is formed by the flanking hills and two rock walls,

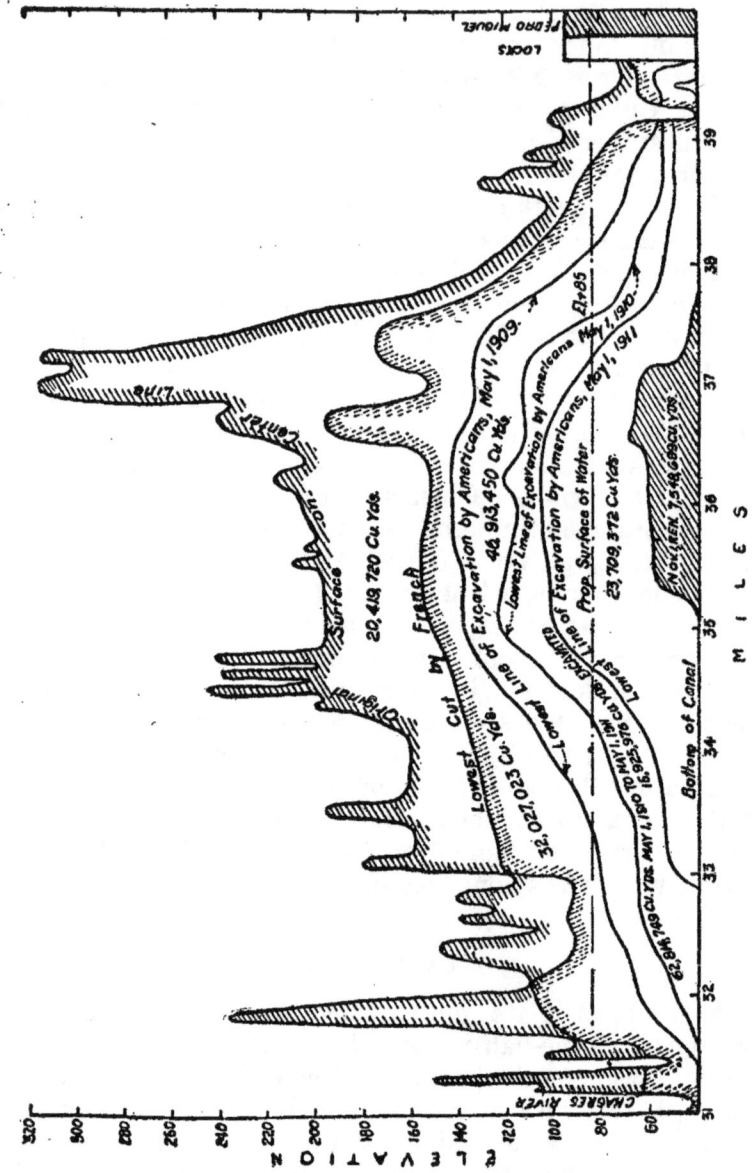

PROFILE OF CULEBRA CUT FROM THE DIKE AT GOMBOA TO PEDRO MIGUEL LOCKS

enclosing a mixture of sand and clay. The top and upstream slopes are heavily riprapped.

The spillway is a concrete-lined opening, 1,200 feet long and 300 feet wide, cut through a hill in the center of the dam, the bottom of the opening being ten feet above sea level. During the construction of the dam, all the water discharged from the Chagres River and its tributaries was carried through this opening. After construction had sufficiently advanced to permit the lake to be formed, the spillway was closed with a concrete dam, fitted with gates and machinery for regulating the water level of the lake, as described below.

The water level of Gatun Lake, extending through the Culebra Cut, is maintained at the south end by an earth dam connecting the locks at Pedro Miguel with the high ground to the westward, about 1,700 feet long, with its crest at an elevation 105 feet above mean tide.

The small lake between the locks at Pedro Miguel and Miraflores is formed by dams connecting the walls of the locks at the latter point with the high ground on either side. The dam to the westward is of earth, about 2,700 feet long, having its crest about 15 feet above the surface of Miraflores Lake. The east dam is of concrete, about 500 feet in length, and forms a spillway for the lake, with crest gates similar to those of the Gatun Dam.

Lake Gatun covers an area of 164 square miles, with a depth in the ship channel varying from 85 to 45 feet. The channel through the lake for the first 16 miles from Gatun is 1,000 feet in width; for the next four miles it is 800 feet, and for the remainder of the distance 500 feet wide. The summit level of the lake extends through the cut and to the Pedro Miguel Locks.

SPILLWAY, GATUN DAM

The Spillway is a concrete lined channel 1,200 feet long and 285 feet wide cut through a hill of rock nearly in the center of the Dam, the bottom being 10 feet above

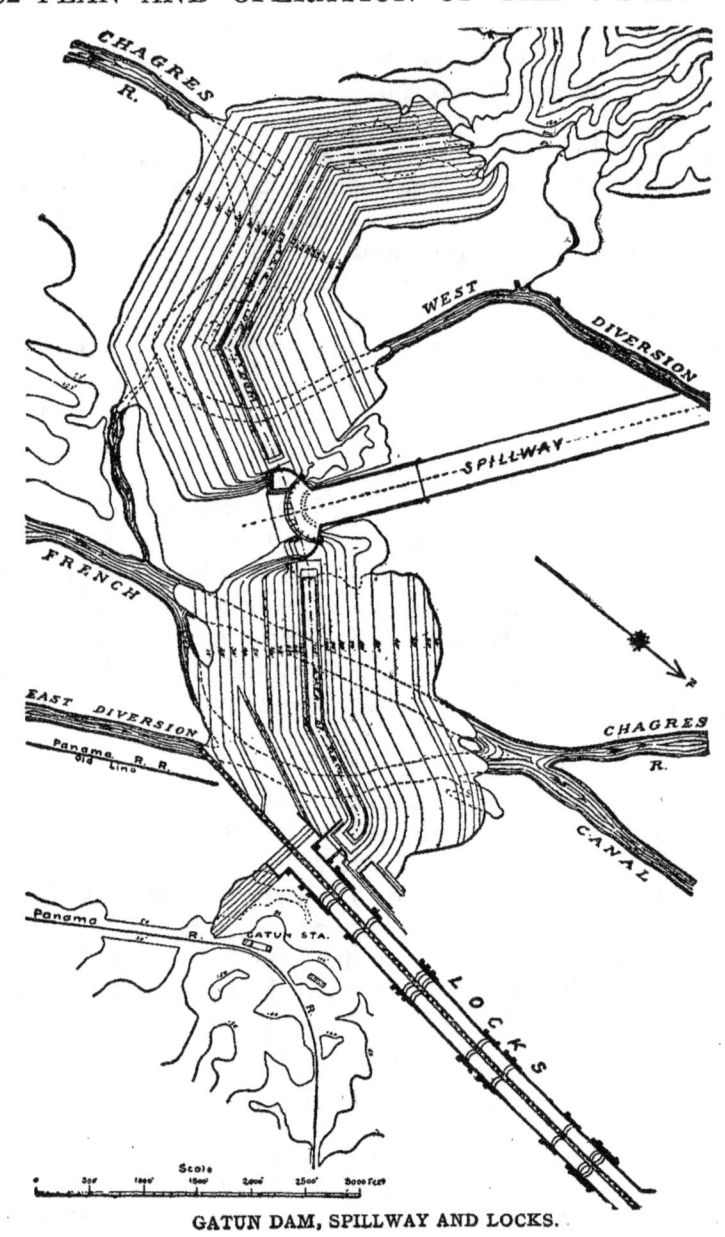

GATUN DAM, SPILLWAY AND LOCKS.

PLAN AND OPERATION OF THE CANAL

sea level at the upstream end and sloping to sea level at the toe. Across the upstream or lake opening of this channel a concrete dam has been built in the form of an arc of a circle making its length 808 feet, although it closes a channel with a width of only 285 feet. The crest of the dam is 69 feet above sea level, or 16 feet below the normal level of the lake which is 85 feet above sea level. On the top of this dam have been placed 13 concrete piers with their tops 115.5 feet above sea level, and between these there are mounted regulating gates of the Stoney type. Each gate is built of steel sheathing on a framework of girders and moves up and down on roller trains placed in niches in the piers. They have been equipped with sealing devices to make them water-tight. Machines for moving the gates are designed to raise or lower them in approximately ten minutes. The highest level to which it is intended to allow the lake to rise is 87 feet above sea level, and it is probable that this level will be maintained continuously during wet seasons. With the lake at that elevation, the regulation gates will permit of a discharge of water greater than the maximum known discharge of the Chagres River during a flood.

HYDROELECTRIC STATION AT GATUN

Adjacent to the north wall of the spillway has been located a hydroelectric station capable of generating through turbines 6,000 kilowatts for the operation of the lock machinery, machine shops, dry dock, coal handling plant, batteries, and for the lighting of the locks and Zone towns and, if desirable, operating the Panama railroad. The building is constructed of concrete and steel, and is of a design suitable for a permanent power house in a tropical country. The dimensions are such as to permit the installation of three 2,000-kilowatt units, and provision is made for a future extension of three additional similar units. It is rectangular in shape, and contains one main operating floor, with a turbine pit and two galleries for electrical equipment. The building, with machinery and electrical equipment has been laid out upon the unit principle, each unit consisting of

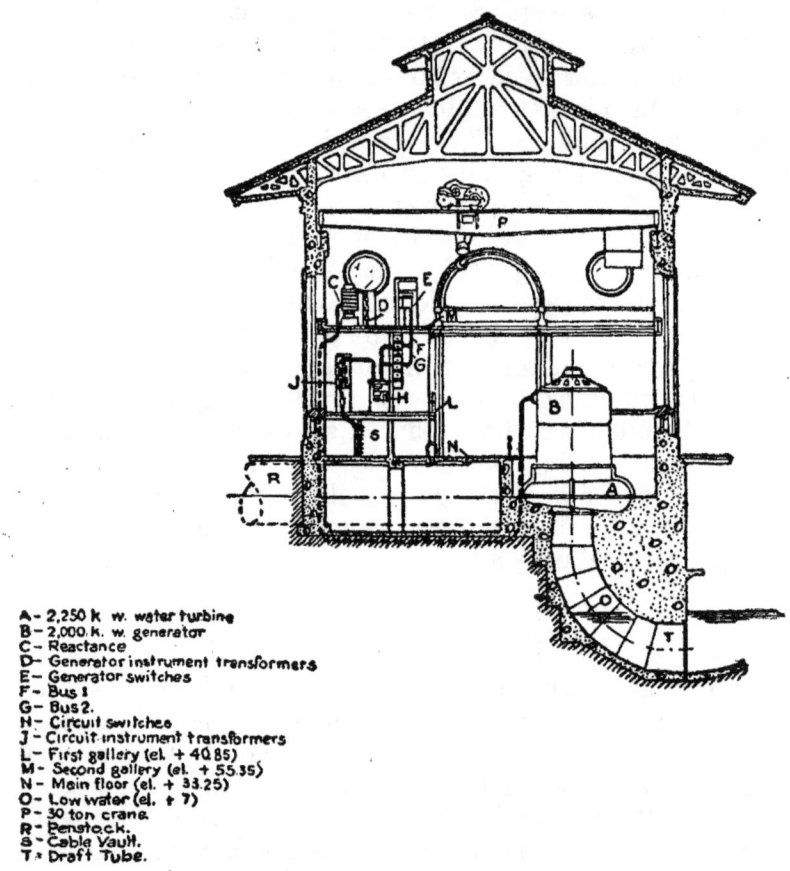

A — 2,250 k. w. water turbine
B — 2,000 k. w. generator
C — Reactance
D — Generator instrument transformers
E — Generator switches
F — Bus 1
G — Bus 2.
H — Circuit switches
J — Circuit instrument transformers
L — First gallery (el. + 40.85)
M — Second gallery (el. + 55.35)
N — Main floor (el. + 33.25)
O — Low water (el. + 7)
P — 30 ton crane.
R — Penstock.
S — Cable Vault.
T — Draft Tube.

THE HYDROELECTRIC STATION AT GATUN.

an individual head gate, penstock, governor, exciter, oil-switch and control panel.

Water supply is taken from Gatun Lake, the elevation of which will vary with the seasons from 80 to 87 feet above sea level, through a forebay which is constructed

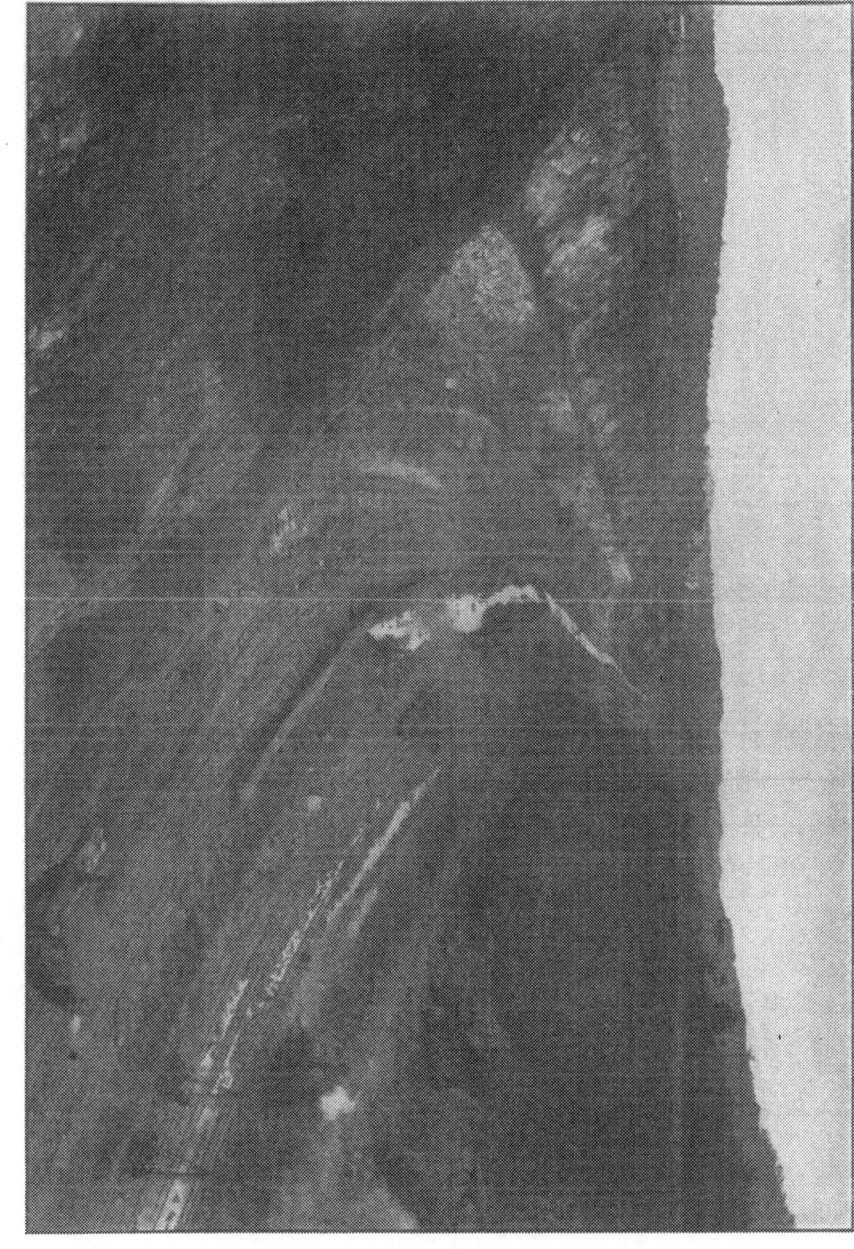

CULEBRA CUT LOOKING SOUTH FROM BEND IN EAST BANK NEAR GAMBOA.

The train and shovel are standing on the bottom of the cut. The water in the drainage canal is about 10 feet below the bottom of the Canal, or at elevation +30.

as an integral part of the curved portion of the north spillway approach wall. From the forebay the water is carried to the turbines through three steel plate penstocks, each having an average length of 350 feet. The entrances are closed by cast iron headgates and bar iron trash racks. The headgates are raised and lowered by individual motors which are geared to rising stems attached to the gate castings. The driving machinery and the motors have been housed in a small concrete gatehouse erected upon the forebay wall directly over the gate recesses and trash racks. The gate house has been constructed for the present requirements of three head gates, and provision made for a future addition of three more units.

WATER SUPPLY OF GATUN LAKE

Gatun Lake impounds the waters of a basin comprising 1,320 square miles. (*See Map, p. 162.*) When the surface of the water is at 85 feet above sea level, the lake will have an area of about 164 square miles, and will contain about 183 billion cubic feet of water. During eight or nine months of the year, the lake will be kept constantly full by the prevailing rains, and consequently a surplus will need to be stored for only three or four months of the dry season. The smallest run-off of water in the basin during the past 22 years, as measured at Gatun, was that of the fiscal year, 1912, which was about 132 billion cubic feet. Previous to that year the smallest run-off of record was 146 billion cubic feet. In 1910 the run-off was 360 billion cubic feet, or a sufficient quantity to fill the lake one and a half times. The low record of 1912 is of interest as showing the effect which a similar dry season, occurring after the opening of the Canal, would have upon its capacity for navigation. Assuming that Gatun Lake was at elevation plus 87 at the beginning of the dry season on December 1st, and that the hydro-electric plant at the Gatun Spillway was in continuous operation, and that 48 lockages a day were being made, the elevation of the lake would be reduced to its lowest point, plus 79.5, on May 7th, at the close of the dry season, after which

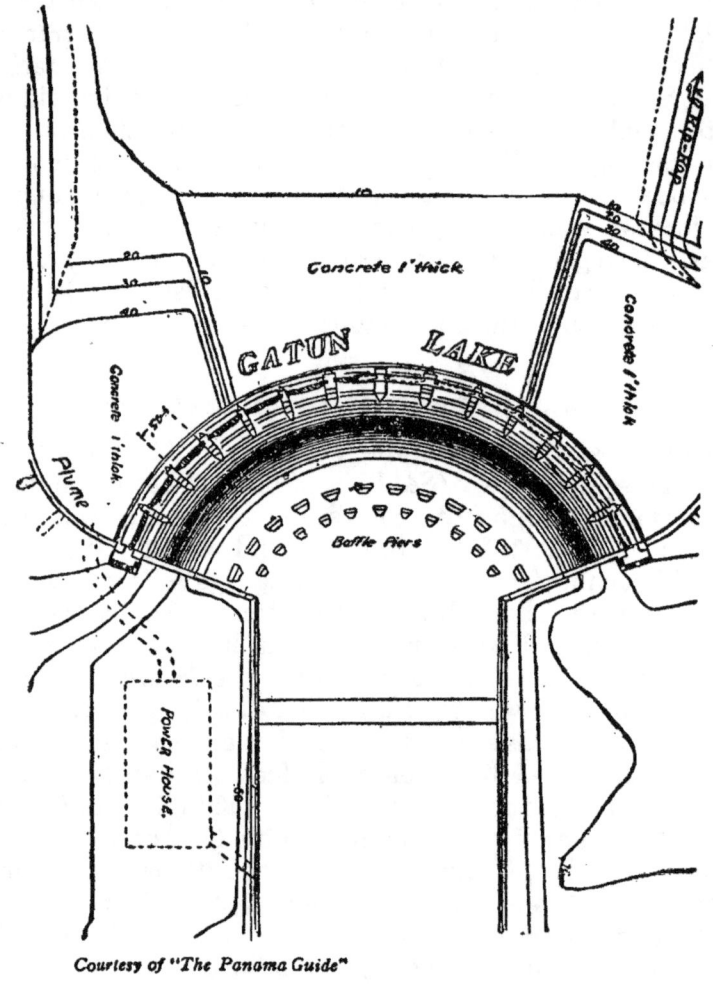

Courtesy of "The Panama Guide"
GATUN DAM SPILLWAY.

it would continuously rise. With the water at plus 79 in Gatun Lake there would be 39 feet of water in Culebra

PLAN AND OPERATION OF THE CANAL

Cut, which would be ample for navigation. The water surface of the lake will be maintained during the rainy season at 87 feet above sea level, making the minimum channel depth in the Canal 47 feet. As navigation can be carried on with about 39 feet of water, there will be stored for the dry season surplus over 7 feet of water. Making due allowance for evaporation, seepage, leakage at the gates, and power consumption, this would be ample for 41 passages daily through the locks, using them at full length, or about 58 lockages a day when partial length is used, as would be usually the case, and when cross filling from one lock to the other through the central wall is employed. This would be a larger number of lockages than would be possible in a single day. The average number of lockages through the Sault Ste. Marie Canal on the American side was 39 per day in the season of navigation of 1910, which was about eight months long. The average number of ships passed was about 1½ per lockage. The freight carried was about 26,000,000 tons. The Suez Canal passed about 12 vessels per day, with a total tonnage for the same year of 16,582,000.

The water level of Gatun Lake, extending through the Cul-

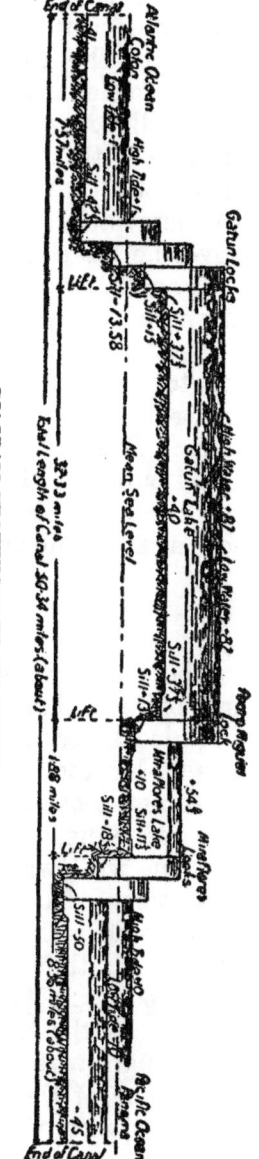

DIAGRAM SHOWING LAKE ELEVATION.

ebra Cut, is maintained at the southern end by an earth dam connecting the locks at Pedro Miguel with the high ground to the westward, about 1,400 feet long, with its crest at an elevation of 105 feet above mean tide. A concrete core wall, containing about 700 cubic yards, connects the locks with the hills to the eastward; this core wall resting directly on the rock surface and being designed to prevent percolation through the earth, the surface of which is above the Lake level.

A small lake between the locks at Pedro Miguel and Miraflores has been formed by dams connecting the walls of Miraflores locks with the high ground on either side. The dam to the westward is of earth, about 2,700 feet long, having its crest about 15 feet above the water in Miraflores Lake. The east dam is of concrete, containing about 75,000 cubic yards, about 500 feet in length, and forms a spillway for Miraflores Lake, with crest gates similar to those at the Spillway of the Gatun Dam.

THE LOCKS

There are twelve locks in the Canal, all in duplicate; three pairs in flight at Gatun, with a combined lift of 85 feet; one pair at Pedro Miguel, with a lift of $30\frac{1}{3}$ feet; and two pairs at Miraflores, with a total lift of $54\frac{2}{3}$ feet at mean tide. The dimensions of all are the same—a usable length of 1,000 feet, and a usable breadth of 110 feet. Each lock is a chamber, with walls and floor of concrete, and water-tight gates at each end.

The side walls are 45 to 50 feet thick at the surface of the floor; they are perpendicular on the face, and narrow from a point $24\frac{1}{3}$ feet above the floor, until they are eight feet wide at the top. The middle wall is 60 feet thick and 81 feet high, with vertical faces. At a point $42\frac{1}{2}$ feet above the surface of the floor, and 15 feet above the top of the middle culvert, this wall divides into two parts, leaving a U-shaped space down the center, which is 19 feet broad at

PLAN AND OPERATION OF THE CANAL

the bottom and 44 feet broad at the top. In this space is a tunnel, divided into three stories or galleries. The lowest of these divisions is for drainage; the middle for the wires that will carry the electric current to operate the gate and valve machinery, which is installed in the central wall, and the upper division forms a passage-way for the operators. The lock chambers are filled and emptied through

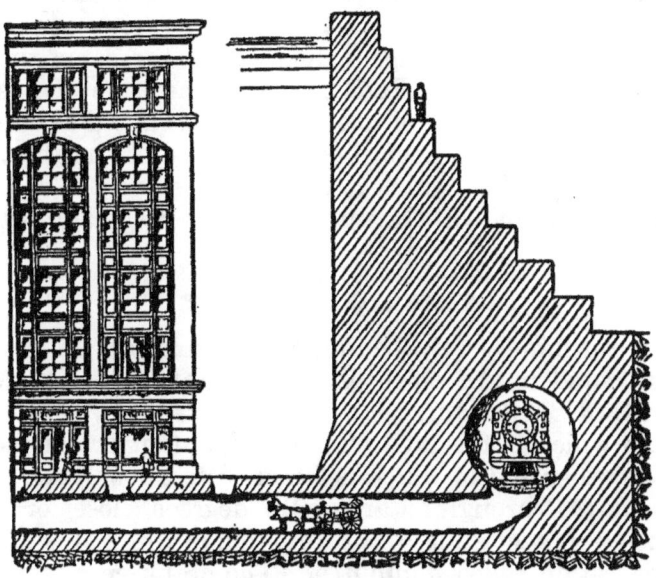

COMPARISON BETWEEN SIDE WALL OF LOCK AND A SIX STORY BUILDING.

lateral culverts in the floors, connecting with main culverts, 18 feet in diameter in the walls, the water flowing in and out by gravity.

The lock gates are steel structures, seven feet thick, 65 feet long, and from 47 to 82 feet high. They weigh from 300 to 600 tons each. Ninety-two leaves are required for the several locks, the total weighing 57,000 tons. Intermediate gates are being used, in order to save water and time, and permit of the division of each lock into two chambers, respectively, 600 and 400 feet long. In the construction of the locks there were used 4,500,000 cubic yards of concrete, which required about the same number of barrels of cement.

The time spent in filling and emptying a lock averages about fifteen minutes, without opening the valves so suddenly as to create disturbing currents in the locks or approaches. The time required to pass a vessel through all the locks is estimated at 3 hours; one hour and a half in the three locks at Gatun, and about the same time in the three locks on the Pacific side. The time of passage of a vessel through the entire Canal is estimated as ranging from 10 to 12 hours, according to the size of the ship, and the rate of speed at which it can travel, since the twenty-four mile passage of Gatun Lake may be made at full speed.

GATE-MOVING MACHINERY

The machinery for opening and closing the miter gates was invented in the office of the Assistant Chief Engineer by Edward Schildhauer. It consists essentially of a crank gear, to which is fastened one end of a strut or connecting rod, the other end of which is fastened to a lock gate. The wheel moves through an arc of 197 degrees, closes or opens the gate leaf, according to the direction in which it is turned. One operation takes 2 minutes. The crank gear is a combination of gear and crank, is constructed of cast steel, is 19 feet 2 inches in diameter, and weighs approximately 35,000 pounds. It is mounted in a horizontal position on the lock wall, turns on a large center pin, and is supported at the rim in four places by rollers. The center pin is keyed into a heavy casting anchored securely to the concrete. The crank-gear has gear teeth on its rim and is driven through a train of gears and pinions by an electric motor in a contiguous room. The motor is remotely controlled by an operator who is stationed at a center control house near the lower end of the upper locks. A simple

PLAN AND OPERATION OF THE CANAL 171

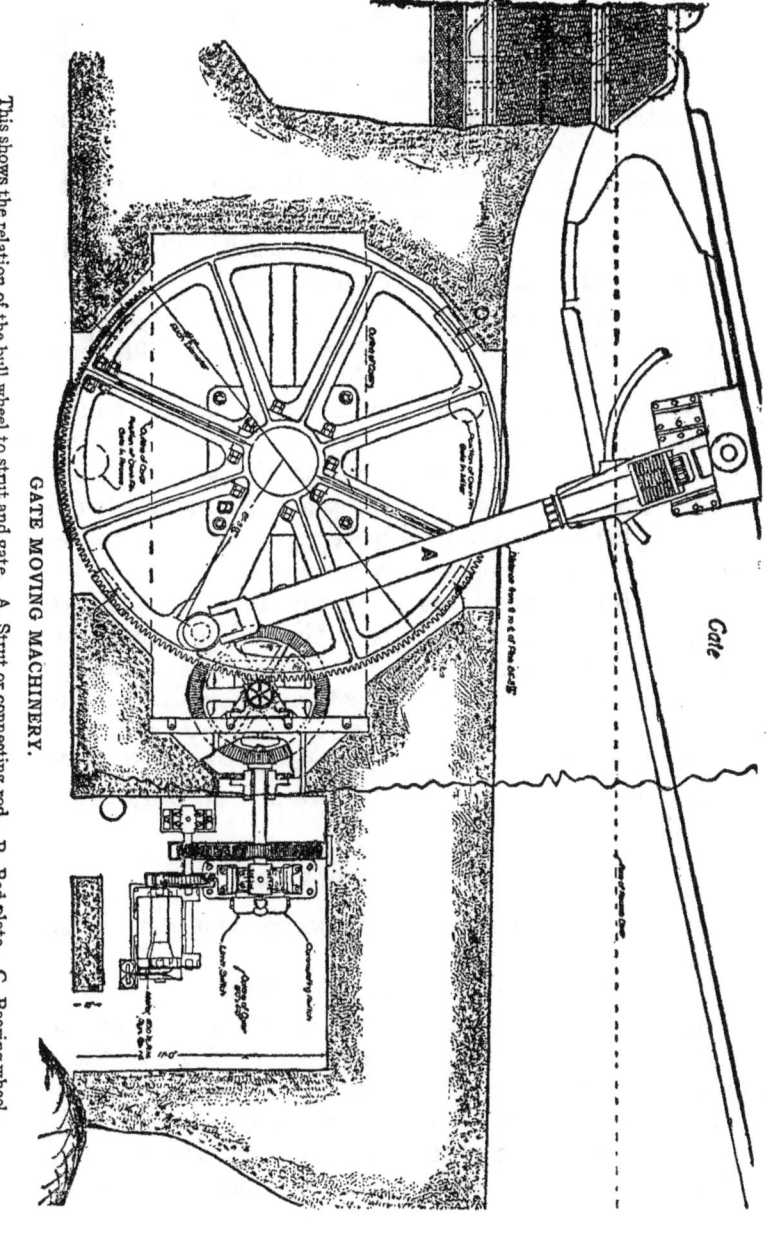

GATE MOVING MACHINERY. This shows the relation of the bull wheel to strut and gate. A. Strut or connecting rod. B. Bed plate. C. Bearing wheel.

pull of a small switch is sufficient to either close or open a 700-ton gate, the operation being perfectly automatic.

No ship is allowed to pass through the locks under its own power, but is towed through by electric locomotives operating on tracks on the lock walls. The system of towing provides for the passing through the locks of a ship at the rate of 2 miles an hour. The number of locomotives varies with the size of the vessel. The usual number required is 4: 2 ahead, 1 on each wall, imparting motion to the vessel, and 2 astern, 1 on each wall, to aid in keeping the vessel in a central position and to bring it to rest when entirely within the lock chamber. They are equipped with a slip drum, towing windlass and hawser which permits the towing line to be taken in or paid out without actual motion of the locomotive on the track. The locomotives run on a level, except when in passing from one lock to another they climb heavy grades. There are two systems of tracks: one for towing, and the other for the return of the locomotives when not towing. The towing tracks have center racks or cogs throughout, and the locomotives always operate on this rack when towing. At the incline between locks the return tracks also have rack rails, but elsewhere the locomotives run by friction. The only crossovers between the towing and return tracks are at each end of the locks, and there are no switches in the rack rail.

PROTECTIVE DEVICES

Several protective devices have been used to safeguard the gates in the locks.

First. Fender chains, 24 in number, each weighing 24,098 pounds, have been placed on the up-stream side of the guard gates, intermediate and safety gates of the upper locks, and in front of the guard gates at the lower end of each flight of locks. They prevent the lock gates from being rammed by a ship that might approach the gates under its own steam or by escaping from the towing loco-

GATUN UPPER LOCKS, EAST CHAMBER.

The view is looking north from the forebay showing the upper guard gates and emergency dam.

motives. In operation, the chain is stretched across the lock chamber from the top of the opposing walls, and when it is desired to allow a ship to pass, the chain is lowered into a groove made for the purpose in the lock floor. It is raised again after the ship passes. The raising and lowering is accomplished from both sides by mechanism mounted in chambers or pits in the lock walls. This mechanism consists of a hydraulically operated system of cylinders, so that 1 foot of movement by the cylinder accomplishes 4 feet by the chain. If a ship exerting a pressure of more than 750 pounds to the square inch should run into the fender, the chain is paid out gradually by an automatic release until the vessel comes to a stop. Thus, a 10,000-ton ship, running at 4 knots an hour, after striking the fender can be brought to a stop within 73 feet, which is less than the distance which separates the chain from the gate.

Second. Double gates have been provided at the entrances to all the locks and at the lower end of the upper lock in each flight, the guard gate of each pair protecting the lower gate from ramming by a ship which might possibly get away from the towing locomotives and break through the fender chain.

Third. A dam of the movable type called an emergency dam has been placed in the head bay above the upper locks of each flight for the purpose of checking the flow of water through the locks in case of damage, or in case it is necessary to make repairs, or to do any work in the locks which necessitates the shutting off of all water from the lake levels. Each dam is constructed on a steel truss bridge of the cantilever type, pivoted on the side wall of the lock approach, and when not in use rests on the side wall parallel to the channel. When the dam is used, the bridge is swung across the channel with its end resting on the center wall of the lock. A series of wicket girders hinged to this bridge are then lowered into the channel with their ends resting in iron pockets embedded in the lock floor. After the girders have been lowered into place, they afford runways for gates which can be let down one at a time, closing the spaces between the wicket girders. These gates form a horizontal tier spanning the width of the Canal and damming the water to a height of 10 feet. Another series of panels is then lowered, and so on until the dam, constructed from the bottom upward, completely closes the channel. When the dam has checked the main flow, the remainder, due to the clearance between the vertical sides of the gates, may be checked by driving steel pipes between the sides of the adjacent panels. These dams are operated in three movements, and the machinery for operating is, therefore, in three classes, gate-moving, raising and lowering the wicket girders, and hoisting the gates on the girders, all driven by electric motors.

CAISSON GATES

To permit examining, cleaning, painting, and repairing the lower guard gates of the locks, and the Stoney gates of the Spillway dam, and for access in the dry to the sills of the emergency dams, there have been provided floating caisson gates of the molded ship type. When their use is required the caissons are towed into position in the forebay of the upper lock, above the emergency dam, or between the piers of the Spillway, and sunk. The caissons are equipped with electric motor driven pumps for use in pumping out the caissons and for unwatering the locks.

ELECTRIC CONTROL OF LOCK MACHINERY

The gates, valves, and fender chains of the locks are operated by electricity, and remotely controlled from a central point; that is, there is a central control station for each of the series of locks at Gatun, Pedro Miguel, and Miraflores. In passing a ship through the locks it is necessary to open and close the miter gates weighing from 380 to 730 tons, to fill and empty lock chambers containing

PLAN AND OPERATION OF THE CANAL

from three and one half to five million cubic feet of water, to raise and lower fender chains weighing 24,098 pounds each, and to tow the vessel through the locks. All these operations, except that of towing, are controlled by one man at a switchboard.

The control system for Gatun Locks is typical. Water is let into the lock chambers or withdrawn from them by means of culverts under the lock floors, which connect with larger culverts in the lock walls, through which water is carried from the higher to the lower levels. The main supply culverts are 18 feet in diameter, and the flow of water through them is controlled by rising-stem gate valves, which can be completely opened or closed in one minute. In the center wall the culvert feeds both lock chambers, and therefore at each outlet into the lateral culverts there is a valve of the cylindrical type, in order that water may be let into or withdrawn from either chamber at will. A complete opening or closing of these cylindrical valves takes ten seconds. The miter gates are never opened or closed with a head of water on either side of them, the chambers being first emptied or filled by means of the valve and culvert system. The time required either to open or close the miter gate is two minutes.

A ship to be raised to the lake level comes to a full stop in the forebay of the lower lock, prepared to be towed through one of the duplicate locks by electric towing locomotives. The water in the lower lock chamber is equalized with the sea level channel, after which the miter gates are opened, the fender chain lowered and the vessel passed into the first chamber, where the water is at sea level. Then the miter gates are closed. The rising stem gate valves at the outlet of the main culverts are closed, while those above are opened, allowing water to flow from an upper level into the lower chamber, which, when filled, raises the vessel $28\frac{1}{3}$ feet, to the second level. This operation is repeated in the middle and upper locks until the ship has been raised to the full height of 85 feet above the level of the sea. At Gatun, in the passing of a large ship through the locks, it is necessary to lower 4 fender chains, operate 6 pairs of miter gates and force them to miter, open and close 8 pairs of rising stem gate valves for the main supply culverts, and 30 cylindrical valves. In all, no less than 98 motors are set in motion twice during each lockage of a single ship, and this number may be increased to 143, dependent upon the previous condition of the gates, valves and other devices.

Each gate leaf, valve, and fender chain is operated by a separate motor mounted near the machinery in chambers in the lock wall, the motors acting through suitable gears (or pump in the fender chain) upon the various machines. In each machinery chamber is erected a starting panel containing contactors by which current will be applied to the motor and these panels are in turn controlled from a main unit in the central control house. Some of the machinery chambers at Gatun are 2,700 feet distant from the point of control; 90 per cent of them are within 2,000 feet, and 50 per cent of the total within 1,200 feet.

The station from which control is exercised over the movement of all the machines is on the center wall at the lower end of the upper flight of locks at Gatun, and similarly placed at Pedro Miguel and Miraflores. It is in a building raised high enough above the top of the wall to allow a towing locomotive to pass under, a height of 16 feet, and to command an uninterrupted view of every part of the locks. In this house is a double control board duplicated to conform to the duplication in locks. The control board is in the nature of a bench or table, 32 inches above the floor, containing a representation, part model and part diagrammatic, of the flight of locks controlled by the respective series of switches. Standing at his switchboard the operator throws the switches, and sees before him in model or diagram the progress of the fender chains as they rise and fall, the movement of the miter gates inch by inch, the opening and closing of the gate valves in the main culverts at every stage, the operation of the cylindrical valves, and, in addition, indication of the gradual rise or fall of the water in the lock chambers. The switches controlling the various motors, together with their indicators, are mounted upon the board in the same relative position as the machines themselves in the lock walls. Some distortion of scale will be allowed, to give room for the switches. The board is not over 4 feet in width, in order that the operator may be able to reach beyond the middle of it, and the length of the board is limited to 30 feet at Gatun, and proportionally at the other locks.

The system is interlocking, so that certain motors can not be started in a certain direction until other motors are operated in a proper manner to obtain consistent operation on the whole, and to avoid any undesirable or dangerous combinations in the positions of valves, gates, or fender chains. In this way and by the use of limit switches the factor of the personal equation in operating the machines is reduced to a minimum, almost mechanical accuracy being obtained. Before the operating pair of valves in the main culverts can be opened, at least one pair of valves at the other ends of the locks, both upstream and downstream, must first be closed. This limits an operator to the act of equalizing water levels between locks, and keeps him from allowing water to flow from, say the lake level to the middle lock past the upper lock, thus preventing a possible flooding of the lock walls and machinery rooms. Interlocks, devoted to the control of action between the gate valves in the main culverts and the miter gates, prevent valves being opened a lock length above or below a miter gate which is being opened or closed, and thus prevent an operator causing a flow of water while the miter gates are being moved. Interlocks for the cylindrical valves guarding the openings from the center wall culvert to the lateral culverts keep those of one side or the other closed at all times, except when it is desired to cross-fill the chambers, when they may be opened by special procedure. An interlock prevents the operator from starting to open a miter gate before unlocking the miter-forcing machine. The miter gates guarded by a fender chain must be opened before the chain can be lowered, and the chain must be raised again before the gate can be closed, or more exactly the switches must be thrown in this order, but the operations may proceed at the same time. The simple interlocks will prevent such a mistake as leaving the chain down through lapse of memory when it should be up to protect the gate.

LIGHTING THE CANAL

The general scheme of lighting and buoying the Canal includes the use of range lights to establish direction on the longer tangents and of side lights spaced about 1 mile apart to mark each side of the channel. The range lights are omitted in Culebra Cut, where their use is hardly practicable, and on four of the shorter tangents on the remainder of the Canal. In the Cut have been placed three beacons at each angle, and between these intermediate beacons in pairs on each side of the Canal. By keeping his ship pointed midway between these beacons, the pilot is able to adhere closely to the center of the Canal. At each tangent it is necessary to have two ranges of two lights each to prolong the sailing line in order that the pilot may hold his course up to the point of turning. These range lights will be situated on land. There are three types, all of reinforced concrete. The more elaborate structures are used on the Gatun locks and dam and in the Atlantic and Pacific Divisions, where they are closer to the sailing lines of the vessels, while simpler structures have been placed in the Gatun Lake, where they are under less close observation. A light and fog signal on the west breakwater in Limon Bay is also included. The illuminants are gas and electricity, the latter being used whenever the light is sufficiently accessible. For the floating buoys, and for the towers and beacons which are in inaccessible places, the system using compressed acetylene dissolved in acetone has been adopted. The buoys are composed of a cylindrical floating body or tank, surmounted by a steel frame which supports the lens at a height of about 15 feet above the water level. The buoys are moored in position along the edge of the dredged channel by a heavy chain and a concrete sinker, and should remain lighted for six to twelve months without being recharged. The candlepower of the range lights varies according to the length of the range, from about 2,500 to 15,000 candlepower. The most powerful lights are those marking the sea channels at the Atlantic and Pacific entrances, they being visible from about 12 to 18 nautical miles. The beacons and gas-buoy lights will have about 850 candlepower. White lights will be used throughout, and, in order to eliminate the possibility of confusing the lights with one another and with the lights on shore, all range lights, beacons, and buoys will have individual characteristics formed by flashes and combinations of flashes of light and dark intervals.

EXCAVATION

The total excavation, dry and wet, for the Canal as originally planned, was estimated at 103,795,000 cubic yards, in addition to the excavation by the French companies. Changes in the plan of the Canal, made subsequently by order of the President, increased the amount to 174,666,594 cubic yards. Of this amount, 89,794,493 cubic yards were to be taken from the Central Division, which includes the Culebra Cut. In July, 1910, a further increase of 7,871,172 cubic yards was made, of which 7,330,525 cubic yards were to allow for slides in Culebra Cut, for silting in the Chagres section, and for lowering the bottom of the Canal from 40 to 39 feet above sea level in the Chagres section. These additions increased the estimated total excavation to 182,537,766 cubic yards. In 1911, a further increase of 12,785,613 cubic yards was made, of which 5,257,281 cubic yards was for slides in Culebra Cut, and the remainder for additional excavation and silting in the Atlantic and Pacific entrances, raising the grand total of estimated excavation to 195,323,379 cubic yards. In 1912 an increase of 17,180,621 cubic yards was made, of which 3,545,000 cubic yards was for slides in Culebra Cut and the remainder for dredging excavation at Gatun locks, silting in the Atlantic entrance, and for the Balboa terminals, and in 1913 came a still further increase of 20,126,000 cubic yards, of which 9,067,000 cubic yards was due to slides and breaks in Culebra Cut, bringing the grand total of estimated excavation to 232,353,000 cubic yards. Deducting Balboa terminal excavation, the total for the Canal proper, according to the estimate of 1913, is about 223,559,000 cubic yards, or nearly double the amount of the original estimate made in the minority report of the International Board of Consulting Engineers in 1906. The points of deepest excavation are in Culebra Cut, 495 feet above the bottom of the Canal at Gold Hill, and 364 feet above at Contractor's Hill opposite. The widest part of the Cut is opposite the town of Culebra, where owing to the action of slides on both banks, the top width is about half a mile. Active excavation work on a large scale did not begin until 1907, when 15,765,290 cubic yards were removed. In 1908, over 37,000,000 cubic yards were removed, and in 1909, over 35,000,000 making a total for the two years of over 72,000,000 yards, or a monthly average for those two years of 3,000,000 cubic yards. In 1910, 31,437,000 cubic yards were removed; in 1911, 31,603,000; in 1912, 30,269,000; and to July 1, 1913, 18,324,637 cubic yards, including both wet and dry excavation, and leaving a total of 25,748,051 yet to be taken out.

SLIDES AND BREAKS

There have been in all 26 slides and breaks in Culebra Cut; 17 covered areas varying from 1 to 75 acres and 9

Photograph, Underwood & Underwood, N. Y.

BERM CRANES AT MIRAFLORES.

These great cranes, which are movable on the tracks at the bottom of the picture, carry electric trolleys which transport the concrete from the mixers to the desired point on the lock walls.

covered areas of less than 1 acre each, making in all a total of 225 acres. One variety of slide is caused by the slipping of the top layer of clay and earth on a smooth sloping surface of a harder material. The largest slide of this character is that known as Cucaracha on the east bank of the Canal just south of Gold Hill. This gave the first French company trouble during the final years of its operations. It first gave the Americans trouble in 1905, and between that date and July 1, 1913, over 12,000,000 cubic yards of material were removed from the Canal because of it. It broke nearly 1,900 feet back from the axis of the Canal and covers an area of 47 acres. Another variety of slide, properly called break, is due to the steepness of the slopes and the great pressure of the superincumbent material upon the underlying layers of softer material. The largest slide or break of this type is on the west side of the Cut at Culebra just north of Contractor's Hill and covers an area of 75 acres. Over 7,000,000 cubic yards of material have been removed from this slide. On the east side of the Cut a similar slide covers an area of about 50 acres, breaking back about 1,300 feet from the center of the Canal. About a half million cubic yards have been taken out of this slide and more remains to be removed. It is estimated that the total amount of material removed from the Canal because of the slides will aggregate between 21,000,000 and 22,000,000 cubic yards.

DRILLING AND BLASTING

Most of the material excavated in Culebra Cut has consisted of rock varying from very soft, which readily disintegrates on exposure to the atmosphere, to very dense rock of great hardness. It has been necessary before excavating this material to drill and blast it. Two kinds of drills have been used—tripod and well—both obtaining their power from a 10-inch compressed air main on the west bank of the Cut which is supplied by three batteries of air compressors placed at equal distances along the 9 miles of the Cut. The usual depth of drill holes has been about 27 feet, three feet deeper than the steam shovels have excavated. The drill holes, placed about 14 feet apart, are loaded with 45 per cent potassium nitrate dynamite in quantities depending upon the character of the rock, and are connected in parallel and fired by means of a current from an electric light plant. The maximum number of drills in use at any one time in Culebra Cut was 377, of which 221 were tripod and 156 well. With these over 90 miles of holes have been drilled in a single month. A pound of dynamite has been used to about every $2\frac{1}{4}$ cubic yards of material blasted, and the quantity used in Culebra Cut during several years has averaged about 6,000,000 pounds a year.

CAPACITY OF STEAM SHOVELS AND DIRT TRAINS

There have been several classes of steam shovels engaged in excavating work, equipped with dippers ranging in capacity from $1\frac{3}{4}$ cubic yards to 5 cubic yards, and a trenching shovel, which has a dipper with a capacity of $\frac{3}{4}$ of a cubic yard. In Culebra Cut excavation the 5-yard dippers have been used almost entirely.

Each cubic yard, place measurement, of average rock weighs about 3,900 pounds; of earth, about 3,000 pounds; of "the run of the Cut," about 3,600 pounds, and is said to represent about a two-horse cart load. Consequently, a five cubic yard dipper, when full, carries 8.7 tons of rock, 6.7 tons of earth, and 8.03 tons of "the run of the Cut."

Three classes of cars were used in hauling spoil—flat cars with one high side, which were unloaded by plows weighing from 14 to 16 tons, operated by a cable upon a winding drum, and two kinds of dump cars, one large and one small. The capacity of the flat cars is 19 cubic yards; that of the large dump cars 17 cubic yards, and that of the small dump cars, 10 cubic yards. The flat car train was ordinarily composed of 20 cars in hauling from the cut at Pedro Miguel, and 21 cars in hauling from the cut at Matachin. The large dump train was composed of 27 cars, and the small dump train of 35 cars.

The average load of a train of flat cars, in hauling the mixed material known as "the run of the Cut," was 610.7 tons (based on a 20-car train); of a train of large dump cars, 737.68 tons, and of a train of small dumps, 562.5 tons.

The average time consumed in unloading a train of flat cars was from 7 to 15 minutes; in unloading a train of large dump cars, 15 to 40 minutes; and in unloading a train of small dump cars, 6 to 56 minutes. The large dump cars were operated by compressed air power furnished by the air pump of the locomotive, while the small dump cars were operated by hand.

The record day's work for one steam shovel was that of March 22, 1910, 4,823 cubic yards of rock (place measurement), or 8,395 tons. The highest daily record in the Central Division was on March 11, 1911, when 51 steam shovels and 2 cranes equipped with orange peel baskets excavated an aggregate of 79,484 cubic yards, or 127,742 tons. During this day, 333 loaded trains and as many empty trains were run to and from the dumping grounds.

The greatest number of shovels in use at one time in the Cut was 43, and the greatest monthly excavation in any single month, in the Cut, was obtained in March, 1911, when 1,728,748 cubic yards of material, mostly rock, were excavated.

To handle this amount of material required the services of 115 locomotives and 2,000 cars, giving about 160 loaded trains per day to the dumps, which on the average were about 12 miles distant, the haul one way varying from about one mile to 33 miles. To serve properly the trains and shovels employed in excavation work in the Cut, although it is less than nine miles in length, about 100 miles of track have been required, or an average of over nine parallel tracks at all points.

BREAKWATERS

Breakwaters have been constructed at the Atlantic and Pacific entrances of the Canal. That in Limon Bay, or Colon harbor, extends into the bay from Toro Point at an angle of 42° and 53′ northward from a base line drawn from Toro Point to Colon light, and is 10,500 feet in length, or 11,700 feet, including the shore connection, with a width at the top of fifteen feet and a height above mean sea level of ten feet. The width at the bottom depends largely on the depth of water. It contains approximately 2,840,000 cubic yards of rock, the core being formed of rock quarried on the mainland near Toro Point, armored with hard rock from Porto Bello. The purpose of the breakwaters is to convert Limon Bay into a safe anchorage, to protect shipping in the harbor of Colon, and vessels making the north entrance to the Canal, from the violent northers that are likely to prevail from October to January, and to reduce to a minimum the amount of silt that may be washed into the dredged channel.

The breakwater at the Pacific entrance extends from Balboa to Naos Island, a distance of about 17,000 feet, or a little more than three miles. It lies from 900 to 2,700 feet east of and, for the greater part of the distance, nearly parallel to the axis of the Canal prism; varies from 20 to 40 feet in height above mean sea level, and is from 50 to 3,000 feet wide at the top. It contains about 18,000,000 cubic yards of earth and rock, all of which was brought from Culebra Cut. It was constructed for a two-fold purpose; first to divert cross currents that would carry soft material from the shallow harbor of Panama into the Canal channel; second, to furnish rail connection between the islands and the mainland.

CHANGE OF LOCATION OF LOCKS

A brief explanatory review of the changes referred to may facilitate a clear understanding of the final plan.

It has been asserted that the abandonment of the Sosa site was in response to a new idea acted upon without due consideration. The facts in the matter are these: In 1905, the present chief engineer visited the Isthmus in the capacity of a member of the Board of National Defenses. In a relevant report, he made the following statement:

"The great objection to the locks at Sosa Hill is the possibility of their destruction by the fire from an enemy's ship. If, as has been suggested to me by officers of this department entitled to speak with authority on the subject, these locks can be located against and behind Sosa Hill in such a way as to use the hill as a protection against such fire, then economy would lead to the retention of the lake. . . . . If, however, Sosa Hill will not afford a site with such protection, then it seems to me wiser to place the locks at Miraflores."

Mature study of the question led to the conclusion that locks at Sosa would not be sufficiently secure, and it was further evident that their transfer to Miraflores would be accompanied by a saving in cost. The latter point, it should be remembered, was that decided upon by the Walker Commission for the site of the tide lock at the Pacific end. So that it appears that this, like all the other features of the plan, has been the subject of the most exhaustive investigation and thought.

CHANGES IN DIMENSIONS

The increase of channel width through one-half the length of Culebra Cut from 200 feet to 300 feet at the bottom, which will enable ships to pass each other in any part of the Cut, was not made on the recommendation of the Commission, but by executive order.

The usable dimensions of the locks were changed at the instigation of the President and on the recommendation of the General Board of the Navy from 900 feet and 95 feet, to 1,000 feet and 110 feet.

On this point Colonel Goethals has said: "It is objected that the size of the locks limits the Canal to vessels which can use them. This is true. The present lock designs provide intermediate gates dividing the locks into lengths of 600 and 400 feet. About 98 per cent of all ships, including the largest battleships now building, can be passed through the 600-foot lengths, and the total lock length will accommodate the largest commercial vessels now building, which, I believe, are 1,000 feet long and 88 feet beam. It is true that ships may increase in size so as to make the present locks obsolete, but the largest ships now afloat can not navigate the Suez Canal, nor the proposed sea level canal at Panama. It must also be remembered that the commerce of the world is carried by the medium-sized vessels, the length of only one of the many ships using the Suez Canal being greater than 600 feet."

It is undoubtedly fortunate that Colonel Goethals' judgment in this matter was not accepted, since during the past two years a great increase in the size of both commercial and war vessels has come about, chiefly noticeable in width. Our new battleships have a beam of 97 feet and upwards, which will leave a clearance in the lock chambers of less than 13 feet in all, or about 6 feet on either side. Commercial vessels now built, and others whose keels have been laid, have a beam of 96 feet, so that it is quite possible that the locks may prove to be too narrow before they are found too short.

The height of the Gatun Dam was decreased, so that its crest stands 30 feet, instead of 50 feet, above the normal level of the lake, which is 85 feet.

This change was made because, with the progress of time and more thorough knowledge of the foundation material, it became quite evident that the larger dimensions were unnecessary, and to build in accordance with them would be a wasteful expenditure of time and money. The reduced weight is sufficient to meet the utmost demands of stability, and the reduced height is ample for the complete retention of the lake, which can never, under any conceivable circumstances, rise to 100 feet above sea level.

COST OF THE CANAL

The present estimated cost of the Canal, which it is improbable that any future conditions will materially affect, is about $375,000,000. No unknown factors, nor hypothetical calculations entered into the preparation of these figures. This estimate is largely in excess of that which formed part of the report of the Board of Consulting Engineers, but which was based on data much less complete than that since rendered available. During the last six years of the work there was an increase in the wage scale and in the cost of material. Wages on the Isthmus exceeded those in the United States from 40 to 80 per cent for the same class of labor. The original estimates were based on a ten-hour day, but Congress afterward imposed upon the Commission the observance of an eight-hour day. The various changes already noted, and others of a minor character, but considerable in the aggregate, increased the quantity of the work to be done by 50 per cent. Despite all this, the unit costs increased no more than 20 per cent. Furthermore, no such system of housing and caring for the employees as was maintained was anticipated by the Board.

In addition, municipal improvements in Panama and Colon, together with advances to the Panama Railroad, approximated $15,000,000, a sum which will eventually be returned to the Treasury of the United States.

APPROPRIATIONS

Payment to the New Panama Canal Company	$40,000,000.00
Payment to Republic of Panama	10,000,000.00
Appropriation, June 28, 1902	10,000,000.00
Appropriation, December 21, 1905	11,000,000.00
Deficiency, February 27, 1906	5,990,786.00
Appropriation, June 30, 1906	25,456,415.08
Appropriation, March 4, 1907	27,161,367.50
Deficiency, February 15, 1908	12,178,900.00

Appropriation, May 27, 1908	$29,187,000.00
Deficiency, March 4, 1909	5,458,000.00
Appropriation, March 4, 1909	33,638,000.00
Deficiency, February 25, 1910	76,000.00
Appropriation, June 25, 1910	37,855,000.00
Appropriation, March 4, 1911	45,560,000.00
Appropriation, August 24, 1912	28,980,000.00
Private Act. Relief of Elizabeth G. Martin	1,200.00
Private Act. Relief of Marcellus Troxell	1,500.00
Private Act. Relief of W. L. Miles	1,704.18
Private Act. Relief of Chas. A. Caswell	1,056.00
Private Act. Relief of Alexandro Comba	500.00
Private Act. Relief of Douglas B. Thompson	1,500.00
Private Act. Relief of Robert S. Gill	2,520.00
Total	$322,551,448.76
Appropriation for Fortifications, March 4, 1911	3,000,000.00
Appropriation for Fortifications, August 24, 1912	2,806,950.00

CLASSIFIED EXPENDITURES TO NOVEMBER 1, 1912

Department of Construction and Engineering	$159,411,558.14
Department of Construction of Engineering Plant	2,868,362.47
Department of Sanitation	15,319,682.40
Department of Civil Administration	5,961,599.68
Department of Law	30,887.52
Panama Railroad, Second Main Track	1,123,477.93
Panama Railroad, Relocated Line	8,866,392.02
Purchase and Repair of Steamers	2,680,112.01
Zone Water Works and Sewers	5,140,506.45
Zone Roadways	1,579,724.67
Loans to Panama Railroad Company	3,247,332.11
Construction and Repair of Buildings	10,188,813.63
Purchase from New Panama Canal Company	40,000,000.00
Payment to Republic of Panama	10,000,000.00
Miscellaneous	4,207,175.37
Total	$270,625,624.40
Expenditures for Fortifications to Nov. 1, 1912	1,685,315.75

The balances carried in expenditure accounts, which are included in the last item above, for water works, sewers, and pavements in the cities of Panama and Colon amounted

PEDRO MIGUEL LOCKS.

The south end of the East Chamber, showing construction of safety and lower gates.

PLAN AND OPERATION OF THE CANAL

altogether to $2,395,358.79. The unexpended balance in the appropriation for sanitation in the cities of Panama and Colon, available for expenditures on water works, sewers, and pavements, was $97,465.64, including transfer of appropriations for quarter ended September 30, 1912.

A careful official estimate has been made by the Canal Commission of the value to the Commission at the present time of the franchises, equipment, material, work done, and property of various kinds for which the United States paid the French Canal Company $40,000,000. It places the total value at $42,000,000, divided as follows:

Excavation, useful to the Canal, 29,708,000 cubic yards	$25,389,240.00
Panama Railroad Stock	9,644,320.00
Plant and material, used, and sold for scrap	2,112,063.00
Buildings, used	2,054,203.00
Surveys, plans, maps, and records	2,000,000.00
Land	1,000,000.00
Clearings, roads, etc	100,000.00
Ship channel in Panama Bay, four years' use	500,000.00
Total	$42,799,826.00

The Canal Zone contains about 436 square miles, about 95 of which will be under the waters of the Canal and Gatun and Miraflores Lakes. It begins at a point 3 marine miles from mean low water mark in each ocean, and extends for 5 miles on each side of the center line of the route of the Canal. It includes the group of islands in the Bay of Panama named Perico, Naos, Culebra, and Flamenco. The cities of Panama and Colon are excluded from the Zone, but the United States has the right to enforce sanitary ordinances in those cities, and to maintain public order in them in case the Republic of Panama should not be able, in the judgment of the United States, to do so.

Of the 436 square miles of Zone territory, the United States owns about 363, and 73 are held in private ownership. Under the treaty with Panama, the United States has the right to acquire by purchase, or by the exercise of the right of eminent domain, any lands, buildings, water rights, or other properties necessary and convenient for the construction, maintenance, operation, sanitation, and protection of the Canal, and it can, therefore, at any time acquire the lands within the Zone boundaries which are owned by private persons. The United States will also control the area to be covered by Gatun Lake which extends beyond the lines of the Canal Zone.

The population of the Canal Zone, official census, is 62,810; of Panama City, 35,368; of Colon, 17,749.

The permanent administration and Canal headquarters building will be on a knoll west of Ancon quarry where it will overlook both the terminal piers and the Canal entrance. It is to have 75,000 square feet of floor space and is to cost not more than $375,000, including $25,000 for that part assigned to permanent records. The quarters for employees attached to the administration building will be erected in the general area adjacent to and northeast of it, and employees connected with the shops, docks, and other terminal facilities at Balboa will be housed in quarters erected in the area surrounding the slope of Sosa Hill and on the fill adjoining the Ancon-Balboa highway. There will be a permanent settlement at Pedro Miguel for employees of the Pacific locks, and one at Gatun for employees of the Atlantic locks. The settlement at Cristobal will be maintained, and possibly the settlement at Ancon. No necessity is apparent for any other than the above five settlements, except for the military forces which will be stationed on the Isthmus.

The piers for commercial use at Balboa are built at right angles to the axis of the Canal, with their ends about 2,650 feet from the center line of the Canal channel. They are about 1,000 feet long, and 200 feet wide, with 300-foot slips between, and with landings for small boats at the head of each slip for the full width between piers. The old French steel wharf, about 1,000 feet long, will be retained for some time in the future, for commercial purposes.

Two wharves and one pier have been constructed at Cristobal, behind a mole and breakwater, built out from shore toward the Canal channel, and paralleling the boundary line between Canal Zone and Panamanian waters. Primarily, these docks are to meet the commercial requirements of the Panama railroad, but should there be enough traffic after the Canal is completed to justify it, four other piers, each about 1,000 feet long, and 209 feet wide, with 300-foot slips between, will be constructed.

The main drydock will be situated at Balboa, and will be capable of accommodating any vessel that can pass through the Canal locks. It will have a usable length of 1,000 feet, a depth over the keel blocks of 35 feet at mean sea level, and an entrance width of 110 feet. The entrance will be closed by miter gates, similar to those used in the locks. The drydock will have a rock foundation, and its sides will be lined with concrete. Its equipment will include a 40-ton locomotive crane, with a travel on both sides.

For vessels of smaller type, an auxiliary drydock will be built at Balboa, in lieu of the marine railways originally contemplated. It will have a usable length of 350 feet, a width at entrance of 71 feet, and a depth over the keel blocks of $13\frac{1}{2}$ feet at mean sea level. It will be provided with a floating caisson. The 40-ton locomotive crane on the main drydock will be utilized for this dock also. The work of providing space for these drydocks, as well as for the new shops, is now under way, and requires the excavation of about 300,000 cubic yards of material from the northwest face of Sosa Hill. The excavated material is used in filling the site for the shops and terminal yard.

On the Atlantic side it is proposed to retain the old French drydock at Mount Hope, which has a usable length of 300 feet, a width at entrance of 50 feet, and a depth over the sill of 13 feet at mean sea level. It was the opinion of the board in charge of the dock projects, that the commercial requirements in sight would not warrant the construction of a drydock at Cristobal capable of accommodating large vessels, in view of the building of a drydock at Balboa, to which any large vessel on the Atlantic side could be taken and returned, in case it was found necessary to dock it for repairs.

The plans contemplate furnishing vessels with fuel, fresh water, and supplies of all kinds. The main coaling plant will be situated on the north end of the island, opposite dock No. 11, Cristobal. It will be capable of handling and storing 200,000 tons of coal, with a possible increase of 50 per cent. One hundred thousand tons of the total normal storage is subaqueous. The plant will have railroad connection with the mainland over a bridge of the bascule type, which will cross the French canal at a point about half a mile south of the Mount Hope drydock. The preliminary work on this plant has been begun by the Panama railroad.

A subsidiary coaling plant will be situated at Balboa, at the outer end of the southeast approach wall of the drydock, having a frontage of 500 feet thereon, adapted for discharging vessels. This plant will be capable of handling and storing 100,000 tons of coal, with a possible increase of 50 per cent. Fifty thousand tons of the total normal storage is subaqueous.

In addition to coal, facilities will be provided at Cristobal and Balboa for supplying shipping, and the Canal works, with fuel oil. In line with this plan, four steel tanks of 40,000 barrels capacity each, have been contracted for in the United States.

The main repair shops will be built at Balboa, and are designed to maintain the following equipment:

1. Lock, spillway, and power plant machinery. 2. Water and land equipment retained for the maintenance of the Canal. 3. Rolling stock and equipment of the Panama railroad. 4. Mechanical apparatus connected with the coaling plants, fortifications, cold storage plant, wireless stations, etc. 5. The making of repairs, etc., required by commercial vessels, and by private individuals and corpora-

tions. 6. The making of such repairs as may be required by vessels of the United States Navy.

In addition to these, a number of subsidiary buildings will be erected. All of the structures will be of permanent construction, with steel frames. The sides and ends will be left open for ventilation and light, protection from sun and rain being afforded by overhanging sheds.

The main metal working shops, including machine, erecting and tool shops, the forge and pipe shop, and the boiler and shipfitters' shop, together with the shed for the storage of steel, will be placed end on between the drydock and repair wharf. The general storehouse, foundry, woodworking shops, subsidiary buildings, and office building, will be erected parallel to the line of the drydock and water front, northeast of the main shops. Two lines of railroad tracks will extend past each end of the main metal working shops, and one track through their center. The main shops will be provided with overhead traveling cranes, the crane runways being extended through each end of the buildings over the railroad tracks. As far as possible, the present machinery will be utilized in the new shops. All of it will be electric driven, including both individual and group drive.

It is proposed to retain the drydock shops, for making repairs on the Atlantic side, until sufficient experience is had to determine the extent and character of repair facilities necessary.

For the handling of the lock gate leaves, as well as for other Canal requirements, and commercial and general wrecking purposes, one, or two, powerful floating cranes will be purchased. For handling vessels of the largest size at Cristobal and Balboa, two high power harbor tugs will be provided, and for the transportation of coal, fuel oil, and fresh water alongside of vessels, a sufficient number of barges and lighters will be placed in service. The steel barges, now in use by the Canal Commission, can be used to good advantage, after the necessary modifications have been made, in the barge and lighter service. A tender for passengers and mail will be furnished at each terminus also, provided the business justifies it.

Some idea of the stupendous nature of the undertaking may be gained by a glance at the following table of statistics of the equipment in use during the construction period:

CANAL SERVICE

Steam shovels:
- 105-ton, 5 cubic yard dippers................................. 15
- 95-ton, 4 and 5 cubic yard dippers............................ 30
- 70-ton, 2½ and 3 cubic yard dippers........................... 33
- 66-ton, 2½ cubic yard dippers................................. 10
- 45-ton, 1¾ cubic yard dippers................................. 11
- 26-ton... 1
- Trenching shovel, ¾ cubic yard dipper......................... 1

    Total... 101

Locomotives:
  American—
- 106 tons... 100
- 105 tons... 41
- 117 tons... 20

    Total.. 161

- French... 104
- Narrow gage, American, 16 tons............................ 33
- Electric.. 9

    Total... 307

Drills:
- Mechanical churn, or well..................................... 196
- Tripod.. 357

    Total... 553

Cars:
- Flat, used with unloading plows............................... 1,760
- Steel dumps, large.. 596
- Steel dumps, small.. 1,207
- Ballast dumps... 24
- Steel flats... 487
- Narrow gage... 209
- Motor... 6
- Pay Car... 1

Pay Certificate... 1
Automatic, electric... 45
Decauville... 224
Special, shops... 12

Total... 4,572

Spreaders... 26
Track shifters... 9
Unloaders... 30
Pile drivers... 14

Dredges:
French ladder... 7
Dipper... 3
Pipeline... 7
Sea-going suction... 2
Clam shell... 1

Total... 20

Cranes... 47
Rock breaker... 1
Tugs... 11
Tow boat... 1
House boats... 3
Clapets... 12
Pile driver, floating... 3
Crane boat... 1
Barges, lighters and scows... 72
Launches... 29
Drill boats... 2
Floating derricks... 2

PANAMA RAILROAD

Locomotives:
Road (12 oil burners)... 36
Switch... 26

Total... 52

Cars:
Coaches... 57
Freight... 1,434

Total... 1,491

Cranes:
- Locomotive... 2
- Wrecking... 2
  - Total... 4

Piledrivers:
- Track.. 1
- Floating... 1
  - Total... 2

Tugboat... 1

Lighters:
- Coal, all steel.. 5
- Cargo, steel and iron.. 8
  - Total... 13

Motor boats... 2
Steam ditcher... 1

SUCCESS OF THE MILITARY MANAGEMENT

The writer confesses to having been one of the sceptics who viewed with misgiving the transfer of the Canal operation to military management, and he acknowledges with pleasure that in every important respect the results have been contrary to his predictions. The work could not have been in better hands. It has been carried on without any hitch or subsidence, and the progress made has excited the admiration and astonishment of engineers throughout the world.

An excellent organization has been established and a strong *esprit de corps* maintained. Health conditions were steadily improved and a gradual increase in the efficiency of labor effected. All classes of employees have been imbued with confidence and courage by the knowledge that their chiefs were moving along clearly cut lines, with well-defined purposes in view. For the first time

THE PACIFIC ENTRANCE TO THE CANAL AT LOW TIDE.

On the extreme left of the picture will be seen the rear tower range light and on the extreme right the front tower. On this tower the high water mark point is marked.

since the enterprise was entered upon, the responsible heads of it were in complete accord with the controlling authorities at Washington.

The plan of organization of the Engineering Department divided all construction work into three topographical districts, each under the charge of an Assistant Engineer with full control and responsibility. These divisions are: The Atlantic Division, extending from deep water to Gatun Lake, and including the Gatun Dam and locks; the Central Division, extending from Gatun to Pedro Miguel, and including the Culebra Cut; the Pacific Division, extending from Pedro Miguel to deep water in the Pacific, and including the dams and locks at the former point and at Miraflores.

CHAPTER XII

MILITARY AND POLITICAL ASPECTS

For more than two hundred and fifty years the various nations of the world have been wrangling over the project of building a canal on the Isthmus of Panama. Diplomats have fought wordy battles and concocted wily schemes to secure a foothold on the Isthmus which would place their governments in an advantageous position either for building a canal or acquiring a strategic position in case one was built by another nation. Spain, England, France, Colombia and the United States have figured as the principals in these diplomatic negotiations. Although there have been other nations involved none have played a part sufficiently noteworthy for mention.

Of course Spain, as the first nation on the ground, was chiefly concerned with the canal project in its early days. Next England, whose traders and freebooters had obtained a foothold on the Spanish main, became a factor in Isthmian politics. The Englishmen had settled in Nicaragua and Honduras, Jamaica and others of the West Indian islands. Of these settlements, perhaps the most important, from a diplomatic point of view, was the English colony in that part of Nicaragua known as the Mosquito Coast. This colony was established in 1740, and some time later became a dependency of Jamaica. This foothold was gradually strengthened by treaty and otherwise, until England was enabled to organize a province there called British Honduras. Diplomatic discussion of this matter between England and Spain again and again resulted to the advantage of England, and her hold upon this territory grew stronger and stronger. In 1860 England was able to obtain an acknowledgment from Nicaragua of the validity of her claim to British Honduras, and became a powerful factor in that part of the Isthmian country.

THE UNITED STATES TAKES A HAND

The United States, although naturally the logical builder of a canal on the Isthmus, was very slow to take advantage of the necessity and opportunity. It was not until about 1835 that any interest in such a project was manifested in this country. In that year the question of a canal was brought up in the Senate, with the result that an emissary was sent to the Isthmus to make an investigation of the matter. This move had no definite results until 1846, when a treaty was negotiated with New Granada by which the United States was given the sole right of transit across the Isthmus between the Atrato River and the Chiriqui Lagoon, either by road, railroad or canal. The limits of this treaty were sufficiently wide to provide a basis for the Panama Railroad concession, secured a few years later.

An attempt was made shortly afterward to negotiate the same privileges with Nicaragua, but complications were immediately encountered because of the fact that England was powerfully entrenched there. Various agents were sent to this country in an effort to conclude a satisfactory treaty. Finally, the negotiations resulted in the signing of a treaty with Nicaragua, guaranteeing that country sovereignty over the territory occupied by the canal which it was proposed to build. As this rather left England out in the cold, she immediately took steps to maintain her strategic position by threatening the seizure of Tiger Island in the Gulf of Fonseca, at the Pacific terminus of the proposed canal.

To block this move the United States, through its agent in Nicaragua, negotiated a treaty with that Republic by which Tiger Island was ceded to the United States, thus creating a difficult situation with England. A diplomatic wrangle immediately ensued, which was settled in 1850 by the unfortunate Clayton-Bulwer Treaty, under which both governments agreed to forego the right to build or fortify an Isthmian canal, or to ally themselves with any Isthmian country for that purpose. Both countries offered protection to any other country which would undertake to build the canal, and guaranteed the freedom of a port at either end of the canal.

This treaty did not apply to British Honduras, and resulted greatly to the disadvantage of the United States.

This state of affairs maintained until after the Civil War in the United States, since that struggle occupied the attention of this country to so great an extent that the matter of building a canal was naturally held in abeyance. In 1866, however, the project again came up for discussion, and the people of the United States came to a clearer realization of the irritating features of the Clayton-Bulwer Treaty, and to desire a greater latitude of action upon the Isthmus of Panama. Various propositions were made looking to the abrogation of the treaty with England, among them being a project to buy Tiger Island. But these came to no definite end. President Grant was the first to advocate the clearcut policy of an American canal under American control, and negotiations were entered into with Nicaragua in 1869 and 1870 with a view to building a canal across the Isthmus.

Soon afterward France entered the field of Isthmian diplomacy, Ferdinand de Lesseps making an attempt to secure an abrogation of our treaty with New Granada, in order that France might have the right to build a canal entirely under French control. The United States applied the Monroe Doctrine and adopted so firm an attitude on this subject, however that the attempt was abandoned.

GROWTH OF DEMAND FOR A CANAL

From this time on the American people turned their eyes more and more strongly to Panama and to the vital

MILITARY AND POLITICAL ASPECTS

necessity of this country for a canal under American ownership. The strong desire for this dates back to 1849 with the rush of the gold miners to California during the great gold strike in that State. Difficulty was experienced in crossing the continent because of a lack of transcontinental railroads and the length and tediousness of the journey by wagon train. A great many of the "forty-niners" chose to take ship to the Isthmus and brave the perils of the jungle and to pay the high rates exacted for crossing there. From this date our Far West grew rapidly in importance, and the necessity for some means of quick transportation, both for the purpose of defense and trade became more and more apparent, until, in 1898, the famous voyage of the Oregon around the Horn brought the crying necessity for a canal before the American people in such a way that public sentiment was aroused and became insistent that a canal should be built and owned by the United States as soon as possible.

THE VOYAGE OF THE "OREGON"

The American people will not soon forget the voyage of the Oregon. At the opening of the war with Spain, when the great Spanish fleet under Admiral Cervera was reported to be speeding across the Atlantic to make an attack upon the American coast, the Oregon, one of the finest ships in our none too large navy, was on the Pacific side. Need of her on the other side of the continent was felt so strongly that orders were telegraphed to her captain to make the long voyage around the Horn at the utmost possible speed. Never before had such a voyage at top speed been made by a battleship. Day by day the people hastened to open their newspapers to see where the Oregon was, and to wonder whether she would be able to make the long voyage without accident and arrive at the scene of action in time. The Oregon did make this memorable voyage without accident and in record-breaking time, and arrived in time to take part in the battle of Santiago. Nevertheless, the lesson taught by the anxiety and suspense endured throughout many days was not soon to be forgotten, and the determination became stronger and stronger that such an emergency must never again arise and that some rapid means of communication between our coasts must be provided. Within two years a new treaty with England called the Hay-Pauncefote Treaty was negotiated, and ratified on December 16, 1901. By the provisions of this treaty the troublesome and annoying Clayton-Bulwer Treaty was abrogated. The United States was empowered to build and control a canal, both in times of peace and war. By this treaty we were forbidden to blockade the canal, but were not forbidden to fortify it, and thus all obstacles to the construction and ownership of a canal across the Isthmus of Panama were cleared away, and a way opened for the enterprise.

SELECTING A LOCATION

The next three years were occupied in selecting a location. Two routes were suggested, one on the location of the French attempt at Panama, and the other through Nicaragua. After careful study and investigation, however, it was decided to adopt the Panama route, as has been set forth at greater length in another portion of this volume.

The negotiations with Colombia, looking to the right to build a canal, have also been detailed at length, as have the dramatic revolution in Panama and the treaty with that country, which closed the diplomatic wrangling of centuries and left the United States free to build a canal under the conditions which we desired.

FORTIFICATIONS

Prominent among the international questions involved by the consideration of the canal has been the question of fortifications. By the Hay-Pauncefote Treaty we were not forbidden to place fortifications on the canal, and in fact no mention of the matter was made. After the signing of the treaty, however, there was a great deal of discussion as to whether or not we had this right. The matter was not definitely settled until 1911, however, when an appropriation of $3,000,000 was made by the House of Representatives for this purpose. Work was begun immediately, and the huge forts which guard the waterway, armed with the latest and largest type of mortars and disappearing rifles, have settled this question for all time.

The questions raised on this subject involved not only our right to fortify the canal, but also the expediency. As on many other questions which have arisen concerning methods of policy connected with the canal, the people of the United States were divided into rival camps on this subject. The opponents of fortifications presented many arguments in support of their position. In the first place it was claimed that no fortification was necessary, inasmuch as the canal could be protected by our fleet. This argument was met by a consideration that in that case our fleet in time of war would be largely tied down to a defense of this important avenue of communication, and would lack the freedom of action which would be most favorable to its success. Further argument along this line was that this would be a far more expensive method of defending the canal than the proposed fortifications, since it would be necessary to provide a fleet of sufficient size to take care of the defense of the canal, in addition to the ships necessary for the defense of our extensive coast line. Many other arguments were brought up by those opposed to fortifications, but these were disposed of along the same logical lines.

The doctrine of non-militarism is the one chiefly expounded by those opposed to canal fortification. Up to the present time our theory of national defense was largely based on the belief that no enemy could successfully attack us because of the ocean lying between. In these days of high speed ships, however, the long stretch of South America, reaching far below us, is practically the only remnant of that isolation. The great length of the voyage around the Horn, together with the fact that no European nation has a foothold in any part of the continent which it could use as a naval base, offers a formidable obstruction to the passage of a hostile fleet. Should the enemy, however, obtain control of the Panama Canal the distance would be shortened by some 8,000 miles, and a powerful fleet would be able to threaten both coasts of the United States at one time, a thing which is now impossible.

Of course, we must be protected from such a possibility. Our army is too small to adequately protect both coasts at the same time, and our land fortifications are too widely separated for adequate defense. With the control of the canal insured to us by powerful fortifications and garrisons, we can concentrate our land forces on that side of the continent which is threatened by an enemy. Thus by means of the Panama Canal we are once more enabled to resume the attitude that we are naturally defended from foreign attack, and that the opening of the Canal is a long step away from militarism instead of in that direction.

Many means of insuring possession to us of the Canal in time of war have been suggested, such as treaties with foreign countries which would assure us that the Canal would not be used against us at such time. These, however, would not be sufficiently trustworthy to satisfy us. A strict neutralization of the Canal would make it possible for the enemy to use the waterway as well as ourselves, an even more unsatisfactory state of affairs. The only possible solution of the problem is that the Panama Canal must be kept open always to our fleet and closed to the fleet of our enemy, and that it must be entirely under our control, unhampered by any other nation. To accomplish this, every possible step must be taken to promptly construct fortifications and military defenses of all kinds, and to establish a garrison sufficiently powerful to insure an adequate defense of this vital point.

PANAMA, PAST AND PRESENT.

Scene showing the repaving of one of Panama's old muddy streets with vitrified brick. Sewers and waterpipes have been laid throughout the city resulting in a great reduction of disease.

The fact that we have fortified the Canal does not in any way conflict with our treaty obligations to maintain a neutral commercial waterway, but we must insist on considering the Canal a part of our coast line, and as such falling under our rightful control as the great highway between our Atlantic and Pacific shores. The sentiment to this end has been growing ever since the Canal project became a concrete one. If a precedent were needed, we have it in the precautions taken by England to guard the approaches to India by means of fortifications at Gibraltar, Cyprus and at Malta, which guard the entrance to the Mediterranean. The Red Sea is protected by fortifications at Aden and on the Island of Perin, and to make matters doubly sure England owns a controlling interest in the Suez Canal. Other nations, furthermore, have pursued similar tactics. Germany has securely fortified the Kiel Canal, and there are other instances of a similar nature.

The control of the Panama Canal is, however, far more necessary to our national security than that of the Kiel Canal to Germany or the Suez Canal to Great Britain, since it is the key to the protection of our many thousands of miles of coast line and the seaports which dot it, and it is only right that we should adopt similar precautions to insure our safety by its adequate defense. One of the chief difficulties with the Clayton-Bulwer treaty was the clause which guaranteed to England a free passage through the Canal in case she was at war with this country, and it was largely on this account that pressure was brought to bear for a repeal of this treaty.

There are two branches of defense which must be considered, namely:—sea and land. The sea defenses will be provided for in the enormous fortifications with their powerful artillery, which are situated at the Atlantic end on both sides of Limon Bay. At the Pacific end the fortifications are placed on the islands which guard the entrance to the Canal. These fortifications serve a double purpose, as they will be the means of keeping a hostile fleet at a distance too great for any bombardment of the locks and machinery of the Canal. They will also serve to protect the exit of our fleet in case it should be necessary to send it through the Canal in the face of a hostile fleet. The second branch of defense of the Canal must provide against an attack by a land force. This will be accomplished by the mobile land garrison, which will be employed to defend the Canal against a landing force from an enemy's fleet, or from an army which would approach to the attack through one of the South American republics.

In the first instance, the proposed garrison of six or seven thousand men would probably be ample to repel any such attack, and the further consideration that it would be very difficult to land any force on the Isthmus in the face of a defending fleet makes this item of little consequence. In case, however, of the expedient of bringing a large army to attack the Isthmus by land, we are in a particularly favorable position to reinforce the garrison by either one of the two oceans, and we can probably put a sufficient force there to insure adequate defense before a hostile army would be able to reach and attack the Canal.

As now planned the land garrison will consist largely of infantry with full artillery, and a small body of cavalry. These men will maintain a permanent garrison, and thorough and detailed plans will be worked out for a complete defense of the Isthmus. With the completion of the Canal the entire Zone, with the exception of the stretch occupied by the Canal itself, together with a few military roads, will be allowed to relapse into the original jungle, and as growth is very rapid in the tropics it will be but a short time until this is again in the wild state and will thus form one of the best defenses against a land force. For this reason the Isthmus will not be open to settlement, but will be maintained strictly as a Government reservation; and no one will be allowed to land there without the express permission of the Government.

In addition to the defenses of the Canal itself, the

enormously strong naval base which we are constructing at Pearl Harbor in the Hawaiian Islands may be counted upon to assist materially in the defense of the Pacific end of the Canal.

CHAPTER XIII

The Results of Opening the Canal

Ever since the project of cutting an Isthmian canal has begun to be talked of in the United States, the question of what the results attained by it would be has been a matter for serious discussion.

As the enterprise neared completion this discussion became more general and of deeper interest to the people at large, especially to those interested in shipping and in transcontinental and foreign commerce. Congressional investigations have been made, and special reports prepared on the subject, until now we are in a position to predict along fairly definite lines what the net results of the opening of the canal will be.

The benefits which will accrue to this country fall into two major classes:—military and commercial. It has long been said that a Panama canal is a commercial convenience and a military necessity. But to the people at large the commercial aspects of the canal are pre-eminent, and they look to it for great results in the reduction of the risks and expenses of commerce.

FROM A MILITARY POINT OF VIEW

From a military point of view the canal will prove of the greatest value. The United States is in a most peculiar position as a world power, on account of the enormous extent of our coast line and the fact that it fronts upon both the Atlantic and the Pacific, upon both of which oceans it is necessary to maintain a powerful naval force. Without the Panama Canal the Atlantic and Pacific fleets are nearly

THE RESULTS OF OPENING THE CANAL

MAP OF ROUTES TO THE ISTHMUS.
This shows the directness of the routes from New York and New Orleans to Colon.

fourteen thousand miles apart, and the seriousness of this matter was best evinced to the American people by the spectacular voyage of the "Oregon" during the Spanish-American war. In other words, it is necessary to maintain two fleets, each one capable of defending the entire eastern or western coast line without assistance from the other side of the continent. This state of affairs is not only expensive, but to a certain extent dangerous, unless we are able to keep both fleets up to a standard of efficiency greater than that of any fleet which could be brought from any eastern or western nation to attack our ports.

By means of the Panama Canal, however, either fleet could be reinforced within a short space of time, and thus the mobility of both fleets will be greatly increased. Furthermore, the Panama Canal with its enormously strong fortifications, its dry-docks, coaling and supply stations, will form a naval base at the sole connecting link between the Atlantic and Pacific oceans. From the standpoint of a military expert this is a most important matter and it has been said that the canal will double the efficiency of our eastern and western fleets. The authorities at Washington were keenly aware of the advantage of such a naval base, and wisely omitted any clause in the Hay-Pauncefote Treaty which forbade us the privilege of fortifying the canal.

COMMERCIAL ASPECTS

So much for the military aspect of the canal. The results of opening the waterway to commerce are far reaching and complex. Since the opening of the first railway to the Pacific, in 1869, shippers have had the choice of rail and water routes for the transportation of their freight from coast to coast, and, in spite of artificial restraints upon the competition of the water routes with the transcontinental railroads, the rates by rail between the two seaboards have been affected by those charged by the carriers by water. The Panama Canal will shorten and improve the intercoastal water route and will greatly increase the influence which the coastwise lines will be able to exert upon the railroad services and rates. The volume of traffic moving coastwise will be greatly enlarged by the canal. Some goods now handled all-rail will move by water or by rail and water lines, and there will necessarily follow a modification of rail rates and a readjustment of the relation of the charges of rail and water lines.

What the actual freight rates between the Atlantic and Pacific seaboards will be, by rail and water lines, after the opening of the Panama Canal, and what shares of the total traffic will move coastwise and by rail, can not be predicted in advance; but inasmuch as the division of intercoastal traffic between the water and rail carriers and the rates charged by the competing ocean and rail routes may be affected by the tolls charged for the use of the Panama Canal, it is desirable that before fixing the tolls as complete information as it is practicable to secure should be obtained concerning the existing traffic and rates of both the water and the rail lines connecting our two seaboards. Accordingly, it is proposed to explain the nature of the traffic now carried by water routes between the two seaboards.

It is well known that only partial information regarding the traffic by rail between the eastern and western sections of the United States is obtainable, but enough facts are known as to the total transcontinental rail tonnage and as to the seaboard and inland origin and destination of that tonnage to give some indication of the probable effects of the Panama Canal upon the traffic and upon the rate policies of the eastern, southern, and transcontinental railroads. It will be possible to present in sufficient detail the traffic and rates of the coast-to-coast carriers by water and to compare the present intercoastal rates by water and rail lines. It will be understood that the conclusions as to the effects which the Panama Canal will have upon the transcontinental traffic and rates of the railroads must be only tentative.

ROUTES AND TRAFFIC BY WATER BETWEEN THE ATLANTIC AND PACIFIC SEABOARDS OF THE UNITED STATES

Shipments between the two seaboards of the United States may move by three water routes that compete with the rail lines connecting the two coasts, (1) the all-water route around South America via Cape Horn for sailing vessels and through the Straits of Magellan for steamers; (2) the route by way of Panama with the transfer of traffic by rail across the Isthmus; and (3) the route via the Isthmus of Tehuantepec, across which, from Puerto Mexico on the Gulf to Salina Cruz on the Pacific, freight is handled by a railroad owned by the Mexican Government.

Traffic carried by rail lines between the Atlantic and Pacific seaboards may move coastwise for a short distance on each seaboard—as from New York to Norfolk or from Portland, Ore., to San Francisco at the beginning or end of the railroad haul across the continent. The only railroad controlling a through route between the Atlantic and Pacific seaboards is the Southern Pacific, which operates the Morgan Line of steamers between New York and New Orleans and Galveston. The steamers of the Morgan Line extend the Southern Pacific route from the Gulf termini of the railroad to New York, and thus enable the Southern Pacific to compete both with the other transcontinental railroads and with the intercoastal water routes around South America and across the Isthmuses of Panama and Tehuantepec. This combined rail and water line of the Southern Pacific is called the "Sunset-Gulf Route."

1. The oldest route between the two seaboards of the United States is the one taken by sailing vessels around Cape Horn. Prior to 1849, however, only an occasional vessel, which was in most instances a whaler, undertook the voyage between the Atlantic and Pacific, but with the discovery of gold at the close of 1848, and for a few years thereafter, there was a very large use of this route. In 1849, 775 vessels cleared from the Atlantic seaboard for San Francisco and all but 12 of them were sailing vessels.

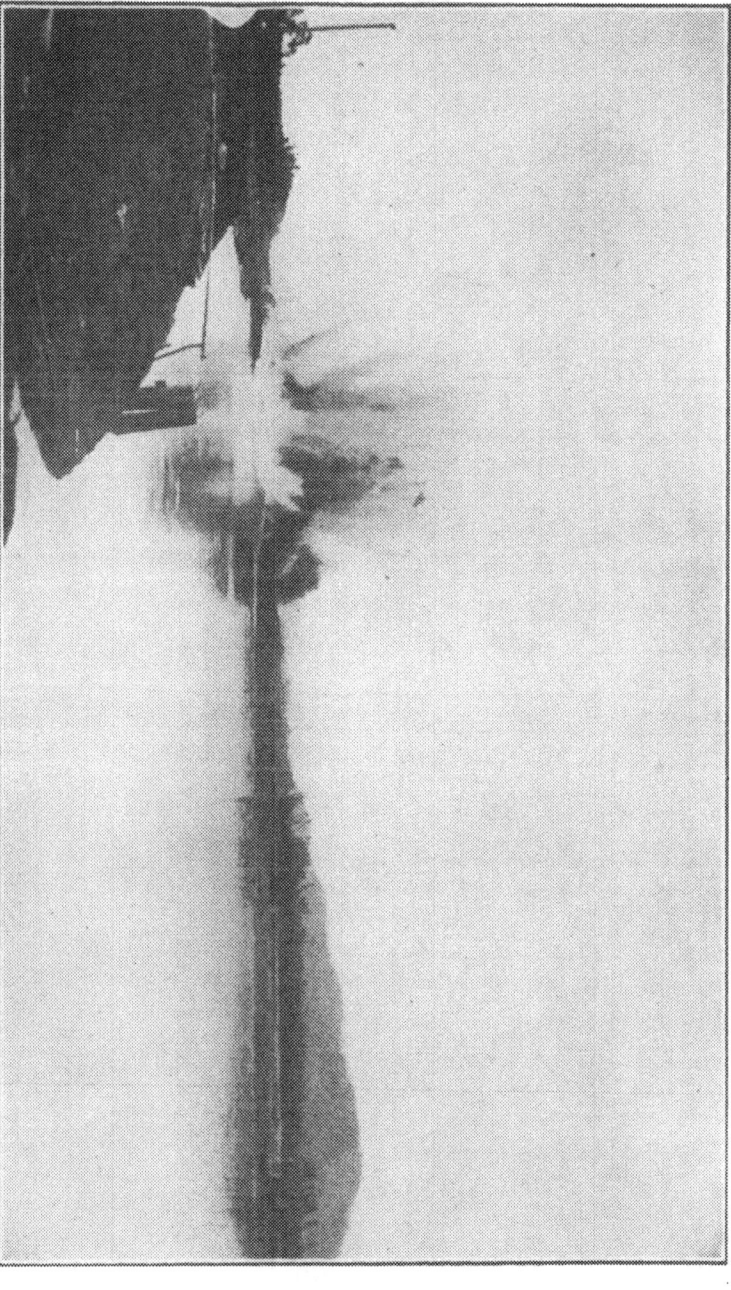

Copyright, The International News Service.

THE WATERS OF THE PACIFIC ENTERING THE PANAMA CANAL.

This photograph shows the blast of 32,750 pounds of dynamite that disposed of the dyke south of the Miraflores locks which separated the waters of the Pacific from the Panama Cut.

The opening of the Panama Railroad early in 1855 caused most of the traffic between the seaboards to abandon the long route around South America, but a considerable number of sailing vessels were annually dispatched between the two seaboards by way of Cape Horn, and a small amount of steam tonnage made use of the Magellan route.

The superiority of steamers over sailing vessels for handling most classes of freight, even for such a long route as that between the two seaboards of the United States around South America, became evident during the 1890's and caused the company which was then operating the principal line of sailing vessels between our two seaboards by way of Cape Horn to sell its sailing vessels and to inaugurate, in 1899, the American-Hawaiian line of steamers run by way of the Straits of Magellan. Early in 1907 the American-Hawaiian line shifted to the route via the Isthmus of Tehuantepec, and since that date practically all of the shipping moving between our two seaboards around South America has consisted of chartered sailing vessels and steamers that handle such bulky cargoes as can be economically shipped by that circuitous route.

2. The Panama route between our two seaboards was opened for traffic at the close of 1848, at the time of the rush to the California gold fields. With the completion of the railroad from Colon to Panama, early in 1855, most of the traffic between our two seaboards moved by way of Panama; and this continued to be the principal highway for transcontinental traffic until 1869, when the connection of the Missouri River with the Pacific coast by the Union and Central Pacific Railroads established the first rail line across the United States. The traffic by way of Panama rapidly fell off after 1869; and, though varying from year to year, remained comparatively small until 1911, when there was a sudden increase in the volume of traffic by water between our two seaboards.

Several causes account for the relative unimportance of the Panama route since 1869. The transcontinental railroads, until recently, have maintained a relentless competitive warfare against the Panama route. The through rail rates between the Atlantic and Pacific seaboards are lower than the rates for shorter hauls to and from the intermediate points in the Rocky Mountain territory; and, until the Government regulation of railroads became effective, the railroad companies quoted shippers such rates as were necessary to keep traffic from taking the Panama route. Moreover, the transcontinental railroads were able to restrict the use of the Panama route through their close relations with the Pacific Mail Steamship Company, which has, for most of the time, been the only regular line between the west-coast ports of the United States and Panama. For a period of 20 years, ending in 1893, the railroads, through the Transcontinental Association, paid the Pacific Mail Steamship Company a fixed monthly sum, or rental, for the freight space available in its steamers, and thus completely controlled the Pacific Mail as a competitor. From 1900 to the present, the Southern Pacific Company has owned a majority of the stock of the Pacific Mail Steamship Company. The history of the relations of the Pacific Mail to the transcontinental railroads and to the Panama Railroad need not be presented in this account of the traffic and rates by the various routes connecting the two seaboards of the United States.* It is sufficient to state that

---

* For the history of the relations of the Panama Railroad to the Pacific Mail Steamship Company and for an account of the connection of the Pacific Mail with the transcontinental railroads, the following references may profitably be consulted:

(1) Opinion of the Interstate Commerce Commission in Railroad Commission of Nevada v. Southern Pacific Company et al. (June 22, 1911), 21 I. C. C. Reports, 329–384.

(2) Statement by Edward A. Drake, vice-president Panama Railroad, to the Committee on Interoceanic Canals, United States Senate, Feb. 11, 1910.

(3) Report of Joseph L. Bristow, special Panama Railroad commissioner, to the Secretary of War, June 24, 1905, upon the Policy to be Pursued in Management of the Panama Railroad Company (Government Printing Office, Washington), also report of Jan. 20, 1908, on the Advisability of the Establishment of a Pacific Steamship Line by the Isthmian Canal Commission (S. Doc. No. 409, 62d Cong., 2d sess.).

(4) Statement by R. P. Schwerin, vice-president and general manager Pacific Mail Steamship Company, to the Committee on Interoceanic Canals, United States Senate, on Senate bill 428, Mar. 10, 1910. Also statement by Mr. Schwerin before same committee, on House bill 21969 Mar. 1, 2, and 3, 1912.

(5) Statement by William R. Wheeler, representative of San Francisco Chamber of Commerce, to Senate Committee on Interoceanic Canals, on House bill 21969, May 27, 1912.

the transcontinental railroads by active competition and by artificial restraint have, until recently, kept the traffic via the Panama route comparatively small.

The development of traffic via Panama has been hampered, not only by the competition and restraint of the transcontinental railroads, but also by two other causes. While the French company was engaged in construction work on the Isthmus from 1882 to 1889, the use of the Panama Railroad by commercial freight was restricted by employment of the railroad for the transportation of materials and supplies used in construction work. Likewise, since 1904, the construction of the canal has limited the volume of commercial freight that could be handled across the Isthmus. The other cause that has checked the growth of traffic via Panama has been the competition of the Tehuantepec route, which, since the beginning of 1907, has afforded a shorter and better transportation route than the one by way of Panama for the traffic between the two seaboards of the United States. The volume of traffic handled via Panama between our two seaboards during recent years has been small and has tended to decline on account of the absorption of the Panama Railroad in Canal work.

3. The Tehuantepec route was opened for traffic early in 1907, when the American-Hawaiian Steamship Company took its steamers off the route via the Straits of Magellan and established regular line services on the Atlantic between New York and Puerto Mexico and on the Pacific between Salina Cruz and Hawaii and the west-coast ports of the United States. In 1906 it made an agreement with the Tehuantepec National Railway, which is owned by the Mexican Government, stipulating that the railway company should receive one-third of the through rate. This agreement also included a guaranty on the part of the Tehuantepec National Railway that the net earnings of the steamship company, per ship ton, should not be less than the earnings had been in 1904, when the steamship company was operating by way of the Straits of Magellan.

This guaranty, however, did not require the Tehuantepec National Railway to reduce its share of the gross receipts of the steamship company to less than 25 per cent. The American-Hawaiian line has been very successful. The fleet of the American-Hawaiian Steamship Company increased from 3 steamers in 1899 to 9 steamers in 1904, and to 17 in 1911. Five new steamers were ordered in 1911. The rapid growth in the traffic of the company has been made possible by the sugar tonnage from Hawaii to the eastern ports of the United States. The freight shipments westbound between our two seaboards are larger than those eastbound, but the exports of Hawaiian sugar have enabled the American-Hawaiian Steamship Company to run its steamers loaded in both directions. Indeed, the exports of sugar from Hawaii have been much larger than the American-Hawaiian Company could handle.

The through route between the two seaboards via the Southern Pacific Railroad from the Pacific coast to Galveston and New Orleans and from those cities to New York by the Southern Pacific Company's steamers (the Morgan Line) was established in 1883. The Sunset-Gulf route immediately began an active warfare against its competitors by rail and by water lines, and secured a large share of the traffic from coast to coast. The transcontinental railroads, other than the Southern Pacific, ran from the Mississippi and Missouri Rivers to the Pacific coast and were primarily interested in the development of traffic between the Middle West and the Pacific coast. The rates by the Sunset-Gulf route from New York to San Francisco were made the same as the rates by the transcontinental lines from St. Louis and Missouri River crossings to the Pacific. Gradually the rates by the through all-rail lines from the Atlantic to the Pacific were made the same as the rates from Chicago, St. Louis, and Missouri River crossings to the Pacific seaboard. This system of blanket rates was worked out by 1896, and has since prevailed on west bound traffic. The establishment of the same rates by the Sunset-Gulf route and by the all-rail lines between the two seaboards allied the Sunset-Gulf route with the all-rail lines as common competitors against the water routes around South America and via the Isthmuses of Panama and Tehuantepec. The control of the Pacific Mail Steamship Company by the transcontinental railroads since 1874, and the ownership of the Pacific Mail by the Southern Pacific from 1890 to the present, enabled the transcontinental railroads, as has been explained, to keep the traffic by the water routes within small proportions, until a few years ago, when the American-Hawaiian Steamship Company, and later the California-Atlantic, developed a relatively large tonnage coastwise via the Tehuantepec and Panama routes. This development of the coastwise business during the last few years has not been seriously opposed by the railroads, doubtless because of the rapid development of the rail tonnage consequent upon the industrial progress of the Intermountain and Pacific Coast States.

The volume of traffic handled between the Atlantic and Pacific ports of the United States by the several water routes has been constantly on the increase for a number of years, showing the rapidly growing need for the canal. The total tons of freight, not including Hawaiian sugar, rose from less than 500,000 tons in 1906 to over 800,000 tons in 1911. If the tonnage of Hawaiian sugar be included, the increase during the six years in total traffic was from 560,000 to 1,104,000 cargo tons. The increase during the four years ending in 1911 was steady and rapid. The decline during 1907 and 1908 is to be accounted for mainly by the San Francisco earthquake and fire.

An important feature is the separation of total traffic into that handled by regular steamship lines and that carried by individual vessels owned or chartered by the shippers. The traffic handled by the regular lines more than trebled during the six-year period, while that carried by individual vessels decreased more than 50 per cent. In 1911, 82.8 per cent of the entire traffic, other than

Hawaiian sugar, was carried by the regular lines, whereas in 1906 only 42.1 per cent was shipped by the established steamship lines.

The volume and variety of the traffic between the two seaboards of the United States have so expanded as to render the services of established steamship lines having regular and frequent sailings more economical than the services of individual vessels carrying full cargoes of single commodities. The traffic manager of the American-Hawaiian line stated to the Interstate Commerce Commission, on January 16, 1907, that—

> We carry practically everything. In the course of a year I think we have at least 90 per cent of the articles that may be named in the transcontinental tariffs and a great many articles not on any tariff that are continually offered and carried.

The traffic carried by way of the Panama route also includes a large variety of commodities. The west-bound freight tariff of the Panama Railroad Steamship Line requires 25 pages to enumerate the several articles upon which individual rates are quoted. The east-bound tariff of the California-Atlantic Steamship Company is a typewritten document of 20 pages.

The freight carried between our two seaboards by way of Panama and Tehuantepec originates and terminates not only at the Atlantic and Pacific ports, but also at interior points. Manifests of the shipments by the American-Hawaiian line enumerate commodities shipped from eastern New York, eastern Pennsylvania, Massachusetts, New Jersey, Vermont, Connecticut, Rhode Island, Maine; also commodities from Syracuse and Buffalo, N. Y., from numerous cities in Ohio, from certain cities in Michigan, and from Chicago, Milwaukee, and St. Louis. These same manifests show that this freight is destined not only to Pacific coast ports, but to inland points, such as Sacramento, Stockton, The Dalles, Ore., Spokane and Everett, Wash., and Reno, Nev.

Most of the bulk cargoes handled in vessels owned or chartered by shippers now move by the disadvantageous routes around Cape Horn or through the Straits of Magellan. The opening of the Panama Canal will make it possible for the individual ship to engage in intercoastal traffic under much better conditions. It is not probable, however, that the percentage of the total traffic handled by individual vessels will increase in the future. It is more probable that the percentage of the entire business handled by lines will increase. Most of the traffic from our Pacific to Atlantic ports carried in individual vessels owned or chartered by the shipper will necessarily consist of cargoes of grain, lumber, and sugar. The sugar traffic is already large and may be expected to become heavier. The shipments of grain from the west coast, especially from Puget Sound ports, to Europe through the canal will be large, but it is not probable that the grain from the northwestern part of the United States will find very much market at the Atlantic seaboard. That section of the United States will in all probability be supplied from the grain fields of the Middle West. Barley from the Pacific Coast States will be required in the Mississippi Valley and Atlantic coast sections of the United States, and may be shipped in vessel cargoes as charter traffic. However, such commodities as wheat, barley, wool, canned salmon, and others of a like character that might advantageously be shipped as full cargoes in chartered vessels will probably be carried eastbound mainly by line vessels, because of the fact that the tonnage of traffic westbound is normally heavier than the tonnage eastbound. Line vessels will seek these bulk commodities as supplemental cargoes eastbound and at low rates. As was stated above, the American-Hawaiian line has developed a profitable business by securing a heavy eastbound tonnage of Hawaiian sugar. In 1911 the Hawaiian line transported 295,800 tons westbound, but only 162,500 tons, other than sugar, eastbound.

The lumber shipments from the Pacific coast through

the canal will comprise a large tonnage, but the destination of most of the traffic will be Europe and not the eastern part of the United States, which will continue to be supplied mainly from the forests in the Southern States. The southern pine and hardwood forests constitute the largest lumber-producing district in the United States at the present time. Shipments are made economically and expeditiously both by all-rail routes to northern markets and also by rail to southern seaports and thence by coastwise vessels.

Upon the opening of the Panama Canal it is probable that manufacturers and other large shippers will employ their own or chartered vessels for shipments of some heavy commodities to Pacific markets. Undoubtedly there will be a good deal of coal shipped westbound in chartered vessels. Fertilizers, heavy iron and steel, and some other commodities may be sent as bulk cargoes in individual ships from time to time. It is probable, however, that most commodities, other than coal and fertilizers, will be shipped by line steamers.

The fact that most of the traffic through the canal between the two seaboards of the United States will be handled by regular steamship lines and that only a minor, and probably a decreasing, percentage of the total will be transported in individual vessels owned or chartered by shippers should be given careful attention in considering, (1) what the policy of the United States should be concerning the prohibition of the use of the canal by vessels controlled by railroads, and (2) concerning the remission or omission of tolls upon vessels engaged in the coastwise business.

1. The policy of denying the use of the canal to vessels owned or controlled by, or affiliated with, railroad companies is advocated by those who favor the policy mainly for two reasons, (*a*) that the competition between the railroad-controlled and the independent steamship lines will be disastrous to the independent lines, and (*b*) that the Government regulation of the rates and services of

THE WEST BREAKWATER, LOOKING SEAWARD FROM TORO POINT.

The illustration shows a dredge at work placing rock on the face of the breakwater which is designed to form a safe harbor for ships entering the Canal from the Atlantic. Similar breakwaters protect the Pacific entrance.

ocean carriers is impracticable and undesirable. If coastwise traffic through the canal were to be handled mainly by individual vessels owned or chartered by shippers, Government regulation would, indeed, be impracticable; but the service of steamship lines operating over established routes is not essentially different from the transportation service of the railroads. Moreover, when several steamship lines operate over the same route or over competing routes they have fixed schedules of rates established by agreement and their rate policy differs in no marked degree from that of competing railroads.

The rates charged by steamship lines differ fundamentally from charter rates, which are highly competitive and fluctuate with the supply of and demand for chartered tonnage. Charter rates fluctuate according to business conditions and could not be and ought not to be subject to Government regulation. The rates of steamship lines, however, are not only made in conferences of the competing lines, but also in many cases are fixed with reference to the rates charged by the railroads with which the steamship lines must compete for traffic. It is thus at least doubtful whether it is good public policy not to regulate the rates and services of coastwise steamship lines. Whether such regulation is wise or unwise, it is at least not impracticable.

2. The question of exempting coastwise shipping from the payment of Panama Canal tolls should be decided with reference to the parties that would be benefited by that policy. If the tolls charged coastwise ships using the canal are added to the rate of freight paid by shippers, the remission of tolls will benefit the shippers and possibly, to some extent, the general public. On the other hand, if the freight rates are not any higher because of the tolls, the exemption of ships from the payment of tolls will not affect the freight rates, and the exemption of the payment of tolls will benefit the steamship company and not the shippers. Charter rates, as has just been stated, are highly competitive and the rates which a shipper must pay to

secure the use of a vessel for a trip through the canal will undoubtedly be increased by the amount of tolls paid. Shippers using vessels which they own or charter will receive the benefit of the exemption of canal tolls. On the other hand, the rates charged by steamship lines, being regulated by agreements among competing companies and being fixed with reference to what the traffic will bear, will presumably be as high as traffic conditions warrant regardless of canal tolls. If the tolls are charged, the operating expenses of the steamship companies will be increased by the amount of the tolls and their net profits will be lessened by the same amount. In other words, free tolls will be a gratuity or a subsidy to the coastwise steamship lines. There are reasons for believing that the rates of the coastwise steamship lines, which will handle from four-fifths to nine-tenths of the water traffic between the two seaboards of the United States, will not be affected by the policy of the United States Government as regards free tolls.

Estimates of the comparative costs of shipment by the methods outlined above as against those via the Panama Canal all point to a saving of at least one-third in favor of the canal. The railroads charge about one-third of the through rate upon all freight carried between the coasts, and this on an average amounts to between $3.00 and $3.50 per cargo ton. Against this there will be merely the charge of $1.20 per net vessel ton exacted for the use of the canal. Inasmuch as a vessel ton is equivalent to 100 cubic feet of space, while a cargo ton is only equivalent to 40 cubic feet of space, these terms must not be confused. As a rule, freight vessels can transport more than two tons of cargo for each net ton of rating, an average of about two tons of freight capacity for each vessel ton. On this basis the tolls as fixed for the canal at present will only amount to about sixty cents per cargo ton, and the saving should be from $2.40 to $2.90 on each ton of cargo as against the railway transfer method.

There are many commodities which will be shipped via the canal which would not bear the double handling made necessary by the old method, either by reason of their fragile nature or the expense of double handling. Among the latter are lumber, coal, ore and such materials which are handled in bulk. This latter consideration will be of the utmost importance in connection with the great ore and nitrate deposits of the western coast of South America.

REDUCTIONS IN SHIPPING RATES

The matter of ascertaining the amount of reduction in costs made possible by the use of the canal is not difficult to determine. When, however, we attempt to investigate the matter of a reduction of charges a more difficult situation confronts us. While the freight rates charged by transcontinental railroads have been a great factor in creating a powerful demand for a canal, in the hope that water competition would result in reducing present rates, it is extremely doubtful if these reductions will bear a true proportion to reductions in costs, although the idea is prevalent throughout the country that such will be the case.

Our industrial history has shown very clearly that it is impossible to compel keen competition. Our railroad companies have pools, conferences, mergers, road understandings and agreements to such an extent that competitive rates do not exist, and the Interstate Commerce Commission is the only means open to the shipper of compelling a reasonable relationship between costs of transportation and rates. The rule of thumb by which railroad rates are fixed is the phrase, "all that the traffic will bear," and it seems likely that this method will also be followed in fixing the steamship rates through the canal, and the rates maintained by the same methods as have been followed in the case of the railroads. All of the great European transport lines are bonded together in rate agreements, and it is probable that the coastwise steamship lines using the Canal will be operated under similar conditions, and the rates between the Atlantic and Pacific coasts will be the same by all rival lines. Of course there will be outside competition by means of privately owned or chartered vessels, but inasmuch as few shippers are able to forward in cargo lots this competition will amount to but a small percentage of the total volume of trade, practically all of which will be handled by the regular transport companies. These rates may be modified, of course, by extending the power of the Interstate Commerce Commission, or some similar body to their regulation, but is is probable that the same conditions which obtain in connection with the transcontinental railroads will reappear in connection with the Canal.

RAILROAD COMPETITION

From this arises the question of competition between the transcontinental railroads and the intercoastal steamship lines. It has been thought that the railroads would be compelled to reduce their rates to a competitive basis with the freight rates charged via the Canal, and it was with the idea of compelling such competition that railway-owned ships were forbidden the use of the waterway. Two sets of conditions are to be apprehended: the first, that rate conferences between the steamship and railroad companies will operate to maintain a non-competitive rate schedule between them; or, in other words, that both will continue to charge as much as the traffic will bear. The second condition is that only about ten per cent of the railroad traffic is billed through from coast to coast, and if the roads should reduce the rate on this class of traffic they would be compelled to adjust the rates to all intermediate points on a similar basis and thus cut heavily into their revenues. On this account it is altogether likely that the railroads will prefer to sacrifice the ten per cent of volume rather than revise all the existing rates on such a basis. Summing up the situation, we must not anticipate a heavy reduction in costs of transportation between the coasts either by ship or railroad. Certain reductions, however, are bound to come, for the reasons that competition cannot be entirely eliminated, and the insistent demands of the public for rates which bear a reasonable relation to the costs of service must be taken into consideration in fixing rates; and there are certain commodities upon which the reduction is sure to be material, and a large number on which some reduction will certainly be made in order to fill the ships which will naturally enter into this business.

The most direct way of estimating what the people of the United States and of the world at large are to gain by the opening of the Panama Canal is to estimate the tonnage which will pass through the canal, and to divide this tonnage among the several classes of trade. It has been estimated that the traffic between the coasts of the United States will amount to only about one-tenth of the ships which pass through the canal, our trade with foreign ports will amount to about one-third, and that one-half of the traffic will be ships which do not touch the ports of the United States at any point, but simply use the canal as a short cut between the Atlantic and the Pacific.

To understand the relation of the now existing trade routes, and those which will come into being with the Panama Canal, a study of a route map is necessary which shows comparative distances on all of the principal trade routes. (*See page 226.*)

RESULTS FAR REACHING

It is difficult to foresee all of the results which will be obtained by the operation of the Canal, for the reason that they are so numerous and so far-reaching. It is probable that in course of time trade, political and banking conditions will be revolutionized to a degree unforeseen. The first effect will naturally be the tightening of the commercial ties between the eastern and western sections of the United

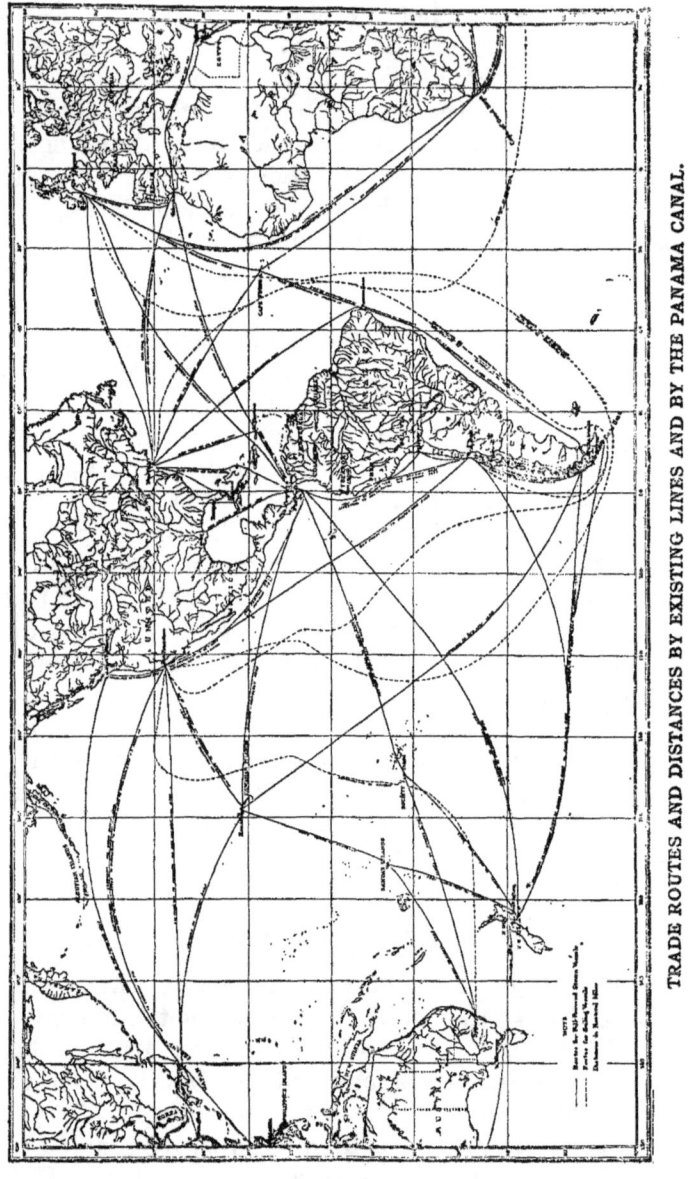

THE RESULTS OF OPENING THE CANAL 227

States, due to the greatly increased facilities for transportation between them. With the increase in commercial relations will naturally come a greater community of interests, not only commercial, but political and social, and a closer welding of East and West.

DISTANCES IN NAUTICAL MILES

SAVED FROM NEW YORK VIA THE PANAMA CANAL ON TRADE ROUTES

San Francisco:
    Magellan.. 13,135
    Panama.. 5,262

        Saved... 7,873

Guayaquil:
    Magellan.. 10,215
    Panama.. 2,810

        Saved... 7,405

Callao:
    Magellan.. 9,613
    Panama.. 3,363

        Saved... 6,250

Iquique:
    Magellan.. 9,143
    Panama.. 4,004

        Saved... 5,139

Valparaiso:
    Magellan.. 8,380
    Panama.. 4,633

        Saved... 3,747

Honolulu:
    Magellan.. 13,312
    Panama.. 6,700

        Saved... 6,612

Manila:
  Suez... 11,589
  *Panama.. 11,548

    Saved..   41

Yokohama:
  Suez... 13,079
  *Panama.. 9,798

    Saved..   3,281

Hongkong:
  Suez... 11,628
  *Panama.. 11,383

    Saved..   245

Melbourne:
  Magellan... 12,852
  Panama... 10,030

    Saved..   2,822

THE CANAL AND THE COMMERCE OF AMERICA

The establishment of a waterway between the two great oceans of the globe will more widely affect the commerce of the world than any single work or event in its history. President Hayes, in 1879, declared that "an interoceanic canal across the American Isthmus will essentially change the geographic relations between the Atlantic and Pacific coasts of the United States and between the United States and the rest of the world." The Panama route will effect much greater economies of time and distance than those that are at present secured by the use of the Suez Canal.

Colquhoun, in his "Key to the Pacific," says: "It will bind together the remote sections of that immense country, assimilate its diverse interests, go far towards solving many

---

* Via San Francisco and the Great Circle.

Copyright, C. H. Graves Co.

GATUN LOCKS.

I. Steel emergency gate for protection of locks in event of accident. J. First lock gate from Gatun Lake, coming from Pacific side. K. Gatun Lake and Canal channel. Lake now 45 feet above sea level. Will be raised to 87 feet during coming rainy season. L. Guide wall where vessels are taken in tow by the motors.

difficult problems, and make the United States still more united. . . . No greater impulse to commerce can be given than this complement to the Suez Canal. It will benefit America in an infinitely greater degree than Europe. . . . It will give an immense impetus to United States manufactures, especially cotton and iron, and will greatly stimulate the shipbuilding industry and the naval power of the United States."

Whilst the Panama Canal must prove an universal boon it will doubtless work to the detriment of some countries and certain industries, at least until after adjustment of the new trade relations. America will always be the greatest beneficiary of the advantages accruing from the use of the waterway and we will briefly consider a few of the changes in conditions that have been brought about by the completion of the enterprise to which so large an amount of American energy, intellect and capital has been devoted.

EFFECT OF THE CANAL ON THE COMMERCE OF THE SOUTH

No region in the United States can feel the immediate benefit of the new route to the same extent as the Southern States and the vast Valley of the Mississippi. The latter territory, the richest in all the world, one and a quarter million square miles in extent, intersected by five thousand miles of navigable waterway, with prolific soil and energetic people, finds new markets and a new outlet for its varied products no longer dependent upon expensive railway transportation. Chicago is nearly the same distance from New Orleans as from New York, but St. Paul, Omaha, Dubuque, Evansville and Denver are nearer to the former point than to the latter. It is quite probable that the present generation will see ocean steamships coming down from Duluth, through the Great Lakes, an inland canal, and the Mississippi River, to the Gulf of Mexico, and passing on to Pacific and Asian ports.

The new gateway to the Pacific will give a tremendous

impetus to the industries of the South. Its raw cotton, which for a decade has been making small gains, under difficult competition with the British East Indies and China, in the Japanese market, is relieved of an onerous handicap. The product of its mills, a coarse fabric, such as is especially adapted to the requirements of South American and Oriental consumers, must enjoy an enlarged demand under stimulating conditions. Heretofore almost all the cotton goods exported from this country to Asia has gone out through New York eastward by way of the Suez Canal.

Alabama coal will find a constant and extensive demand at Panama, which will become the greatest coaling port in the world. Birmingham, where iron can be produced more cheaply than at any other place on the earth, will find new markets in South America and Asian countries for its output. The steel, machinery, and various hardware of Tennessee and other Southern States, which have been reaching Australia and China during the past few years under the most disadvantageous conditions of shipment, can be sent through the Canal to these and other destinations at a cost which may defy competition. The large lumber and wood manufacturing industries of the South will be obviously benefited to a great extent by the creation of a short route to the western coasts of Central and South America.

GREAT BENEFITS TO OUR PACIFIC STATES

The immense saving in the journey from our eastern ports to the Pacific Coast will revolutionize the trade of the latter region. Von Schierbrand says:* "It has been computed that on a single voyage of a 1,500-ton sailing vessel between Port Townsend, Seattle or San Francisco and Boston, New York or Philadelphia, the saving effected in wages, repairs, insurance, provisions, and freight charges, by reason of the Panama Canal will aggregate between

---

*America, Asia and the Pacific. Wolf von Schierbrand. New York, 1904.

$8,000 and $9,500." Many raw products of our Pacific Coast, which can not bear the cost of long railroad hauls, are made available to eastern markets at prices profitable to the producer and the manufacturer. This applies particularly to building lumber and furnishes a partial solution to the problem with which the rapidly disappearing forests of our middle and eastern states are confronting us. The economies effected in the transportation of the cereal and fruit products of California and other western regions may easily be imagined. Millions of pounds of fish were sent annually in ice across the continent, aside from the enormous quantities that went to Europe in English sailing vessels round Cape Horn. All this passes through the Canal.

The Canal is the means of enabling the people of the Pacific Coast to buy more cheaply and to secure better prices for their products. By breaking the monopolistic power of the railroads it will lead to the agricultural development of the unoccupied sections of this territory, to a vast increase in its population and to the creation of world-wide markets for its products.

A BOON TO THE NORTHEASTERN TERRITORY

The industries of the northeastern section of the United States, that is to say the territory lying to the east of Pittsburg and to the north of the James River, consist mainly of the manufactures of iron and steel, machinery, tools, etc., and textiles, coal mining, and shipbuilding. The exports of manufactured cotton from this and other parts of the United States go principally to ports in Asia and Oceania, where their chief competitor is the product of the British mills. It is not necessary to expatiate upon the advantage which the short route will give to us in this trade. The countries of South America expend about $80,000,000 annually in the purchase of cotton goods. At present, however, little more than five per cent of this large sum is paid for American cloth, but the facilities for shipping economically that will be created by the Canal must have, among other results, that of giving to the manufacturers of our Northeastern and Southern States a very large share of this desirable business.

It is hoped that by the use of a new type of steel river barge of large capacity and small draft the coal of Pennsylvania and the Southern mines may be shipped direct to Panama at a cost of one dollar per short ton. This would allow of its being sold at three dollars, a figure sufficiently low to preclude successful competition. The ability to supply cheap fuel would not only accrue to the benefit of our coal mining interests, but would, where other considerations balanced, decide shipmasters in favor of the Panama route, for the contract price of steam coal at Port Said is about six dollars and the current price about ten dollars per ton.

OUR ADVANTAGE OVER FOREIGN COMPETITORS

The principal exporting competitors of the United States in the markets for the manufactures of iron and steel are Great Britain, Germany and Belgium. European producers can reach the west coast of South America, and the oriental countries in general, more readily than can our manufacturers, but the Canal will entirely subvert the condition in the favor of the latter. Few of our industries are likely to receive such an expansive impulse from that event as those dependent upon iron and steel for their material and the section which will benefit most in that respect is the coal and ore region of the South.

One of the most certain consequences of the increased American trade due to the waterway between the Atlantic and Pacific oceans will be the great extension of the merchant marine and the expansion of the shipbuilding industry of the country. The Canal will have the effect of largely increasing the coasting trade of the United States and all the vessels engaged in it must be built in American yards. Aside from this the increased foreign trade under conditions that will make the shipping business once more profitable, must lead to the construction of a large additional number of American vessels, and the considerable benefiting of American shipbuilders, who find great difficulty in competing with those of Europe on account of our higher wage scales.

A large shipbuilder responded to an inquiry by the Isthmian Canal Commission with the following statement: "In my judgment the opening of the Isthmian Canal and the development of its traffic would stimulate American shipbuilding to the extent of an increased demand for vessels to be used in trade affected by said canal. As a rule increased demand develops increased sources of supply and the cost of product is invariably reduced in proportion of increased business to fixed expenses of any manufacturing establishment, and therefore the canal would in this case tend to enable shipbuilders to construct ships more economically and more surely to compete with foreign builders."

The foregoing are only a few illustrative examples of the benefits to certain portions of the United States conferred by the Panama Canal. Anything approaching a comprehensive statement of the matter would fill a large volume.

THE EFFECT ON OUR FOREIGN COMMERCE

But to gain a full view of all that will be accomplished it is necessary to go farther afield. Up to within the last few years the American people have been so largely occupied with the development of the enormous natural resources of this country they have had little time or necessity for the development of foreign trade, and the commerce of the world at large is carried on by European nations. This state of affairs cannot exist indefinitely, however, and our foreign trade is now growing very rapidly. In spite of this present great total, however, the effect of the Panama Canal will be to multiply it enormously. For instance, our percentage of the great trade with the western coast of South America is extremely small. The shipments from southern Chile of nitrate, copper and iron ores, etc., amount to an enormous tonnage each year. Of this the United States gets less than one-fifth. Grain shipments from western South America are also heavy, and practically all of this goes to Europe. With the Canal open the United States will be so much nearer than Europe that a large portion of this trade should eventually be diverted to the eastern coast of the United States, where our great manufacturing plants are located. The same conditions apply to Australia and New Zealand, with which we will be on a par with Europe so far as distance is concerned by the use of the canal, and our Atlantic coast will be 4,000 miles nearer Australia by Panama than by Suez. New York will be 5,000 miles nearer New Zealand by Panama than around the Cape of Good Hope.

Our traffic with the Far East, China and Japan, will likewise be greatly benefited by the new route, although not to such a great extent, as both China and the Philippines will be equally distant from New York via both the Panama Canal and the Suez Canal. From the standpoint of a reduction of distance the Panama Canal will undoubtedly benefit us to a very great extent.

The other considerations of costs of fuel, supplies, facility for repairs, etc., have been taken care of by the establishment of the great supply stations at Panama.

THE EFFECT ON OUR SHIPPING INTERESTS

The question of American shipping has been a sore point for many years. In fact, the American flag has almost disappeared from the world's merchant marine. There have been various causes for this, chief among them the high cost of labor, which has put the cost of building ships in the United States up to a prohibitive figure and made it far cheaper to buy ships abroad and operate them under a foreign flag than to build here. Recent legislation admitting foreign built ships to American registry, together with the admission of necessary parts free of duty, looks to the remedy of this matter, and we shall probably see an enormous increase in the American registry within the next few years. Ships, however, which are engaged purely in the coastwise trade must still be built in the United States to obtain the privilege of American registry.

WILL THE CANAL PAY

The question of whether or not the Canal would pay has been one which has agitated the American people for some time. The maximum rate which has been authorized by Congress for canal tolls is $1.25 per ton on freight, and $1.50 per passenger, although these rates may be reduced by the President in case they are higher than necessary to produce the amount required for operation and maintenance, which will amount to about $4,000,000 annually. If we take into account the interest upon the investment at the rates at which the Canal bonds have been placed, the tolls must produce another $10,000,000 per year, or a total of $14,000,000 annually for the Canal to be self-supporting. It is not likely from the outlook that the Canal will pay for some years to come.

Copyright, C. H. Graves Co.

GATUN LOCKS.

A. Completed sea level section of canal, seven miles long, from Atlantic Ocean to Gatun Locks, where by a series of three locks vessels are raised to Gatun Lake 85 feet above sea level. B. Small area of land to be dredged away as soon as Gatun Locks are completed. C. Electric towing motor, four of which will tow each vessel entirely through the locks. They run on cog rail along the lock walls. D. Lock gate under construction. E. Floor of first lock from Atlantic side. Note holes in floor for admitting the water. F. Lock for vessels coming from Pacific side. G. Base on which concrete posts will be erected for electric lights. A row of lights on all sides of the locks will make operation at night as safe as day. H. Incline from locks of different levels up and down which the towing motors run on cog rails.

APPENDICES

APPENDIX I*

GREAT CANALS OF THE WORLD

Ship canals connecting great bodies of water, and of sufficient dimensions to accommodate the great modern vessels plying upon such waters, are of comparatively recent production and few in number. The one great example of works of this character which has been a sufficient length of time in existence and operation to supply satisfactory data as to cost of maintenance and operation and practical value to the commerce of the world is the Suez Canal, and for this the available statistics begin with the year 1870, while its new and enlarged dimensions only date from the year 1896. For the Sault Ste. Marie Canal, connecting Lake Superior with Lake Huron, statistics date from 1855. Statistics of the Welland Canal date from 1867, though the canal in its enlarged form has been in operation only since 1900. The other great ship canals of the world are of much more recent construction, and data regarding their operation therefore cover a comparatively brief term, and in some cases are scarcely at present available in detail.

The artificial waterways which may properly be termed ship canals are nine in number, viz.:

(1) The Suez Canal, begun in 1859 and completed in 1869.

(2) The Cronstadt and St. Petersburg Canal, begun in 1877 and completed in 1890.

(3) The Corinth Canal, begun in 1884 and completed in 1893.

---

* The following matter is largely quoted from the monograph under this title issued by the Department of Commerce and Labor, Washington, D. C.

(4) The Manchester Ship Canal, completed in 1894.

(5) The Kaiser Wilhelm Canal, connecting the Baltic and North Seas, completed in 1895.

(6) The Elbe and Trave Canal, connecting the North Sea and Baltic, opened in 1900.

(7) The Welland Canal, connecting Lake Erie with Lake Ontario.

(8 and 9) The two canals, United States and Canadian, respectively, connecting Lake Superior with Lake Huron.

THE SUEZ CANAL

The Suez Canal is usually considered the most important example of ship canals, though the number of vessels passing through it annually does not equal that passing through the canals connecting Lake Superior with the chain of Great Lakes at the south. In length, however, it exceeds any of the other great ship canals, its total length being 90 miles, of which about two-thirds is through shallow lakes. Work on the canal was begun on April 25, 1859. Political, labor and financial troubles delayed the completion of the enterprise, however, and the formal opening of the canal was not until November, 1869.

The material excavated was usually sand, though in some cases strata of solid rock from 2 to 3 feet in thickness were encountered. The total excavation was about 80,000,000 cubic yards under the original plan, which gave a depth of 25 feet. In 1895 the canal was so enlarged as to give a depth of 31 feet, a width at the bottom of 108 feet and at the surface of 420 feet. The original cost was $95,000,000, and for the canal in its present form slightly in excess of $120,000,000.

By the concessions of 1854 and 1856 the tolls were to be the same for all nations, preferential treatment of any kind being forbidden, and the canal and its ports were to be open to every merchant ship without distinction of nationality. The formal neutralization of the canal oc-

GREAT CANALS OF THE WORLD

curred in 1888 by the Suez Canal Convention, but was not fully assented to until April 8, 1904.

The canal is without locks, being at sea level the entire distance. The length of time occupied in passing through the canal averages about eighteen hours. By the use of electric lights throughout the entire length of the canal passages are made with nearly equal facility by night or day. The use of these lights, the growth in canal dimensions, the increase in the number and size of passing stations or "lay-bys" and the straightening of curves have reduced the average time required to pass through the canal from 48 hours 58 minutes in 1870 to 17 hours 1 minute in 1911.

The canal has accommodated the following traffic service since its opening:

	Vessels.	Gross Tonnage.
1870	486	654,915
1875	1,494	2,940,708
1880	2,026	4,344,519
1890	3,389	9,749,129
1895	3,434	11,833,637
1900	3,541	13,699,237
1905	4,116	13,134,105
1910	4,533	16,581,898

The tolls charged are $6\frac{3}{4}$ francs per ton for vessels carrying cargo, and $4\frac{1}{4}$ francs for vessels in ballast. Steam vessels passing through the canal are propelled by their own power.

THE CRONSTADT AND ST. PETERSBURG CANAL

The canal connecting the Bay of Cronstadt with St. Petersburg is described as a work of great strategic and commercial importance to Russia. The canal and sailing course in the Bay of Cronstadt are about 16 miles long, the canal proper being about 6 miles and the bay channel about 10 miles, and they together extend from Cronstadt, on the Gulf of Finland, to St. Petersburg. The canal was opened in 1890 with a navigable depth of $20\frac{1}{2}$ feet, the original depth having been about 9 feet; the width ranges from 220 to 350 feet. The total cost is estimated at about $10.000,000.

THE CORINTH CANAL

The next of the great ship canals connecting bodies of salt water in the order of date of construction is the Corinth Canal, which connects the Gulf of Corinth with the Gulf of Ægina. The canal reduces the distance from Adriatic ports about 175 miles and from Mediterranean ports about 100 miles. Its length is about 4 miles, a part of which was cut through granite soft rock and the remainder through soil. There are no locks. The width of the canal is 72 feet at bottom and the depth $26\frac{1}{4}$ feet. The work was begun in 1884 and completed in 1893 at a cost of about $5,000,000. The average tolls are 18 cents per ton and 20 cents per passenger.

THE MANCHESTER SHIP CANAL

The Manchester Ship Canal, which connects Manchester, England, with the Mersey River, Liverpool, and the Atlantic Ocean, was opened for traffic January 1, 1894. The length of the canal is $35\frac{1}{2}$ miles, the total rise from the water level to Manchester being 60 feet, which is divided between four sets of locks, giving an average to each of 15 feet. The minimum width is 120 feet at the bottom and average 175 feet at the water level; the minimum depth 26 feet, and the time required for navigating the canal from five to eight hours. The total amount of excavation in the canal and docks was about 45,000,000 cubic yards, of which about one-fourth was sandstone rock. The lock gates are operated by hydraulic power; railways and bridges crossing the route of the canal have been raised to give a height of 75 feet to vessels traversing the canal, and an ordinary canal whose route it crosses is carried over it by a springing aqueduct composed of an iron caisson resting upon a pivot pier. The total cost of the canal is given at $75,000,000. The revenue in 1911, according to the Statesman's Year-Book. was £580,841, and the working expenses, £305,977.

THE KAISER WILHELM CANAL

Two canals connect the Baltic and North seas through Germany, the first, known as the Kaiser Wilhelm Canal, having been completed in 1895 and constructed largely for military and naval purposes, but proving also of great value to general mercantile traffic. Work upon the Kaiser Wilhelm Canal was begun in 1887, and completed, as before indicated, in 1895. The length of the canal is 61 miles, the terminus in the Baltic Sea being at the harbor of Kiel. The depth is $29\frac{1}{2}$ feet, the width at the bottom 72 feet, and the minimum width at the surface 190 feet. The route lies chiefly through marshes and shallow lakes and along river valleys. The total excavation amounted to about 100,000,000 cubic yards, and the cost to about $40,000,000. The saving is 200 miles in the Kattegat passage, and the time of transit occupies from eight to ten hours.

THE ELBE AND TRAVE CANAL

A smaller canal known as the Elbe and Trave Canal, with a length of about 41 miles and a depth of about 10 feet, was opened by the Emperor of Germany, June 16, 1900.

It was under construction for five years, and cost about $5,831,000, of which Prussia contributed $1,785,000 and the old Hanse town of Lubeck $4,046,000. This canal is the second to join the North Sea and the Baltic, following the Kaiser Wilhelm Canal (or Kiel Canal), built at a cost of $37,128,000. The breadth of the Elbe and Trave Canal is 72 feet; breadth of the locks, 46 feet; length of locks, 261 feet; depth of locks, 8 feet 2 inches. It is crossed by 29 bridges, erected at a cost of $1,000,000. There are seven locks, five being between Lubeck and the Mollner

See (the summit point of the canal) and two between Mollner See and Lauenburg-on-the-Elbe. The canal is able to accommodate vessels up to 800 tons burden; and the passage from Lubeck to Lauenburg occupies 18 to 21 hours. The first year it was open (June, 1900, to June, 1901) a total of 115,000 tons passed through the canal.

ELECTRIC TOWING

At this point it may be noted that the Germans began experiments during 1900 with electric towing on the Finow Canal between Berlin and Stettin. A track of 1-meter gauge was laid along the bank of the canal, having one 9-pound and one 18-pound rail laid partly on cross-ties and partly on concrete blocks. The larger rail served for the return current, and had bolted to it a rack which geared with a spur wheel on the locomotive. The locomotive was 6 feet 10 inches by 4 feet 10 inches, mounted on four wheels, with a wheel base of 3 feet 6 inches, and weighing 2 tons. It was fitted with a 12-horsepower motor, current for which was furnished by a 9-kilowatt dynamo, driven by a 15-horsepower engine. The current was 500 volts, transmitted by a wire carried on wooden poles 23 feet high and about 120 feet apart. The boats were about 132 feet long and 15 feet 6 inches beam, and carried from 150 to 175 tons on a draft of 4 feet 9 inches.

SHIP CANALS CONNECTING THE GREAT LAKES OF NORTH AMERICA

Three ship canals intended to give continuous passage to vessels from the head of Lake Superior to Lake Ontario and the St. Lawrence River are the Welland Canal, originally constructed in 1833 and enlarged in 1871 and 1900; the St. Mary's Falls Canal at Sault Ste. Marie, Mich., opened in 1855 and enlarged in 1881 and 1896, and the Canadian Canal at St. Mary's River, opened in 1895. In point of importance, measured at least by their present use,

A CYLINDRICAL VALVE MACHINE, MOTOR AND LIMIT SWITCH.

This machine is one of many which are used to regulate the flow of water to the locks. All valves are controlled from a central operating station on each of the three sets of locks. The limit switch automatically shuts off the power and stops the motor when the valve is entirely open or shut.

the canals at the St. Mary's River by far surpass that of the Welland Canal, the number of vessels passing through the canals at the St. Mary's River being eight times as great as the number passing through the Welland, and the tonnage of the former nearly forty times as great as that of the latter. One of the important products of the Lake Superior region, iron ore, is chiefly used in the section contiguous to Lake Erie, and a large proportion of the grain coming from Lake Superior passes from Buffalo to the Atlantic coast by way of the Erie Canal and railroads centering at Buffalo. The most important article in the westward shipments through the Sault Ste. Marie canals, coal, originates in the territory contiguous to Lake Erie. These conditions largely account for the fact that the number and tonnage of vessels passing the St. Mary's River canals so greatly exceed those of the Welland Canal.

The Welland Canal connects Dalhousie on Lake Ontario and Port Colburne on Lake Erie on the Canadian side of the river. It was constructed in 1833 and enlarged in 1871 and again in 1900. The length of the canal is 27 miles, the number of locks 25, the total rise of lockage 327 feet, and the total cost about $26,000,000. The canal will accommodate vessels of 14 feet draught.

THE SAULT STE. MARIE CANALS

The canals at Sault Ste. Marie, Michigan, and Ontario are located adjacent to the falls of the St. Mary's River, which connects Lake Superior with Lake Huron, and lower or raise vessels from one level to the other, a height of 17 to 20 feet. The canal belonging to the United States was begun in 1853 by the State of Michigan and opened in 1855, the length of the canal being 5,674 feet, and provided with two tandem locks, each being 350 feet in length and 70 feet wide, and allowing passage of vessels drawing 12 feet, the original cost being $1,000,000; the final, $4,000,000. The United States Government, by consent of the State, began in 1870 to enlarge the canal, and by 1881 had increased its length to 1.6 miles, its width to an average of 160 feet, and its depth to 16 feet; also had built the Weitzel lock, 515 feet long and 80 feet wide, 60 feet at gate openings, with a depth of 17 feet on the sills, which was located 100 feet south of the State locks. The State relinquished all control of the canal in March, 1882. In 1887 the State locks were torn down and replaced by a single lock known as the Poe, 800 feet long, 100 feet wide, with a depth of 22 feet of water on the sills. This lock was put in commission in 1896. The canal was also deepened to 25 feet. In 1908 began the widening of the canal above the locks and the construction of a new lock 1,350 feet long between gates and having a draught of $24\frac{1}{2}$ feet at extreme low water. The Canadian canal, $1\frac{1}{8}$ miles long, 150 feet wide, and 22 feet deep, with lock 900 feet long, 60 feet wide, with 22 feet on the miter sills, was built on the north side of the river during the years 1888 to 1895 at a cost of $7,900,000. The commerce passing through the canals is larger than that of any other canal in the world; the total tonnage of the American canal in 1910 was 49,856,123, while that of the Suez Canal was only 23,054,901.

LAKE BORGNE CANAL

The Lake Borgne, Louisiana, Canal was formally opened in August of 1901. It affords continuous water communication with lakes Maurepas, Pontchartrain, and Borgne, the Mississippi Sound, Mobile, and the Alabama and Warrior rivers, and the entire Mississippi River system, and has an important bearing as a regulator of freight rates between these sections. The effects of the canal may be briefly summed up as: Shortening the distance between New Orleans and the Gulf points east of the Mississippi; bringing shipments from the Gulf coast direct to the levees at New Orleans; saving the trans-shipment of through freights, with a consequent reduction in freight rates; enabling sea-

GREAT CANALS OF THE WORLD 247

going vessels, drawing 10 to 12 feet of water, to come within 20 miles of New Orleans, saving all such craft the cost of tonnage, and shortening, by 60 miles, direct water communication between New Orleans and the deep water of the Gulf. In addition to these effects may be enumerated the cheapening of coal for consumption at New Orleans. Coal had hitherto been floated down the rivers from Pittsburgh, a distance of 2,100 miles. The canal opened up the coal fields in the interior of Alabama for New Orleans consumption and reduced coal prices considerably, giving an additional advantage to domestic industries and to steamers purchasing bunker coal. The canal is 7 miles long and from 150 to 200 feet in width. Bayou Dupre forms a portion of the canal. The lock chamber is 200 feet long, 50 feet wide, and 25 feet deep, and connects the canal with the Mississippi River.

THE CHICAGO SANITARY AND SHIP CANAL

The Chicago Sanitary and Ship Canal connects Lake Michigan at Chicago with the Illinois River at Lockport, a distance of 34 miles. It was cut for the purpose of giving to the city of Chicago proper drainage facilities by reversing the movement of water, which formerly flowed into Lake Michigan through the Chicago River, and turning a current from Lake Michigan through the Chicago River to the Illinois River at Lockport and thence down the Illinois River to the Mississippi. The canal, which is practically a sewer, is flushed with water from Lake Michigan, and its waters are pure within a flow of 150 miles. Its capacity, not fully utilized at first, is 600,000 cubic feet per minute, sufficient to renew the water of the Chicago River daily. Indeed it has been proved that the Illinois is purer than the Mississippi at their junction.

The minimum depth of the canal is 22 feet, its width at bottom 160 feet, and the width at the top from 162 to 290 feet, according to the class of material through which it is cut. The work was begun September 3, 1892, and completed and the water turned into the channel January 2, 1900. The flow of water from Lake Michigan toward the Gulf is now at the rate of 360,000 cubic feet per minute, and the channel is estimated to be capable of carrying nearly twice that amount. The total excavation in its construction included 28,500,000 cubic yards of glacial drift and 12,910,000 cubic yards of solid rock, an aggregate of 41,410,000 cubic yards. In addition to this the construction of a new channel for the Desplaines River became necessary in order to permit the canal to follow the bed of that river, and the material excavated in that work amounted to 2,068,659 cubic yards, making a grand total displacement in the work of 43,478,659 cubic yards of material which, according to a statement issued by the trustees of the sanitary district of Chicago, would, if deposited in Lake Michigan in 40 feet of water, form an island 1 mile square with its surface 12 feet above the water line.

All bridges along the canal are movable structures. The total cost of construction, including interest account, aggregated $34,000,000, of which $21,379,675 was for excavation and about $3,000,000 for rights of way and $4,000,000 for building railroad and highway bridges over the canal.

The Illinois and Michigan Canal, which formerly carried off most of the waste of the city, is used by small craft, and the new drainage canal also may be used for shipping in view of the federal government's improvements of the rivers connecting it with the Mississippi for the construction of a ship canal for large vessels. The canal also made possible the development of enormous hydraulic power for the use of the city.

THE HENNEPIN CANAL

The Illinois and Michigan Canal has been supplemented by the Illinois and Mississippi Canal, more commonly known as the "Hennepin." It completes a navigable waterway from the Mississippi River to Lake Michigan. The first appropriation for the project was made in 1890; work was begun in 1892 and the canal formally opened, October 24, 1907.

Starting at the great bend of the Illinois River, $1\frac{3}{4}$ miles above Hennepin, this barge canal follows the Bureau Creek valley to the mouth of Queen River on the Rock River, and then proceeds by the Rock River and a canal around its rapids at Milan to its mouth at Rock Island in the Mississippi River. The canal is 80 feet in width at the water line, 52 feet in width at the bottom, and seven feet in depth. The greater part of the water comes from the Rock River, which is dammed by a dam nearly 1,500 feet long between Sterling and Rock Falls, Illinois.

OTHER CANALS

In addition to the ship canals previously mentioned, there are a number of other important waterways worthy of mention. The great North Holland Canal, cut in 1845 from Amsterdam to Helder, a distance of 51 miles, to avoid the shoals of the Zuyder Zee, has a depth of 20 feet, a width of 125 feet at the surface, and carries vessels of 1,300 tons burden, and is described as "the chief cause of the great prosperity of Amsterdam."

The Caledonian Canal, which connects the Atlantic Ocean and North Sea through the north of Scotland, is 17 feet in depth, 50 feet in width at the bottom, and 120 feet at the surface, with a surface elevation at the highest point of 94 feet above sea level. The canal proper is 250 miles long, and the distance between the terminals over 300 miles. It saves about 400 miles of coasting voyage round the north of Great Britain through the stormy Pentland Firth. The cost has been stated at $7,000,000, including repairs; and the annual income is between $35,000 and $40,000.

The Canal du Midi, cut through France from Toulouse, on the Garonne River, to Cette, on the Mediterranean, a distance of 150 miles, is 60 feet wide, 6½ feet deep, has 114 locks, and is, at its highest point, 600 feet above the level of the sea. Its cost was $3,500,000, and it is navigable for vessels of 100 tons.

In India the canals, constructed primarily for irrigation purposes, at a cost of about $15,000,000, are utilized to a considerable extent for inland navigation. In Germany the canals, aside from the Kaiser Wilhelm, are 1,511 miles in length, and the canalized rivers 1,452 miles. In France the length of the canals in operation is 3,021 miles.

CANADIAN CANALS

The canal systems of European countries and of Canada differ from those of the United States in that they are operated in conjunction with, and made complemental to, the railway systems of those countries. Canada's six great systems of government canals afford, with the St. Lawrence River connections, important inland communications. The total length of the canals in operation is 262 miles, but the aggregate length of continuous inland navigation rendered available by them is nearly 3,000 miles. The amount expended in the construction and maintenance of these canals, including the Sault Ste. Marie Canal, is over $100,000,000.

The St. Lawrence River canal system from Lake Superior to tide water overcomes a difference of about 600 feet and carries immense quantities of grain from the West to Montreal, the chief port of summer trade on the Atlantic. These canals have a minimum depth of 14 feet on the sills and are open to Canadian and American vessels on equal terms.

Numerous smaller canals bring Ottawa into connection with Lake Champlain and the Hudson River via Montreal. Over this route travel the logs and lumber of Ontario,

Quebec and New Brunswick. One group of canals, the Trent Valley system, shorten the distance from Lake Superior to the sea. They connect Lake Ontario with Georgian Bay (an arm of Lake Huron) via Lake Simcoe. Surveys have been made with a view to connecting the Georgian Bay, through the intervening water stretches, with the Ottawa River system and thus with Montreal. In 1903 all tolls were removed from Canadian canals.

CANALS OF THE UNITED KINGDOM

In the United Kingdom the length of canals belonging to railways is 1,144 miles, and that of canals not belonging to railways 3,310 miles. The paid-up capital (from all sources) of the independent canals in 1905 amounted to £36,973,503, according to the board of trade returns. Including railway-owned canals, this amount exceeded £47,000,000. The annual traffic runs about 43,000,000 tons, comparing unfavorably with the amount carried by the railways. The improvement and development of these internal waterways is regarded by the chamber of commerce as a matter of urgent necessity.

CANALS OF THE UNITED STATES

The canals of the United States still used for commercial purposes are 38 in number, with an aggregate length of 2,443 miles, the total cost of their construction being about $200,000,000. The most important of these, aside from that connecting the Great Lakes, of course, is the Erie Canal, 387 miles in length, with 72 locks and a depth of 7 feet. Next in length is the Ohio Canal from Cleveland, Ohio, to Portsmouth, Ohio, 317 miles in length, with 150 locks and a depth of 4 feet. Next in length is the Miami and Erie Canal, from Cincinnati to Toledo, 274 miles in length, with 93 locks and a depth of $5\frac{1}{2}$ feet. The Pennsylvania Canal, from Columbia to Huntingdon,

Pa., is 193 miles in length, with 71 locks and a depth of 6 feet. The Chesapeake and Ohio Canal, from Cumberland, Md., to Washington, D. C., is 184 miles in length, with 73 locks and a depth of 6 feet. The Lehigh Coal and Navigation Company's Canal, from Coalport to Easton, Pa., is 108 miles in length, with 57 locks and a depth of 6 feet. The Schuylkill Navigation Company's Canal, from Mill Creek, Pa., to Philadelphia, Pa., is 108 miles in length, with 71 locks and a depth of $6\frac{1}{4}$ feet. The Illinois and Michigan Canal, from Chicago, Ill., to La Salle, is 102 miles in length, with 15 locks and a depth of 6 feet, and the Champlain Canal, from Whitehall, N. Y., to West Troy, is 81 miles in length, with 32 locks and a depth of 6 feet.

COST OF MAINTENANCE AND OPERATION OF CANALS

There are no locks on the Suez Canal, but the channel is through drifting sand for a great part of its length. The entrance to the harbor of Port Said on the Mediterranean intercepts the drift of sand discharged from the Nile and carried along the coast by the easterly current. The maintenance of the Suez Canal therefore requires a large amount of dredging and consists mainly of this class of work. The operating expenses are also large, the great traffic involving heavy costs for pilotage. The general expenses for administration have necessarily been greater for the Suez Canal than for the Kiel or Manchester canals, on account of the distance of the work from the point of central control, a disadvantage which will also attend the operation of the Panama Canal. The annual cost of maintenance and operation of the Suez Canal in 1911 was $6,600,000, or about $733,000 per mile.

The cost of maintenance and operation of the Kiel Canal for 1910 was $12,000 per mile; of the Manchester, $39,000 per mile. These canals have locks and other mechanical structures, and therefore might be expected

Photograph, Underwood & Underwood, N. Y. LOCK GATE OPERATING MACHINERY.

The great gear wheel, known as a "bull wheel," is connected with one leaf of the gate on the right by means of a strut so that revolving the bull wheel by means of an electric motor through a train of gears results in opening or closing the gate.

to have a higher cost of maintenance than the Suez Canal, which has none, but this appears to be more than offset by reduced cost of maintaining the prism and more economical central control. The traffic being light on these canals, the cost of pilotage and port service is small.

APPENDIX II

Economic Effects of Ship Canals

Much has been written concerning the ship canals of the world as great works of engineering; much, too, on their political and military importance; but of the part they have played in the great economic changes, the result of the marvelous development of transport industries during this last half century, it is not so easy to find definite or satisfactory accounts. At the same time vague and indefinite statements frequently made indicate that their economic importance has been significant; and, in fact, it is only as they are influential in this way that they become commercially profitable undertakings. The attempt is here made to trace with some degree of precision these economic effects, showing how, in consequence of the canals, important changes have been made in business machinery, in business methods, in producing and marketing commodities, and in general economic development.

The ship canals do not form a connected part of the world's transportation system, and in consequence the economic results of each are, in the main, independent of all other canals. Furthermore, the economic importance of the different canals presents the widest variations. Each opens the way for the creation of many and extensive carrying routes; but, while the influence of some has been merely local, the consequences of others have been felt throughout the commercial and industrial world. These conditions suggest the natural method of treatment to be a consideration of each canal separately, tracing so far as possible the particular economic effects that have resulted from its existence.

AMSTERDAM CANAL

In a country as well supplied with smaller canals as Holland is, it was natural that the idea of a ship canal should present itself to Amsterdam, when the shallowness of the Zuyder Zee and other difficulties of approach were causing her to lose trade to her rival, Rotterdam. The idea soon took practical form, and in 1826 the Helder Canal, with an 18-foot channel, offered an easier approach to the Dutch port. With the development of the shipping industry the dimensions of this canal became inadequate after a few decades, while its length (50 miles) and the difficult entrance in the passes of the Texel proved additional disadvantages. To maintain the commercial position of Amsterdam the construction of a new and larger canal, built by the shortest line to the sea, was decided on, and in 1876 the North Sea Canal, terminating at Ymuiden, $15\frac{1}{2}$ miles in length and 23 feet in depth, was opened for use.

The effect of the new canal on the commerce of Amsterdam was instantaneous. For twenty years the tonnage statistics for shipping at that port had shown an almost complete stagnation, while at Rotterdam the shipping had trebled. In six years after the new canal was opened the tonnage entering and clearing at Amsterdam had more than doubled, rising from 802,000 tons in 1876 to 1,734,000 tons in 1882.

Extensive enlargements and improvements were early decided upon, and the Amsterdam Canal can now be used by all but a few of the largest sea-going passenger vessels. Ymuiden has become one of the leading fishing ports in Europe.

THE SUEZ CANAL

In December, 1858, a company was formed to undertake M. de Lesseps' audacious scheme of connecting the Mediterranean and Red seas; in the following spring work was commenced, and in 1869 the Suez Canal opened a new water route to the East.

It takes but a glance at the statistics of traffic to notice the enormous difference between the trade that has developed through the Suez Canal and that of the canals already considered. Beginning in 1870, with 486 vessels, having a tonnage of 436,000 tons, there was a steady increase until 1875, when it had reached nearly 1,500 ships and over 2,000,000 tons. After a few years of quiescence came a second period of rapid increase, from 1880 to 1883, in the latter year the figures of 3,300 ships and 5,800,000 tons being reached. Since then there has been a slowly increasing tonnage, reaching the maximum figure of 8,700,000 tons in 1891, but falling off somewhat since that year. In 1896 the figures were 3,409 ships with a tonnage of 8,594,307.

EFFECT OF SUEZ CANAL ON SHIPPING

The development of a trade of such an extent and value by a new route could not but have an important and far-reaching influence on the economic interests of the world. Perhaps the most striking results of the opening of the canal route to the East were those on the machinery of trade—meaning by this term both the material appliances and the business organization of trade. One effect might have been in part anticipated. The new route saved nearly 3,000 marine leagues on the voyage from the ports of western Europe to the East, or almost half the distance to Bombay. The obvious result of the use of the new route would be that half of the vessels engaged in the Eastern trade would be out of employment. In fact, however, the change came more indirectly. Sailing vessels did not find it advantageous to use the canal, and continued on the old route around the Cape of Good Hope. But the canal, by making practicable the use of steamships in the oriental trade, brought about an even greater revolution in the character of the shipping business to the East. By the

Cape route coaling places were few, and the facilities for coaling expensive. The consequence was that the enormous expense of coaling at these out-of-the-way places, with the loss of freight room for the extra space needed for coal, made the use of steamers unprofitable. But by the canal route a steamer could coal at Gibraltar, Malta, Port Said, and Aden, where coal could be furnished at moderate rates, while the space saved from coal could be used to carry a larger cargo. Accordingly, a large number of new iron screw steamers were soon constructed for the trade with the East, and replaced a large percentage of the sailing vessels. It has been estimated that 2,000,000 tons of vessels were thus thrown out of employment, and the effect of this can be seen in the immediate reduction in the tonnage of sailing vessels. In 1869 the sailing tonnage in the British foreign trade was 3,600,000 tons; in 1876 it was but 3,230,000 tons.

GREAT ORIENTAL STEAMSHIP COMPANIES

In the construction of the new steamers for the canal trade two lines already in existence—the Peninsular and Oriental Steamship Company and the Messageries Compagnie—took prominent parts. But new companies also were rapidly organized, which built steamers and established new lines to the East, among which may be noted the British India Steam Navigation Company, the Clan Line, the Austro-Hungarian Lloyds Company, the Italian Steam Navigation Company, and the Rubbotino Company, of Genoa. It is not possible to get at the amount of shipbuilding made necessary by the change in the kind of ships used in the Eastern trade, but some idea of the importance of the change may be seen by noting the fact that the total steam tonnage in the British foreign trade increased from 650,000 tons in 1869 to 1,500,000 tons in 1876. It would, of course, be possible to learn the number and tonnage of ships now engaged in the trade between Europe and the

East, but to account for all of this by the Suez Canal would be to exaggerate its effects. Improvements in marine engines and in the construction of steamers make much longer steamer voyages possible to-day than were possible in 1870, as is shown by the lines to Australia and across the Pacific Ocean. It is, therefore, certain that if no Suez Canal had been built, there would have been by this time steamers in the Eastern trade; but the change would have come at a much later period, and sailing vessels would continue to carry a large, perhaps a dominant, share of the traffic. The effect of the Suez Canal was to make the transition from sail to steam sharp and decisive, and to bring it about in the decade 1870–1880.

AN ANTICIPATED EFFECT NOT REALIZED

One change in the shipping industry that was expected from the construction of the Suez Canal has not been realized. It was predicted that the geographical advantage given to the Mediterranean ports by the new route would soon enable them to regain the position they had held in the Middle Ages as the carriers of Eastern produce to the markets of Europe. In England it was felt that the canal would seriously threaten British maritime supremacy, but the results have been otherwise. It was only in England that the capital was at hand to build the large screw steamers which alone could profitably use the canal, and from the start three-fourths of the vessels using the canal have been British.

But while the carrying trade is still in British vessels a much larger and a growing share of the traffic is carried from the East directly to the Continent, and England has declined in relative importance as a warehousing and distributing point for Eastern goods. Under the old *régime* of sailing vessels around the Cape, when voyages from India took a good part of a year, and the time of arrival could not be calculated on within a month or two, it was necessary that large stocks of goods should be kept on hand to enable dealers to meet the varying demand for their goods. Steamers by way of the Suez Canal make the voyage in thirty days and the time of their arrival can be regulated within a day. Shorter voyages and punctuality of arrivals make it possible for local dealers both in England and on the Continent to order directly from the East and the change in the method of this business rendered useless to a large extent the immense warehouses at London, Liverpool, and other English ports.

DIRECT EXPORTS FROM INDIA TO EUROPE

This change in the direction of trade has not been simply the transfer of the distributing points from England to the Mediterranean ports of southern Europe. The towns of Italy, Greece, and southern France have been almost as greatly disappointed in their expectations of becoming trade centers as in their hopes of controlling the shipping trade to the East through the operation of the Suez Canal. To be sure there has been a heavy increase in Indian exports to Italy, Austria, and Russia; and the Mediterranean ports, notably Genoa, have increased in importance. But the most striking feature of the change in the direction of Indian exports lies in the increased traffic to France, Holland, Belgium, and, above all, to Germany. The statistics of Indian exports to these countries show that there is no longer any one country preeminent as a distributing point for Eastern produce, but that all Europe trades directly with the East. Nevertheless, with this great change in the character of the Indian export trade the imports of European goods to India continue, as in the days before the canal, to come almost entirely from England.

The termination of the warehouse distribution system of England was one of the forces which led to the disappearance of the class of merchant princes who had hitherto monopolized the Eastern trade. The system of bank discounts and commercial loans, by enabling men of ability to secure capital at low rates of interest, also played a large part in driving out of trade the old houses doing business on their own capital, from which they expected large rates of interest. But as long as large stocks of goods had to be kept on hand for six months or more at a time, it was difficult for the new business man to get the credit that would enable him to supplant the old-established houses in the Eastern trade. When, however, the new route by the Suez Canal, by bringing steamers into use, enabled a cargo to be sold and delivered within a month after the order had been sent, the advantages on the side of the man working with borrowed capital were decisive.

As a result of the opening of the Suez Canal, sailing vessels, warehouses, merchant princes, dealers in six months' bills found their old occupations slipping away. The old modes and channels of business were altered and new adjustments had to be made. In the meantime the confusion and disturbances in the business world were so great that the London *Economist* has said that they constituted one great general cause for the universal commercial and industrial depression and disturbance of 1873.

EFFECT ON EASTERN PRODUCE

The effect of the opening of the Suez Canal and the new route to the East on the production and marketing of Eastern produce is by no means so easy to trace as the effects on the machinery of trade. If all the necessary statistical material were at hand it would be an almost endless task to disentangle from the complex results of complicated causes the exact changes that have been due to the canal. It is possible, however, to see the effects produced by the canal in the case of a few leading com-

THE FRONT TOWER ON APPROACH WALL OF GATUN LOCKS.

These range lights are used to guide ships in the channel of Gatun Lake and aid them in reaching the entrance to the locks at night.

modities, and in other respects the general tendency of the new route can be recognized.

EFFECT ON CERTAIN COMMODITIES

A few commodities will serve to show that not every article in the Eastern trade has been affected by the new route and the new methods of business brought about by it. The exports of Indian cotton have remained at about the same figure since the opening of the canal, showing that for that article the sailing vessel and the Cape route provided as cheap a road as the canal route. The exports of Indian wool and of spices have increased to some extent, but with nothing to indicate that the increase is greater than would have taken place in the ordinary development of trade. The exports of tea from India show an astonishing increase from 11,000,000 pounds in 1870 to 120,000,000 in 1893-94. But with an article of such high value the direct effects of the canal through cheaper freight rates can have had little influence here, though indirectly the increased Indian production may be due in part to the easier communication with the West that was made possible by the canal. In the earlier arrival of the new season's teas the influence of the canal in shortening the time from India to England is clearly evident. Tea imports to England in July, 1870, were 711,000 pounds; in July, 1871, 4,000,000 pounds; in July, 1872, 23,000,000 pounds—the enormous increase being the direct result of the use of steamers via the canal in place of sailing vessels and the long Cape voyage.

Rice is a commodity the trade in which has been subject to important changes as a direct result of the use of the canal route to the East. Rice is a staple Italian cereal and a leading article of Italian export. It had formerly been imported into European countries by the Cape route, but by the canal route Eastern rice was enabled to reach markets in southern Europe formerly inaccessible, and even to be sold in Italy itself, much to the displeasure of the Italian producers. In the six years following the opening of the Suez Canal the export of Indian rice doubled and has continued to increase since. It constitutes the largest single item in the export trade of India.

INDIA AS A WHEAT-EXPORTING COUNTRY

The creation of the wheat export trade of India is due directly to the opening of the Suez Canal route to Europe. Efforts had been made to carry wheat around the Cape, but the liability to heat during the long voyage and the loss from weevil in the cargo made all such attempts unsuccessful. The possibility of carrying wheat by the new and shorter route was soon demonstrated, and a trade was established that has grown until India has become the second wheat-exporting country in the world. In 1870 the wheat exports of India were 130,000 bushels; in 1876, over 4,000,000 bushels; in 1883, 35,000,000 bushels; in 1891, 50,000,000 bushels.*

Under ordinary conditions the Indian product is an important item in the wheat market of the world. It will be observed that the great increase in this Indian export trade did not begin until after the year 1876. The extension at that time came about through the reduction in freight rates made possible by improved steamers. It is nevertheless true that the establishment of the wheat-export trade of India and the possibility of any such trade's existing at all is to be ascribed to the Suez Canal.

On the imports into India the direct influence of the Suez Canal seems to be striking in the case of but one commodity—petroleum from the Russian oil fields at Batoum. Before the discovery of these fields the imports of oil into India were insignificant. The value of such imports in 1869 was about $110,000 and in 1876 had risen

---

* According to statistics of 1911, India stood third among the wheat-producing countries of the world. The United States stood first, with 621,338,000 bushels; Russia in Europe, second, with 447,016,000 bushels; and British India, third, with 371,646,000 bushels.

only to $175,000. But when the Batoum oil fields were discovered, an extensive trade to India, via the Suez Canal, immediately developed. In 1880 the imports of oil into India were 6,500,000 gallons, valued at $1,360,000; in 1885 this had risen to 26,300,000 gallons; in 1890, to 51,800,000 gallons, and in 1893, to 86,600,000 gallons. For a considerable period the Indian demand absorbed more than half the total product of the Russian oil wells, and to-day it takes more than a quarter of their output. As the distance from Batoum to India around Africa is as great as that from the American oil fields, it does not seem possible that any of this Russian oil would have found its way to India by the Cape route. Some trade might have arisen by the overland route to India, which, when railroad connections from the Caspian Sea to India are complete, would have become important, but the oil imports of India as they stand to-day are made possible only by the existence of the canal route.

If the question be asked, What is the total significance of the Suez Canal on the production and marketing of commodities? the answer can be given only in general terms. A superficial observer might base an estimate on the increase in Indian trade with Europe from $280,000,000 in 1870 to $700,000,000 in 1894.* If, however, it is borne in mind that this increase has been at a less proportionate rate than that from 1850 to 1870 without the canal, and if the large extensions of the foreign trade of Australia, South Africa, Argentina, and the United States within the last twenty years are also remembered, it must be evident that other and more general causes than the opening of the canal have affected the development of India. On the other hand, to limit the effects of the canal to those results which can be directly traced, such as the development of the trade in rice, wheat, and petroleum, is to err by understatement. The greater ease of communication by the

* In the year ending March 31, 1912, the total European trade of India amounted to $750,000,000.

canal route has brought much more Western life into personal contact with the East, and this has had much to do with the development not only of the foreign trade of the Eastern countries, but also of their internal resources.

To recapitulate: The construction of the Suez Canal has led to the immediate and rapid development of the use of steamers in the Eastern trade, has brought about the disuse of most sailing vessels in that trade, has caused the decline of the warehouse distribution system of England, and the rise of a direct trade between the East and the consuming countries of Europe. The shorter and more direct route has also made possible the wheat export trade of India, and the trade in oil from Batoum to India, and has doubled the rice exports of the latter country. The canal has also been one of the many factors in other important economic changes, among which may be mentioned the crisis of 1873 and the general development of trade and industry in the East.

APPENDIX III*

HISTORY OF TRAFFIC ON GREAT CANALS

The traffic of the Suez Canal during the first two years was relatively small, for the reason that the Suez route is not a practicable one for sailing vessels. At the time of the opening of the canal, most of the freight between Europe and the countries on and beyond the Indian Ocean was carried in sailing vessels. Steamers had to be built for the Suez route, and, being much less efficient than freight steamers are to-day, they but gradually took the traffic with the Far East and Australasia from the sailing vessels and the Cape of Good Hope route.

The increase in the traffic of the Suez Canal, however, was relatively large during the first decade, the net tonnage of the vessels that passed through the canal amounting to 2,000,000 in 1875 and to 3,000,000 in 1880. During the following ten years the traffic rose to 6,800,000 net tons, the gain for the decade being 126 per cent. This was a decade of rapid expansion of the commerce of Great Britain and other European countries with India, the Orient, and Oceania; and the Suez Canal secured, in competition with the Cape Route, a steadily increasing share of that commerce.

The third decade of the operation of the Suez Canal, 1890-1900, was one of only moderate traffic development. Serious business depressions in different parts of the world during this decade checked the rate of commercial expansion. From 1890 to 1900 the Suez traffic, net vessel tonnage, rose from 6,800,000 to 9,738,000 tons, the absolute

---

* The following paragraphs on the traffic history of canals are extracted from the report of Emory R. Johnson, Special Commissioner on Panama Canal Traffic and Tolls.

increase being less than 3,000,000 tons and the rate of increase 43.2 per cent—only a third of the rate that had prevailed from 1880 to 1890.

Since 1900, the traffic of the Suez Canal has risen rapidly. The net tonnage in 1910 was 16,581,000, 70.2 per cent above the figures for 1900. In 1911, the net tonnage advanced to 18,324,794 tons, or to 69.3 per cent above the figure for 1901. Europe and the eastern part of the United States are building up a large commerce with the countries east of the Suez Canal. The countries of the Indies, Oceania,

TRAFFIC OF THE SUEZ CANAL, 1870-1911

Years	Gross Tonnage	Number of Vessels	Total Passengers
1870	654,915	486	26,758
1871	1,142,230	765	48,422
1875	2,940,708	1,494	84,446
1880	4,344,519	2,026	101,551
1885	8,985,411	3,624	205,951
1890	9,749,129	3,389	161,352
1895	11,833,637	3,434	216,938
1900	13,699,237	3,441	282,511
1905	18,310,442	4,116	252,691
1906	18,810,713	3,975	353,881
1907	20,551,982	4,267	243,826
1908	19,110,831	3,975	218,967
1909	21,500,847	4,239	213,122
1910	23,054,901	4,533	234,320
1911	25,417,853	4,969	275,651

and the Orient are entering upon the development of their resources and industries with the increasing assistance of western capital; and the consequent expansion of the commerce of those countries is indicated by the rapid growth of the traffic of the Suez Canal.

The frequent enlargements in the dimensions of the canal have permitted the use of larger ships and have favored the growth of traffic. The draft allowed vessels in the canal was increased in 1890 from 24 feet 7 inches to 25 feet 7 inches, in 1902 to 26 feet 3 inches, in 1906 to 27 feet, and in 1908 to 28 feet. By 1915, when the present improvements shall have been completed, vessels drawing between 31 and 32 feet will be permitted to use the canal. The average size of the vessels that passed through the Suez Canal in 1911 was more than four times the average in 1870 and more than double the average in 1885, the mean tonnage per vessel being 898 net tons in 1870, 1,509 tons in 1880, 2,033 tons in 1890, 2,830 tons in 1900, 3,658 tons in 1910, and 3,685 tons in 1911. The number as well as the size of the vessels has increased rapidly each decade, with the exception of the ten years from 1890 to 1900 when the growth in the world's commerce was at a slackened pace. In 1911, nearly 5,000 vessels—4,969—made use of the canal, an average of nearly 14 per day for each of the 365 days of the year.

The number of passengers through the Suez Canal varies from year to year. The total for 1911—275,651—was somewhat less than the figures for 1900. The maximum for any one year was reached in 1906, when, at the time of the war with Japan, Russia took a large number of naval vessels and troops through the canal.

TRAFFIC ON THE KAISER WILHELM CANAL

Vessels totaling 7,231,458 net tons, not including war vessels or ships in the service of the canal administration, passed through the canal. The increase since 1896, the first full year of the canal's operation, had been 312 per cent, and the increase during the last decade 70.7 per cent. In 1910, 43,328 vessels passed through the canal, 83.4 per cent of them being vessels flying the German flag. Steamers contributed 76 per cent of the total tonnage, while sailing vessels and unrigged craft made up the remainder. The average tonnage of the steamers was but 278 net tons, and that of sailing and unrigged vessels only 71.6 tons. Only 46.1 per cent of the total number of merchant vessels using the canal were steamers, though they comprised 76 per cent of the net tonnage. The small coasting vessels operated on the North and Baltic seas make large use of the canal and account for most of its traffic.

TRAFFIC ON THE MANCHESTER SHIP CANAL

Though the traffic of the Manchester Ship Canal has been less than was estimated, there has been a steady increase. In 1911, 5,217,812 tons of freight used the canal, as compared with 925,659 tons in 1894, the first year of operation. The gain during the decade 1900 to 1910 was 61.3 per cent, although the high figure of 1907, owing to the subsequent commercial depression, had not yet been reached in 1910. The increase during the decade ending in 1911 was 77.3 per cent, more freight being handled in that year than during any previous year in the history of the canal.

Of the total traffic in 1911, 4,894,670 tons consisted of sea-borne traffic, this being an increase of 82.3 per cent over the year 1901. The barge traffic of the canal in 1911 totaled 323,142 tons, and was less than was carried during the later nineties. In view of the connection of the Manchester Canal with as many as 14 barge canals, the barge traffic is surprisingly small.

The total number of vessels entering the canal in 1911 was 6,409 with a net register tonnage of 2,869,641. Since the opening of the canal the annual number of vessels entering has increased 40.8 per cent, and the net tonnage 298.3 per cent. During the last decade the number of vessels entering increased 27.9 per cent, and the net tonnage 97.2 per cent. The Royal Commission on Canals and Waterways after reviewing the traffic from 1898 to 1905 concludes that "these figures show a rapid and satisfactory progress, and prove what can be done by energy and courage, and with a large expenditure of capital, in favorable circumstances, to create trade."

The officials of the canal company have, however, repeatedly expressed dissatisfaction with the growth of traffic

Courtesy of "Popular Mechanics." VESSEL BEING TOWED THROUGH LOCKS BY ELECTRIC LOCOMOTIVES.

In order to avoid risk of accident to the lock gates through a misunderstanding of signals between a ship's bridge and engine room, no ship will be allowed to use her own power in the locks. As she approaches the lock entrance two electric locomotives are run out on the guide walls at either side, cables are attached and the ship is drawn into the lock where two more locomotives may be coupled to the stern to draw the vessel through the lock.

which so far as facilities are concerned might have been more rapid. The chairman of the board of directors at the general meeting of the company on February 17, 1910, spoke as follows:

> If more patriotism could somehow be infused into the mercantile and manufacturing community of this district we should soon have a large expansion of traffic. What I mean with regard to imbuing the mercantile and manufacturing community with local patriotism is this: That they should be determined in every case to back up their own part. If shipowners were made to believe that when they take the risk of running lines of steamers to and from Manchester they would have the whole-hearted sympathy and support of the whole mercantile community we should go ahead very much faster. Self-interest is the dominant factor in business, and it is on that ground that I mainly appeal to the mercantile and manufacturing community. It is sheer folly to send their goods by rival routes merely because they, for the time being, in competition with the Ship Canal, come down to the Manchester Ship Canal cost. But I appeal also on higher grounds. Surely the men of Manchester are not going to incur the stigma of being unable to put the finishing hand to their great work. They have attained celebrity all over the world for converting their inland town into one of the great seaports of the Kingdom. Are they going to clinch their effort by showing the whole world they are determined that their own port, and not rival ports, shall have every ton of traffic they can influence? Manchester men are generally believed to be too far-seeing and thorough to do things by halves; and the serious question for our undertaking is "Are they going to live up to their reputation?"

The chairman's words point to the chief traffic difficulty of the canal. From the very beginning it has had to compete with the railroads which previously carried nearly all the freight to and from the Manchester district. During the promotion of the canal their policy was to block its construction; and, failing in this, their policy has been to cut their rates to the basis of canal charges in order to hold as much of the traffic as possible and to compel the canal company to operate as a losing venture to its stockholders. The chief competition centers about the traffic to and from the points around Manchester not directly on the canal. Upon such traffic, the canal charges, plus railroad rates, plus handling charges, must compete with the through railroad rate to Liverpool and the handling charges at that terminal. Shipments directly to and from Manchester are sometimes handled by rail from and to coast ports, when the railways are able to provide shippers and consignees with sidings and to offer them favorable through rates.

This competition with rail carriers indicates, however, that the commercial value of the canal is not fully measured by the extent of its traffic. The favorable railroad rates to the coast ports are directly due to the ship canal, and much of the industrial growth of the Manchester district is directly due to the canal. The Royal Commission on Canals and Waterways asserts that "it is true that this undertaking has not as yet proved sufficiently remunerative to enable dividends to be paid on ordinary share capital. It has, however, fulfilled the object of greatly increasing the commercial prosperity of Manchester. The trade of Manchester was, in the period immediately before the construction of the canal, in a depressed condition. Works were being closed, there was no extension, and the value of property was going down. Since the canal was opened there has been a large increase in the net annual ratable value in Manchester, and there are other signs of increased wealth and prosperity." The report also states "this benefit or indirect return has already been sufficiently abundant to justify the great outlay on the canal. Moreover, the net revenue shows a steady increase, and provides a direct return on a growing proportion of the capital."

The inland city, Manchester, has not only maintained itself as an industrial center, but has become the fourth port in England. The population of Manchester, not including the increase due to the extension of its area to surrounding towns, rose from 644,873 in 1901 to 714,427 in 1910, or 10.79 per cent. The population of Liverpool meanwhile increased from 704,134 to 746,566, or 6.03 per cent. The shipping of Manchester (entrances and clearances) increased from 3,001,000 tons in 1900 to 4,564,000 in 1910, or 52 per cent; those of Liverpool grew from 18,477,000 to 21,828,000, or 18.1 per cent; those of Hull from 6,732,000 to 9,885,000, or 46.8 per cent, and those of London from 30,500,000 to 36,030,000, 18.1 per cent. The shipping using the port of Manchester consists mainly of freight vessels, as the large ocean-going passenger ships dock at coast ports. Nevertheless the increase during the decade 1900-1910, of 65.8 per cent in the seaborne traffic of the Manchester Ship Canal and of 55.8 per cent in the net tonnage of vessels annually entering and clearing the port of Manchester through the canal, does not compare unfavorably with the gain in the shipping at the other great ports of Great Britain. It will be recalled that the traffic of the Suez Canal during that decade increased 70.2 per cent. It is significant that during the decade ending in 1911 the net tonnage of shipping using the Suez Canal increased 69.3 per cent, while during the same period the total freight traffic of the Manchester Canal increased 77.3 per cent, and its seaborne traffic made a gain of 82.3 per cent.

TRAFFIC ON THE AMSTERDAM CANAL

The gross tonnage of the vessels using the Amsterdam Canal increased from 1,401,128 in 1877 to 8,583,066 in 1911, and the number of vessels during the same period increased from 3,376 to 28,799. During the decade 1901 to 1911, the gross tonnage increased 50.6 per cent and the number of vessels 196 per cent. Of the total gross tonnage in 1911, 7,968,257 tons were of seagoing vessels, the remainder, or 614,809 gross tons, were of fishing and other small craft. In that year there were 4,650 seagoing and 24,149 fishing and other small vessels locked through the locks at Ymuiden. The gross tonnage of the seagoing vessels using the canal increased 43.4 per cent during the decade ending with 1911, although the number of seagoing vessels annually using the canal increased but 4.5 per cent.

Of the total vessels locked at Ymuiden in 1911, 14,548 were locked inward and 14,251 outward.

The gross tonnage entering Amsterdam in 1911 aggregated 3,573,498 gross tons, and was 39.1 per cent in excess of the entrances in 1901 and 316 per cent greater than it was in 1877. In 1911 83.2 per cent of the entire gross tonnage locked inward at the North Sea locks moved through the canal to Amsterdam; but owing to the large number of fishing boats and small vessels engaged in local traffic only 16.2 per cent of the total number of vessels that passed the locks were entered at Amsterdam.

APPENDIX IV

The Canal System of India

In a few of the colonies of the world, notably India and Ceylon, irrigation works of great value have been constructed by the colonial governments. While these have been costly, the expense has been entirely borne from colonial funds or from loans which are borne by the colonial government, and the cost has been many times repaid by the increased production of the irrigated areas. It has been estimated that the value of a single year's crop produced in the irrigated sections of India in excess of that which would have been produced without irrigation more than equals the entire cost of the irrigation system.

THE IMPORTANCE OF CANALS IN INDIA

The irrigating system of India is described by Sir John Strachey as follows:

"In India the very existence of the people depends upon the regular occurrence of the periodical rains, and when they fail through a wide tract of country, and, still worse, when they fail in successive years, the consequences are terrible. The greater part of India is liable periodically to this danger, but the country is so vast that it never happens that all parts of it suffer at the same time. Improvements in the economic condition of the people, especially more diversity of occupation, can alone bring complete safeguards and render general famine, in its extremest form, through a great tract of country impossible. But this must be a long and gradual process. Meanwhile it had been found by experience that although the entire prevention of famines, the most destructive of all calamities, is beyond the power of any government, we can do much to mitigate them by removing obstacles which hinder commercial intercourse and which diminish the productiveness of the land. The instruments by which we can do this are roads, railways, and canals. . . .

IRRIGATION CONSTANTLY REQUIRED IN PARTS OF INDIA

"In northern India, even in good seasons, artificial irrigation is a necessity for the successful cultivation of many of the more valuable crops, and when there is a general failure of the periodical rains there is no other means by which drought and scarcity can be prevented. A large portion of northern India is now protected by canals of greater magnitude than exist in any other country of the world. . . .

"Little of the old irrigation works of our predecessors is retained in the existing canals. Practically all of these have been made by ourselves, and the often-repeated statement, prompted, I believe, by that strange inclination to depreciate their own achievements which often besets Englishmen, that the old canals have been more profitable than those constructed by ourselves has not the least foundation of truth."

A NEW ERA IN IRRIGATION

The year 1878, which saw the close of the most disastrous famine, opened a new era in irrigation. It was at last recognized that such famines would probably continue to occur at no great intervals of time, and that the cost of relief operations must be met, not by increasing the permanent debt of the country, but by creating a fund of famine relief and famine insurance. For this purpose it was fixed that there should be an annual provision of 1,500-000 rupees to be spent on (1) Relief, (2) Protective Works, (3) Reduction of Debt. Among protective works the first place was given to works of irrigation. These in turn were divided into three classes: (i) Productive Works, (ii) Protective Works, (iii) Minor Works.

The productive works are those which may reasonably be expected to be remunerative, and they include all the larger irrigation systems. The capital cost is provided from loan funds, and not from the relief funds previously mentioned. In the seventeen years ending 1896–97 the capital expenditure on such works was 10,954,000 rupees, including a sum of 1,742,000 rupees paid to the Madras Irrigation Company as the price of the Kurnool-Cuddapah, Canal, a work which will never be financially productive, but which nevertheless did good service in the famine of 1896–97 by irrigating 87,226 acres. In the famine of 1877–78 the area irrigated by productive canals was 5,171,000 acres. In the famine year 1896–97 the area was 9,571,000 acres, including an area of 128,087 acres irrigated on the Swat River Canal in the Punjab. The revenue of the years 1870–80 was nearly 6 per cent on the capital outlay. In 1897–98 it was 7.5 per cent. In the same seventeen years 2,099,000 rupees were spent on the construction of protective irrigation works, not expected to be directly remunerative, but of great value during famine years. On four works of this class were spent over 1,500,000 rupees, which, in 1896–97, irrigated over 200,000 acres, a valuable return then, although in an ordinary year their gross revenue does not cover their working expenses.

In the seventeen years ending 1896–97, 827,214 rupees were spent on the minor works for which capital accounts have been kept, and during the last of that time they yielded a return of 9.13 per cent. In the same year the irrigation effected by minor works of all sorts showed the large area of 7,442,000 acres. Such are the general statistics of the outlay. The Government may well be congratulated on having secured in that year of widespread drought so large an area of irrigated territory. Since that time progress has been steady.

CANALS OF THE PUNJAB

Beginning with the Punjab province, in which most progress has been made, the great Sutlej Canal, which irrigates the country to the left of that river, was opened in 1882, and the Western Jumna, perhaps the oldest in India, was extended into the dry Hissar and Sirsa districts, and generally improved so as to increase by nearly half its area of irrigation between 1878 and 1897. This is sufficient to secure the territory forever from famine.

The Bari Doab Canal, which irrigates the Gardaspur, Amritsar and Lahore districts, has been enlarged and extended so as to double this irrigation. The Chenab Canal, the largest in India, and the most profitable, was begun in 1889. It was designed to command an area of two and one-half million acres, and to irrigate annually somewhat less than one-half that area. It flows through land which, in 1889, was practically a desert. Colonization began in 1892, and nine years later the canal was watering nearly two million acres. The population at that time was 800,000, consisting chiefly of thrifty, prosperous peasants, with occupancy rights in holdings of about twenty-eight acres each.

The Jhelum Canal was opened October 30, 1901. It is a smaller work than the Chenab, but it is calculated to command over a million acres, of which at least one half will be watered annually.

A smaller work, but one of great interest, is the Swat River Canal in the Peshawar Valley. It was never expected that this would be a remunerative work, but it was considered expedient for political reasons in order to induce the turbulent frontier tribes to settle down into peaceful agriculture.

A scheme greater than any so far mentioned is that of the Sind Sagar Canal, projected from the left bank of the Indus opposite Kalabagh to irrigate 1,750,000 acres at a cost of 6,000,000 rupees. Another great canal scheme proposed from the right bank of the Sutlej would irrigate about

600,000 acres, commanding Montgomery and Multan districts, at a cost of 2,500,000 rupees. These three last projects would add 2,774,000 acres to the irrigated area of the province, and as they would flow through tracts almost uninhabited they would offer a most valuable solution for the congestion in some districts of Northern India.

In addition to these great perennial canals, much has been done since 1878 in enlarging and extending the so-called "inundation canals' of the Punjab, which utilize the flood waters in the rivers during the monsoon season and are dry at other times. By these canals large areas throughout most of the Punjab are brought under cultivation, and the area thus watered has increased from about 180,000 to 500,000 acres since 1878.

CANALS IN SIND

Upon inundation canals such as these the whole cultivation of Sind depends. In 1878 the area was 1,500,000 acres. In 1896–97 it had increased to 2,484,000 acres. This increase was not due to famine in Sind, for that rainless province depends always on the Indus as Egypt does on the Nile, and where there is no rainfall there can be no drought. But the famine prices obtained for agricultural produce doubtless gave an impetus to cultivation. In Sind, too, there is room for much increase of irrigation. It has been proposed to construct two new canals, the Canal Jamrao and the Shikaarpur, and to improve and extend three existing canals, Nasrat, Naulakhi and Dad. The total cost of these five projects, some of which are now in progress, was estimated at 1,586,000 rupees, and the extension of irrigation at 660,563 acres.

THE GANGES CANAL

In the basin of the Ganges, the commissioners appointed to report on the famine of 1896–97, found that in the territory between the Ganges and the Jumna little was left to be done beyond the completion of some distributary channels. The Ganges Canal, the East India Company's great work, constructed between 1840 and 1854, before there was a mile of railway over India, still holds first place among later irrigation work both for boldness of design and completeness of execution. It is a lasting monument to the genius of Sir Proby Cautley, an officer of the Bengal Artillery, and a born engineer.

Since 1870 consideration has been given to projects for irrigating the fertile province of Oudh, by means of a great canal to be drawn from the river Sarda. Water is here in abundance and the land is well adapted for irrigation, but as there is considerable rainfall it is doubtful whether this scheme would prove remunerative, and a large section of the landowners have hitherto opposed it as likely to waterlog the country.

PROTECTIVE WORKS

Among the four protective works of irrigation, which, as previously stated, irrigated over 200,000 acres in 1896–97, one of the most important is the Betwa Canal in the parched district of Bundelkhand. This canal has cost over 400,000 rupees, and causes an annual loss to the state in interest and working expenses of 20,000 rupees. The value of crops raised on the area, however, has justified its construction.

A similar canal from the river Ken in the same district has been constructed. Proceeding farther east we find very satisfactory progress in the irrigation of Southern Behar effected by the costly system of canals drawn from the river Sone. In 1877–78 these canals irrigated over 240,000 acres. Rapid progress was not expected here, and 792,000 acres was calculated as the maximum that could be covered with the water supply available. In the five years preceding 1901 and 1902 the average irrigated area was 463,181 acres, and during the latter year the area was 555,156 acres, the greatest maximum ever obtained.

CANAL SYSTEM OF ORISSA

The canal system of Orissa was likewise not expected to be remunerative, since in five years out of six the local rainfall is sufficient for the rice crop. In 1878-79 the area irrigated was 111,250 acres, and the outlay up to date was 1,750,000 rupees. In 1900-01 the area was over 200,000 acres, the highest ever attained, and the capital outlay amounted to 2,623,000 rupees. It should be stated in favor of these canals that, although the irrigation is not of annual value, they supply important water communication through a province which, from its natural configuration, is not likely soon to be intersected by railways. If, moreover, such a famine as that of 1866-67 were again to occur in Orissa, there would be no question of the value of these splendid canals.

IRRIGATION IN THE MADRAS PRESIDENCY AND MYSORE

In the Madras Presidency, and in Mysore, irrigation has long assumed a great importance, and the engineering works of the three great deltas, Godavari, Kistna and Cauvery, the outcome of the genius of Sir Arthur Cotton, have always been quoted as showing what a boon irrigation is to a country. In 1878 a total area of irrigation in the Madras Presidency amounted to about 5,000,000 acres. The irrigation of the eight productive systems was 1,680,000 acres, and the revenue, 789,000 rupees. In 1898 there were ten of these systems with an irrigation area of 2,685,000 acres, and a revenue of 1,163,000 rupees.

In the three great deltas, and the small southern delta that depends on the Srivaikuntam weir over the river Tumbraparni, extension and improvement works have also been carried on. The Sangam and Pennar systems depend on two weirs on the river Pennar in the Nellore district, the former about eighteen miles above the latter just below the town of Nellore. The former irrigates on the left; the latter on the right bank of the river. This district suffered severely in the famine of 1870-78, and the irrigation works were started in consequence. The Barur tank system in the Salem district was also constructed after this famine, but as yet it has not fulfilled expectations.

THE PERIYAR SCHEME

The Periyar scheme has for its object both the addition of new irrigation, and the safeguarding of that which exists in the district of Madura, playing water by means of a large number of shallow tanks drawing their supply from a very uncertain river, the Vaigai, which takes its rise on the eastern slopes of the Ghat range of mountains. Just opposite this river, on the western base of the range, is the source of the river Periyar. The rainfall on the west is greater than that on the east, and the surplus waters of the Periyar used to find their way through a short torrent course to the sea, rendering no small service by the way. Its upper waters are now stemmed by a masonry dam, 178 feet high, forming a large lake, at the eastern end of which is a tunnel 5,700 feet long, piercing the watershed and discharging 1,600 cubic feet per second down the eastern side of the mountains into the river Vaigai. No bolder work of irrigation has been carried out in India, and the credit is due to Colonel J. Pennycuick, C. S. I. The dam and tunnel works were unusually difficult of construction, as the country was roadless and uninhabited except by wild beasts, and a breeding place for fever and cholera.

THE RUSHIKULYA CANAL

The Rushikulya Canal was not expected to be remunerative, but is considered a valuable protection against famine. It consists of weirs over the river Gulleri, Mahanadi and Rushikulya in the backward province of Ganjan south of Orissa. From these weirs flow canals altogether about 127 miles in length, which, in connection with two large reservoirs, are capable of irrigating 120,000 acres. In 1901 the works, though incomplete, already irrigated over 67,000 acres.

OTHER WORKS

In addition to all these vast engineering systems, southern India contains a number of minor works of irrigation, some utilizing springs in the sandy beds of rivers, others utilizing the rainfall of a half square mile ponded up in a valley. In other cases tanks are fed from neighboring streams, and great ingenuity is displayed in the methods used to prevent the precious water from being wasted.

The canals of Sind have already been mentioned. Elsewhere in the Bombay presidency, in the Deccan and Gujart, there are fewer facilities for irrigation than in other parts of India, and the rivers are, for the most part, of uncertain volume. The cost of storage works is also great. In ordinary years the black soil can raise fairly good crops of cotton, millet and maize without artificial watering. The most important irrigation works in this region are Mutha and Nira canals in the Poona district.

In Upper Burmah three productive irrigation works were planned at the opening of the present century—the Mandalay, the Shivebo and the Mon canals, of which the first was estimated to cost over 320,000 rupees and to irrigate 22,000 acres. The area estimated to be watered by the whole three projects is 262,000 acres, located in the only part of Burmah that is considered liable to famine.

RECOMMENDATIONS OF THE IRRIGATION COMMISSION

In 1901 the government of India appointed a commission to examine throughout all India what could further be done to alleviate the horrors of famine. It had previously been the custom of the government not to borrow money for the execution of irrigation works unless there was a reasonable expectation that within a few years they would give a return of 4 or 5 per cent of the capital outlay. But in 1901 a different attitude was assumed. It was found that although some irrigation works (especially in the Bombay Deccan) would never yield a direct return of 4 or 5 per cent, still in a famine year they might be the means of producing a crop which would go a long way toward reducing the necessity of famine relief. In the Sholapur district of Bombay, for instance, about three years' revenue was spent on relief during the famine of 1901, when an expenditure of ten years' revenue on irrigation works might have done away for all future time with the necessity for this greater outlay. After further careful study of every part of India the Irrigation Commission published an exhaustive report. While emphatically asserting that irrigation alone could never prevent famine, they recommended an outlay of £45,000,000 spread over a period of twenty-five years.

PRESENT OUTLOOK

Up to 1913 the net revenue has remained fairly constant at $3,000,000 a year. During the four years ending 1910–11 the capital outlay increased from $172,500,000 to $197,500,000, while the total area irrigated and the net receipts showed little change and consequently the percentage of profits fell from 6.74 to 6.33. Punjab is the province where the existing canals are the most necessary and also the most remunerative and it is there that the most important work is now under construction. This is known as the Triple Canal in the Upper Jhelum, the Upper Chenab and the Lower Bari Doab, which will be completed in 1915 at a cost of $40,000,000. In the United Provinces a series of minor canals have been constructed for the protection of Bundelkhand against famine, while a large scheme is under consideration to increase the supply of the Ganges and Jumna Canals from the overflow of the Sarda River at Oudh. These projects involve the expenditure of nearly $30,000,000.

APPENDIX V*

CANALS IN CHINA

There are several features of the canal system of China, especially of the Imperial or Grand Canal, which can be studied with profit by the people of the United States. One of these is the use of the canal for the production of food in addition to its uses as a means of transportation. Allied to this is the use of the muck which gathers at the bottom of the waterway for fertilization. Another is the use of every particle of plant life growing in and around the canal for various purposes.

The Chinese secure a vast quantity of food of one sort or another from their canals. To appreciate the exact situation with respect to the waterways, it must be realized that the canals of China cover the plain country with a network of water. Leading from the Grand Canal in each direction are smaller canals, and from these lead still smaller canals, until there is hardly a single tract of 40 acres which is not reached by some sort of ditch, generally capable of carrying good-sized boats. The first reason for this great network is the needs of rice cultivation. During practically all of the growing season for rice the fields are flooded. Wherever a natural waterway can be made to irrigate the rice fields it is used, but, of course, from these to the canals or larger rivers there must be waterways. Where natural streams can not thus be adapted the Chinese lead water in canals or ditches to the edge of their fields and raise it to the fields of rice by the foot-power carriers which have been described so often by tourist writers. However the water

---

* Report of United States Consul Anderson, Hangchau, China.

is supplied to the rice, it is evident that there must be a waterway leading to the field and back to a principal stream, which is generally a branch canal. These waterways naturally take up a considerable portion of the land, and the Chinese make as profitable use of them as of the land itself.

The first use of the waterways is for fishing. The quantity of fish taken from the canals of China annually is immense. The Chinese have no artificial fish hatcheries, but the supply of fish is maintained at a high point by the fact that the flooded rice fields act as hatcheries and as hiding places for the young fish until they are large enough to look out for themselves. In the United States this fish-propagation annex to the canals is probably neither possible nor needful in view of the work done by the State and National bureaus, but in China it is nothing less than providential.

CHINESE CANALS SUPPLY FERTILIZER

Along the canals in China at any time may be found boatmen gathering muck from the bottom of the canal. This muck is taken in much the same manner that oysters are taken by hand on the Atlantic coast. In place of tongs are large bag-like devices on crossed bamboo poles which take in a large quantity of the ooze at once. This is emptied into the boat, and the process is repeated until the boatman has a load, when he will proceed to some neighboring farm and empty the muck, either directly on the fields—especially around the mulberry trees, which are raised for the silkworms—or in a pool, where it is taken later to the fields. From this muck the Chinese farmer will generally secure enough shellfish to pay him for his work, and the fertilizer is clear gain. The fertilizer thus secured is valuable. It is rich in nitrogen and potash and has abundant humus elements. This dredging of the canals for fertilizers is the only way by which the Chinese have kept their canals in reasonably good condition for centuries.

The fertilizer has paid for itself both ways. Recently there were complaints filed at Peking that the ashes from the steam launches plying on the canal were injuring the muck for fertilizing purposes, and the problem has been considered a serious one by the Chinese Government.

In addition to securing fertilizers from the canals, and thus keeping the canals in condition, the farmers' help keep them purified by gathering all floating weeds, grass, and other vegetable debris that they can find upon them. Boatmen will secure great loads of water plants and grasses by skimming along the surface of the canal. The reeds growing along the canals are used for weaving baskets of several grades, and for fuel. In short, no plant life about the canal goes to waste.

UTILIZATION OF SWAMP LAND

Where there are so many canals there is more or less swamp ground. In China this is utilized for the raising of lotus roots, from which commercial arrow-root is largely obtained. There is no reason why much of the waste swamp land in the southern portion of the United States should not be used for a similar purpose, and the commercial returns from a venture of this sort in that part of the country ought to be satisfactory. Where the canals of China widen, by reason of natural waterways, or for other reasons, the expanse of water not needed for actual navigation is made use of in the raising of water nuts of several varieties, especially what are known as water chestnuts. These nuts are raised in immense quantities. They are, strictly speaking, bulbs rather than nuts. They are rich in arrow-root and are prolific, an acre of shallow water producing far more than an acre of well-cultivated soil planted in ordinary grain or similar crops. These nuts, also, could be produced to advantage in the United States where there is land inundated for the growing season to a depth which will give ordinary water plants a chance to thrive and which is not capable of being drained for the time being. The nuts or bulbs are toothsome when roasted, and are wholesome, but probably would be more valuable in the United States for the manufactured products which can be secured from them.

There are duck farms all along the canals in China. These are profitable. Chinese canals, as a rule, considering the population upon them and their varied uses, are cleaner than canals in the United States. There are few if any factories to contaminate them. The Chinese use of certain sewage for fertilization also prevents contamination to a great extent. The canal water is used for laundry, bath, and culinary purposes indiscriminately. A canal in the United States could never be what it is in China, but the Chinese have a number of clever devices and ideas in connection with canals which can be adopted in the United States with profit.

THE ANCIENT GRAND CANAL OF CHINA

The Grand Canal system in China has existed in almost its present shape since about the time Columbus discovered America. The Grand Canal itself, extending from Hangchau to Peking, is about a thousand miles long. Much of it is banked with stone, and all of it is in such condition that with the expenditure of a little money the system could be put upon a modern and effective basis. As it is, the canal handles practically all the internal trade of China, and this trade is far greater than its foreign trade. The coming of railroads will affect the canals somewhat, but not so much as may be imagined, for the railroads will very largely build up a trade of their own. A little money will make China's canal system in the future what it has been in the past, the greatest on earth.

www.ingramcontent.com/pod-product-compliance
Lightning Source LLC
Chambersburg PA
CBHW082106230426
43671CB00015B/2621